Spring Web Flow 2 Web Development

Master Spring's well-designed web frameworks to develop powerful web applications

Sven Lüppken

Markus Stäuble

PACKT PUBLISHING

BIRMINGHAM - MUMBAI

Spring Web Flow 2 Web Development

First published: March 2009

Production Reference: 1120309

Published by Packt Publishing Ltd.
32 Lincoln Road
Olton
Birmingham, B27 6PA, UK.

ISBN 978-1-847195-42-5

www.packtpub.com

Cover Image by Vinayak Chittar (vinayak.chittar@gmail.com)

Credits

Authors
Sven Lüppken
Markus Stäuble

Reviewers
Luca Masini
Xinyu Liu

Senior Acquisition Editor
David Barnes

Development Editor
Shilpa Dube

Technical Editors
Dhiraj Bellani
Reshma Sundaresan

Copy Editor
Sumathi Sridhar

Indexer
Rekha Nair

Production Editorial Manager
Abhijeet Deobhakta

Project Team Leader
Lata Basantani

Project Coordinator
Leena Purkait

Proofreader
Laura Booth

Production Coordinator
Aparna Bhagat

Cover Work
Aparna Bhagat

About the Authors

Sven Lüppken holds a degree in Computer Science, which he passed with distinction. He is currently employed as a Java Software Developer at CBC Cologne Broadcasting Center GmbH, one of the leading broadcasting and production companies in Germany and a part of Media Group RTL Germany. Sven started programming in C and C++ at the age of sixteen and quickly fell in love with the Java programming language during his studies. When he got the chance to write his diploma thesis about object-relational mapping technologies, he accepted at once. Since then, he has integrated Hibernate and the JPA in many projects, always in conjunction with the Spring Framework.

I would like to dedicate my first book to my fiancée Frauke. Thank you for having always been supportive and understanding when I was spending my evenings and weekends writing this book. I would also like to thank Markus for giving me the opportunity to write this book, I'm very grateful to him. Some of my friends provided me with invaluable feedback, ideas, and criticism: Dr. Thomas Richert, Alexandre Morozov, and Oliver Fehrentz. Thanks guys!

Special thanks to my parents, who have supported and encouraged me my entire life. Thank you so much!

Markus Stäuble is currently working as a CTO at namics (Deutschland) GmbH. He has a Master's degree in Computer Science. He started programming with Java in the year 1999. After that, he has earned much experience in building Java enterprise systems, especially web applications. He has a deep knowledge of the Java platform and the tools and frameworks around Java.

There are many people who supported the writing of this book. But there is especially one person whom I want to say thank you, my wife Maria Elena. She greatly supported the writing and gave me the power and energy to finish this book.

About the Reviewers

Luca Masini was born in Florence in 1971. He is a senior software engineer and architect. He has been heavily involved from his first days in the Java world as a consultant for the major Italian banks, developing integration software and as a technical leader in many of the flagship projects. He worked for the adoption of Sun's J2EE standards in environments where COBOL was the leading language, and then he shifted his eyes toward open source, in particular IoC containers, ORM tools, and UI frameworks. As such, he adopted early products like Spring, Hibernate, and Struts, giving customers a technological advantage. Now he is working in enterprise ICT to simplify application development, thanks to Java EE 5, simplified standard, build tools, and project archetypes.

He also worked in the review of *Google Web Toolkit GWT Java AJAX Programming*, by Packt Publishing.

I would like to thank my son Niccolò.

Xinyu Liu had his graduate educations at the George Washington University. As a Sun Microsystems certified enterprise architect and developer, he has intensive application design and development experience across JavaEE, JavaSE, and JavaME. He is a writer for **Java.net** and **Javaworld.com** on various topics, including JSF, Spring Security, Hibernate Search, and Spring Web Flow. He also has a physics PhD background with several publications in both high energy and condensed matter fields.

Table of Contents

Preface

Spring Web Flow is an open-source web development framework and part of the Spring product portfolio. Its primary purpose is to define the (work) flow of a web application. The flow is independent of the implementation and thus the infrastructure of your application. This enables developers accustomed with Spring Web Flow to write powerful and re-usable web applications that are easy to maintain and enhance. Along with the Spring Web Flow distribution, additional libraries are shipped. These libraries make it easier for developers to improve their applications with compelling AJAX functionality. It also includes Spring Faces, which combines Spring Web Flow with the powerful JavaServer Faces technology to create feature-rich graphical user interfaces. You will find explanations about all this and much more in this book.

What this book covers

Chapter 1: Introduction gives an introduction to the world of Spring Web Flow. Additionally, the chapter covers important definitions that you need to know to understand the following chapters.

Chapter 2: Setup for Spring Web Flow 2 shows how to install Spring Web Flow and create the first small application. It also shows the usage of the examples that are provided in the Spring Web Flow distribution.

Chapter 3: The Basics of Spring Web Flow 2 covers all the basics that are essential to build applications with Spring Web Flow. It also explains all the essential things about the flow definition file.

Chapter 4: Spring Faces gives an overview and also a detailed explanation on the usage of Spring Faces with Spring Web Flow. For better understanding, it also explains the essential basics around JavaServer Faces.

Chapter 5: Mastering Spring Web Flow covers advanced topics, for example, the usage of subflows and the new Spring JavaScript library that ships with Spring Web Flow for the first time. The chapter also covers an in-depth look into the flow definition file.

Chapter 6: Testing Spring Web Flow Applications covers the important topic of testing applications that are developed with Spring Web Flow. It shows the integrated support of JUnit (`http://www.junit.org`) and includes step-by-step instructions showing how to test your applications.

Chapter 7: Security shows how to secure applications that are developed with Spring Web Flow using Spring Security.

Appendix A: flow.trac – The Model for the Examples describes the classes in the sample project, `flow.trac`. These classes are used in the examples of this book.

Appendix B: Running on the SpringSource dm Server explains how to run a Spring Web Flow application on the SpringSource Application Platform (AP).

What you need for this book

For the examples in this book, we have used the following software packages:

- Java Development Kit (JDK) 6
- Spring Web Flow 2.0.x
- Eclipse 3.4.x and NetBeans 6.1
- Apache Tomcat 6.0.18
- Apache Ant 1.7.1 / Apache Ivy 2.0.0 RC1
- Apache Maven 2.0.9
- Microsoft® SQL Server 2008 Express Edition
- Microsoft® SQL JDBC Database Driver 1.2
- Hibernate Core 3.3.1 GA, Hibernate Annotations 3.4.0 GA, and Hibernate EntityManager 3.4.0 GA
- SpringSource dm Server 1.0.x

Who this book is for

This book is targeted at Java web application developers who work with Spring Web Flow. This book is a must-read for those who wish to bridge the gap between the popular web framework and the popular application framework, and also for those who want to create powerful and re-usable web applications. It requires prior knowledge of Spring.

Conventions

In this book, you will find a number of styles of text that distinguish between different kinds of information. Here are some examples of these styles, and an explanation of their meaning.

Code words in text are shown as follows: "Next, we define a custom view resolver with a special `viewClass` property."

A block of code will be set as follows:

```
<dependency>
   <groupId>org.springframework.webflow</groupId>
   <artifactId>org.springframework.js</artifactId>
   <version>2.0.5.RELEASE</version>
</dependency>
```

When we wish to draw your attention to a particular part of a code block, the relevant lines or items will be shown in bold:

```
<end-state id="success" commit="true" />
<end-state id="failedView" view="failedView.jspx" />
```

Any command-line input or output is written as follows:

```
mvn clean compile war:exploded
```

New terms and **important words** are shown in bold. Words that you see on the screen, in menus, or dialog boxes for example, appear in our text like this: "If you click on the **Next** button, a request to the server will be sent which renders a new web site using Tiles."

[Warnings or important notes appear in a box like this.]

[Tips and tricks appear like this.]

Reader feedback

Feedback from our readers is always welcome. Let us know what you think about this book—what you liked or may have disliked. Reader feedback is important for us to develop titles that you really get the most out of.

To send us general feedback, simply drop an email to `feedback@packtpub.com`, and mention the book title in the subject of your message.

If there is a book that you need and would like to see us publish, please send us a note in the **SUGGEST A TITLE** form on `www.packtpub.com` or email `suggest@packtpub.com`.

If there is a topic that you have expertise in and you are interested in either writing or contributing to a book, see our author guide on `www.packtpub.com/authors`.

Customer support

Now that you are the proud owner of a Packt book, we have a number of things to help you to get the most from your purchase.

Downloading the example code for the book

Visit `http://www.packtpub.com/files/code/5425_Code.zip` to directly download the example code.

The downloadable files contain instructions on how to use them.

Errata

Although we have taken every care to ensure the accuracy of our contents, mistakes do happen. If you find a mistake in one of our books—maybe a mistake in text or code—we would be grateful if you would report this to us. By doing so, you can save other readers from frustration, and help us to improve subsequent versions of this book. If you find any errata, please report them by visiting `http://www.packtpub.com/support`, selecting your book, clicking on the **let us know** link, and entering the details of your errata. Once your errata are verified, your submission will be accepted and the errata added to any list of existing errata. Any existing errata can be viewed by selecting your title from `http://www.packtpub.com/support`.

Piracy

Piracy of copyright material on the Internet is an ongoing problem across all media. At Packt, we take the protection of our copyright and licenses very seriously. If you come across any illegal copies of our works in any form on the Internet, please provide us with the location address or web site name immediately so that we can pursue a remedy.

Please contact us at `copyright@packtpub.com` with a link to the suspected pirated material.

We appreciate your help in protecting our authors, and our ability to bring you valuable content.

Questions

You can contact us at `questions@packtpub.com` if you are having a problem with any aspect of the book, and we will do our best to address it.

1
Introduction

Nearly every day you read about a new release of a framework for developing web based applications. The Spring Framework is no exception. What makes **Spring Web Flow** (**SWF**) (second version, unless explicitly mentioned otherwise) special is that this framework not only solves one part of the tasks that have to be done in the development of a web application, but also helps you organize the flow (the order in which pages are called) inside your web application. Additionally, it manages the storage of data. However, to build a complete web application, you need more than Spring Web Flow. Therefore, we will also explain how to integrate Spring Web Flow with other frameworks.

> This book is neither a reference documentation, nor does it replace the reference documentation of the Spring Web Flow Framework. If you are interested in the reference documentation, we strongly recommend the reference from SpringSource. It is available online at the **Uniform Resource Locator** (**URL**) `http://static.springframework.org/spring-webflow/docs/2.0.x/reference/html/index.html`. If you need more information about the Spring Framework, visit the web page of the framework at the URL `http://www.springframework.org`.

> If you need more help with your daily development of frameworks from the **Spring Portfolio, please** visit `http://www.springsource.org/`. The site provides more information about all of the different frameworks. If the available reference documentation is insufficient for your needs, you can search the forums that are offered on that page. The start page for the forums is `http://forum.springsource.org/`.

Besides the theoretical basics of the Spring Web Flow Framework, we will show you many examples in the later chapters. For the examples, we have chosen a bug-tracking application because it is common to have a bug tracker inside a software project. We developed some model classes, which we will use in all our examples. All the classes are shown in the Appendix A1: *flow.trac – The Model for the Examples*. You can use the classes under the Apache License Version 2.0. For more information about the license, please visit `http://www.apache.org/licenses/LICENSE-2.0.html`.

In this chapter, we will give a brief introduction to the essential modules of the complete Spring Framework stack: Spring, Spring MVC, and Spring Web Flow. Then we will explain the Spring Web Flow elements: flow, view, and conversation. This will be followed by the new features and modules of Spring Web Flow 2.0.

Three cornerstones: Spring, Spring MVC, and Spring Web Flow

Before we start explaining and writing an application with the Spring Web Flow Framework, we want to give you a small overview of the essential modules of the complete Spring Framework stack. You should know these for writing an application based on the Spring Web Flow Framework. The three cornerstones are:

- Spring Framework
- Spring MVC
- Spring Web Flow

We will visualize the three cornerstones in the following figure:

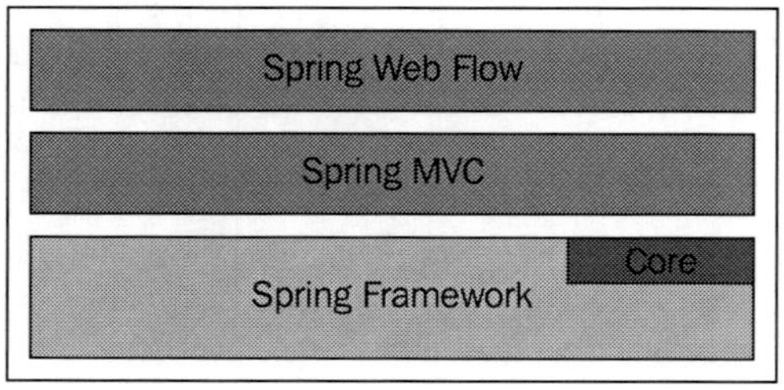

Spring Framework

The Spring Framework is the base for all other modules (frameworks) inside the Spring portfolio. It was initially developed as a dependency injection container (this principle is also known as **inversion of control**). Besides the dependency injection, the second cornerstone of the Spring Framework is **aspect-oriented programming** (**AOP**).

The current version of the Spring Framework is far more than that. It is the base for a complete stack for building enterprise Java applications.

Spring MVC

Spring **Model–View–Controller** (**MVC**) is the base for web framework from SpringSource. It provides a complete implementation of the widely known Model–View–Controller pattern.

Spring Web Flow

Spring Web Flow is the framework that is covered in this book. It is possible to use Spring Web Flow without Spring MVC, but the integration with this framework is seamless.

What is Spring Web Flow

Whenever you read about Spring Web Flow on the Internet, you will find the expression **conversational**—you can use Spring Web Flow to create conversational web applications.

But what does that expression mean? It means that a user can interact with the application in a quite natural way. The application asks for information. After you have entered it, you can send it back to the application, which processes the data. In most cases, the application asks for more information.

For example, take an application with a wizard-like interface. Usually, wizard-like applications consist of multiple pages that are displayed one after the other. You can enter some information and then proceed to the next page, where you can enter additional information. If you think you've made mistakes, you can always go back to the previous page. Take a look at the data you have entered and correct them if they are wrong. Although you can go back any time you like, you can use the application only in the way the authors intended it to be used. You are working in a predefined *flow* with a specific goal, such as ordering a book or creating a new user account.

Although you can definitely write applications with this behavior using different technologies (even with pure Spring MVC), Spring Web Flow makes it very easy to create flows. Flows created by Spring Web Flow are not only decoupled from the applications logic, but are also re-usable in different applications. A **flow** in Spring Web Flow is a sequence of steps, that is, with *states* and *transitions* between them. There are also *actions* that can be executed on various points, for example, when the flow starts or a web page is rendered.

We have already mentioned that each flow exists for the purpose of reaching a defined goal. This means that you can use Spring Web Flow for all kinds of web applications with a predefined outcome such as user registration or login forms.

> **Use the latest version of Spring Web Flow 2**
>
> We started writing this book with an early version of Spring Web Flow. While writing, some minor versions of Spring Web Flow were released (for example: 2.0.3, 2.0.4, and 2.0.5). It is highly recommended to use the latest available version of the framework. To see the fixes, you can look into the bug tracker for the Spring projects available at `http://jira.springsource.org`.

The elements of Spring Web Flow: flow, view, and conversation

Around the Spring Web Flow Framework there are three important words, which have to be defined:

- Flow
- View
- Conversation

Flow

A flow is a self-contained business process representing a real-world use case. Typically, a flow consists of some views, and the data is stored inside a conversation. From a more technical viewpoint, a flow encapsulates a re-usable sequence of steps that can be executed in different contexts.

First, the flow describes the order and the requirements when the views are shown. Additionally, actions can be executed. Between the executions of a flow, a conversation holds the data of the user.

View

A **view** in Spring Web Flow is a single page that visualizes information.

Conversation

In traditional web applications, you have the scopes: `request`, `session`, and `application`. Many use cases in a web application consist of more than one page. Therefore, you need more than the `request` instance to store the data. A `request` is often not enough, and a `session` is too much. For this case, Spring Web Flow introduces the concept of a **conversation**.

For better understanding, we will visualize the conjunction of these three important concepts in the following figure:

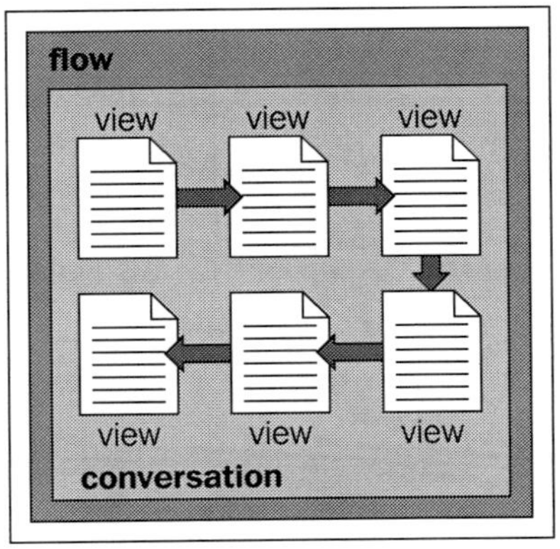

The Spring Web Flow elements: an example

Now that we have described the three cornerstones—flow, view, and conversation, we want to explain the three elements and their relationship in a small example.

Imagine we have a portal where the user has to log in to see the content of the portal. We have the following three pages: `login.xhtml`, `portal.xhtml`, and `error.xhtml`. The `login.xhtml` is the page that is shown if the user is not logged into the portal. If the user is successfully logged in, the `portal.xhtml` page is shown. If the login fails, the `error.xhtml` page is shown. The following figure shows an example page flow:

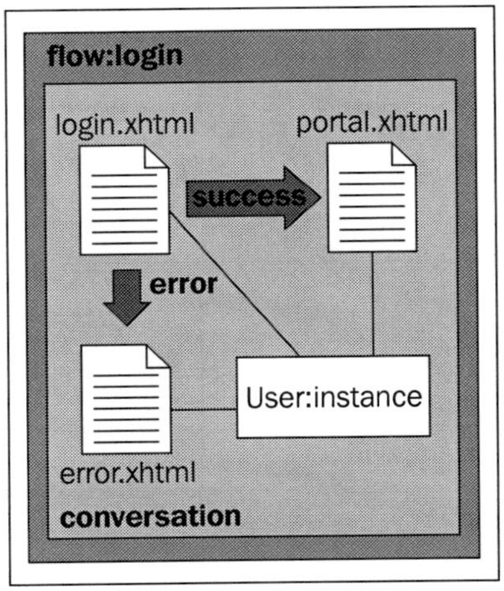

The flow describes both the circumstances: a successful login and an unsuccessful login. Moreover, the transitions between the pages are described. The single pages (`login.xhtml`, `portal.xhtml`, and `error.xhtml`) are the views inside the flow. The conversation holds the data until a flow is executed. In the given example, the conversation stores the instance of an example class, `User`.

The new major release: Spring Web Flow 2.0

In mid-2008, Version 2.0, the new major version of Spring Web Flow was released. The following list shows a few main features of the new version:

- A domain-specific language for defining re-usable controller modules called flows
- An advanced controller engine for managing conversational states
- First-class support for using Ajax to construct rich user interfaces
- First-class support for using JavaServer Faces with Spring

If you download the Spring Web Flow 2.0 distribution (`http://www.springframework.org/download`), you will get the following four modules:

- Spring Web Flow
- Spring Faces
- Spring JavaScript
- Spring Binding

The following figure visualizes the structure for the 2.0.3 distribution of Spring Web Flow:

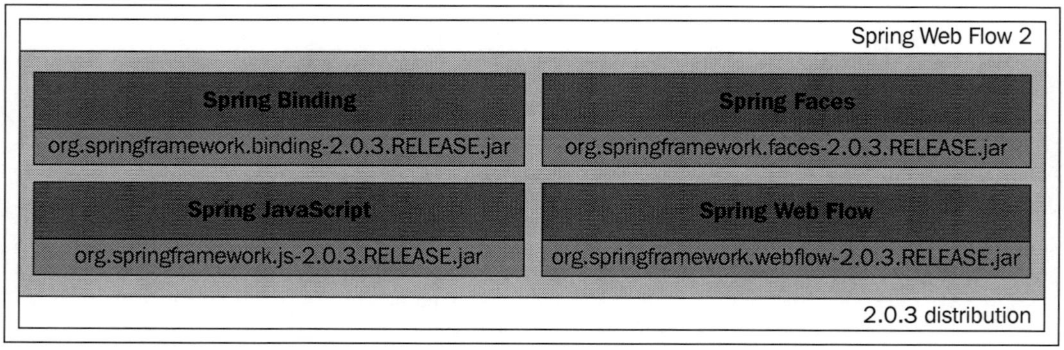

Spring Web Flow

Spring Web Flow is a framework in itself. It manages the handling of the flow with its conversation and views.

Spring Faces

Spring Faces is the module that connects Spring Web Flow with the **JavaServer Faces** (**JSF**) technology.

Spring JavaScript

Spring JavaScript is an encapsulation to add functionality on the client side to **HyperText Markup Language** (**HTML**) elements, for example, to add **Asynchronous JavaScript and Extensible Markup Language** (**AJAX**) features to the elements.

Spring Binding

Spring Binding is a library that helps you to bind data to the elements. This library is used internally by Spring Web Flow.

Introduction to a new version

To those readers who are familiar with the older version of Spring Web Flow, we want to give a small overview on what has really changed from Version 1.

The following concepts were added to the mentioned release of the Spring Web Flow Framework:

- Automatic model binding
- Support for a new expression language
- Flash scope is now a real Flash scope
- Spring Faces
- Flow managed persistence
- External redirects

A complete list of features is shown in Chapter 12 of the reference documentation of Spring Web Flow 2. This documentation is available online at `http://static.springframework.org/spring-webflow/docs/2.0.x/reference/html/ch12.html`.

Automatic model binding

In Version 1 of Spring Web Flow, you had to manually do the binding for your model classes. For this version, the class `FormAction` (package `org.springframework.webflow.action`) exists. The most notable methods are `setupForm` and `bindAndValidate` (see the following example).

```
<view-state id="display" view="sampleView">
        <render-actions>
            <action bean="formAction" method="setupForm"/>
        </render-actions>
        <transition on="submit" to="show">
            <action bean="formAction" method="bindAndValidate"/>
        </transition>
</view-state>
```

The new release of Spring Web Flow now supports an automatic `model` binding through the usage of the `model` attribute inside the `view-state`.

Support for a new expression language

In Spring Web Flow 1, only **Object-Graph Navigation Language** (**OGNL**) is supported as an **Expression Language** (**EL**) within the flow definition files. Now support for the Unified EL is added. OGNL, of course, is still supported.

Flash scope is now a real flash scope

In Version 1 of Web Flow, the `flash` scope lived across the current request and into the next request. This is similar to the `view` scope inside the Version 2 of Spring Web Flow. In Web Flow 2, the `flash` scope is cleared after every view render. Now the `flash` scope is consistent with other web frameworks.

Spring Faces

The integration of `JavaServerFaces` is significantly improved with Ajax-enabled, custom **JavaServer Faces (JSF)** `UICommand` components, and an event-driven, action-binding approach. The name of the module is Spring Faces.

Flow managed persistence

Inside a web application, you have to deal with data: you have to read them from a database and store them to a database. Spring Web Flow offers the concept of **flow managed persistence**. With this feature, a flow can create, commit, and close an object persistence context for you. The framework integrates with both the object persistence technologies: Hibernate and **Java Persistence API (JPA)**. (For more information on Hibernate Framework, visit `http://www.hibernate.org`; for more information on JPA read the Java Persistence FAQ from Sun available at `http://java.sun.com/javaee/overview/faq/persistence.jsp`.)

External redirects

The external redirects inside Spring Web Flow 1 were always relative to the context. Now in Spring Web Flow 2, if the redirect begins with a slash, it is considered to be *servlet relative*, rather than context relative. URLs without a leading slash are still considered *context relative*.

Summary

This chapter covers a brief overview of the new major release of Spring Web Flow. We mentioned the use of a bug-tracking application for the examples, which we will show in the following chapters.

In this chapter, we also explained the three frameworks: Spring, Spring MVC, and Spring Web Flow. The three cornerstones of Spring Web Flow—flow, view, and conversation—were also explained using practical examples. For the example, we assumed a login to a portal. Last, but not the least, we showed you the new features that are offered by Spring Web Flow 2. In the following chapter, we will explain how to install Spring Web Flow 2 and show an example that you can run on your local machine. With this example, you will get an idea of how to build your own web application using Spring Web Flow 2.

2

Setup for Spring Web Flow 2

Now that we have covered the basics, it is time to actually write the first real application with Spring Web Flow. The typical example most books cover is the (in)famous *Hello World* example. We thought you would like something more sophisticated, so we decided to show you how you can design and implement a very simple login form. But first, we will explain how to install the Spring Web Flow 2 distribution on your computer. We will also show you which tools exist for you as a developer, and how you can integrate Spring Web Flow with your **Integrated Development Environment** (**IDE**). This will make it much easier to actually implement the example application.

There are certain prerequisites for the installation of a Spring Web Flow application, which we want to show you in this chapter as well. When you write your own application, you just have to take a look at this chapter and you will find all the information you need to start coding.

Installation of Spring Web Flow 2

Spring Web Flow 2 is available as a free download on the Spring project web site at `http://www.springsource.com/download/community?project=Spring Web Flow`. Additionally, as Spring Web Flow is an open source project, you can download the most up-to-date sources from the projects source code repository. While the core Spring project uses **CVS** (**Concurrent Versions System**) to manage the source code, Spring Web Flow uses Subversion (see `http://subversion.tigris.org` for more information on Subversion). Downloading the sources gives you an inside look at how Spring Web Flow really works, and even permits you to contribute to the project. If you are interested in using the source, you can find information on how to access the repository at `http://sourceforge.net/svn/?group_id=73357`. As you can see a little later in this chapter, the source code is also included in the binary distribution, in case you do not need the latest sources.

There are two variants of the Spring Web Flow distribution. You can either download it with all of the dependencies (`spring-webflow-2.0.5.RELEASE-with-dependencies`), or without any dependencies (`spring-webflow-2.0.x.RELEASE`). We'll explain the differences between the two distributions while looking at the folder layout of the extracted archive.

Inside the distribution

In this chapter, we will give you an overview of the binary distribution of Spring Web Flow. After you've downloaded the files from the location mentioned in the previous section, you can use your favorite ZIP tool to unzip the distribution file. The folder layout looks like the one shown in the following screenshot in both the distributions:

In the `dist` folder, you can find the actual distribution of Spring Web Flow. It includes the JAR files that you can use in your applications. Using these libraries, you can have access to all the features that Spring Web Flow offers developers.

The `docs` folder includes documentation of the project. In this folder, you can find a reference guide in both HTML and **Portable Document File** (**PDF**) formats that covers the most important topics of Spring Web Flow.

The sources of Spring Web Flow and all related projects (such as requirements for building web applications and even the sources of the reference guide), as well as example applications are included in the `projects` folder.

The `src` folder provides you with the JAR files, which include the source code. You can use these, for example, in Eclipse to attach the source code.

> You can use the *F3* key on your keyboard on Spring Web Flow classes to jump into the source code. You will find this very useful when debugging applications.

In the distribution with dependencies, you can find an additional folder called `ivy-cache` in the `projects` folder:

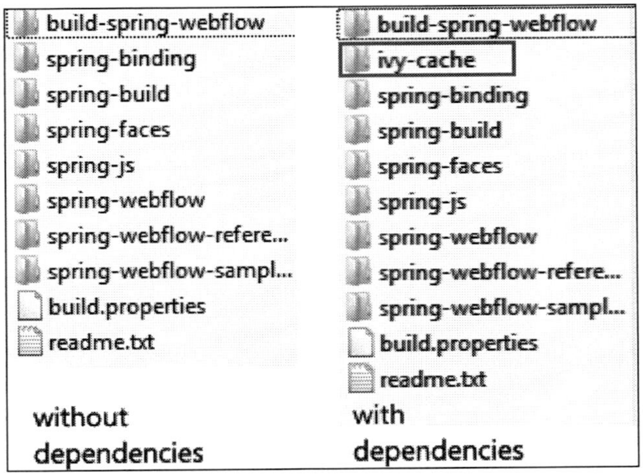

This folder makes it easier to build examples of Spring Web Flow (explained later in this chapter) wherein proxy servers or firewalls prohibit protocols other than say HTTP or **HyperText Transfer Protocol Secure** (**HTTPS**). As explained a little later, for each example in the distribution, the Amazon S3 protocol is used for the download. As you already have the dependencies of the examples, Ant (or its optional dependency manager, Ivy) doesn't have to download them from the Internet again.

> As mentioned above, the distribution includes the reference documentation written by the Spring Web Flow developers. You can find additional information on the web site of the project (`http://www.springframework.org/webflow`). It explains the purpose of Spring Web Flow, and points to blog entries of the project's developers. Sadly, there is not much information available on the Internet. If you find a bug in Spring Web Flow, you can use the project's bug-tracking system at `http://jira.springframework.org/browse/SWF`. If you need help with a specific problem in your application, you can ask the Web Flow developers and other users using the project's forum, which you can access using the following URL: `http://forum.springsource.org/forumdisplay.php?f=36`.

The examples inside the distribution

If you download the distribution of the Spring Web Flow Framework, it includes the source code for five example projects. All examples implement the same web application. The differences between the sample applications would be in the technical fundaments used in them. The example application is a web application that simulates the booking of a hotel. The name of the demo hotel-booking application is **Spring Travel**. The application is available for online browsing at `http://richweb.springframework.org/swf-booking-faces/spring/intro`. The following screenshot shows the sample screen of the Spring Faces reference application.

After the extraction of the latest distribution of Spring Web Flow 2, you should see a `projects` folder. Inside this folder, you will find a root example folder, `spring-webflow-samples`. The layout of this folder should appear as shown in the following screenshot:

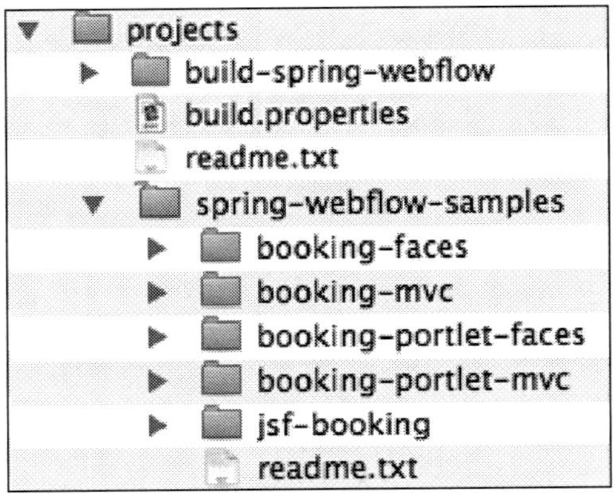

As mentioned earlier, each of the five example applications (each folder inside the `spring-webflow-samples` folder is an application) implements the same web application, **Spring Travel**. The technology base used is described in the following table:

Name of the folder	Description of the technical base used in the example
`booking-faces`	The Spring Travel application using the following technologies: Spring MVC, Spring Web Flow, Spring Faces, and Spring Security working together with **JavaServer Faces** (**JSF**) and Facelets
`booking-mvc`	The Spring Travel application using the following technologies: Spring MVC, Spring JavaScript, Spring Web Flow, and Spring Security working together with **JavaServer Pages** (**JSP**) and Tiles
`booking-portlet-faces`	The Spring Travel application based on `booking-faces` for a Portlet environment
`booking-portlet-mvc`	The Spring Travel application based on `booking-mvc` for a Portlet environment
`jsf-booking`	The example `jsf-booking` is to show you the solution for the integration of JSF and Spring with the Spring Faces module; the example uses the *JSF-centric* approach for the integration; the artifacts from JSF such as JSF controller model, JSF managed beans, and JSF navigation rules are used; Spring is used for the realization of the service layer; this example is only for comparison between a normal JSF application and a JSF application with Spring Faces and Spring Web Flow 2

Building the examples from the source code

The examples inside the distribution are provided as source files. This section explains how to build those examples.

The requirements to build the examples are:

- Apache Ant Version 1.7 or higher (if you need more information about Apache Ant, or you want to download the latest release, visit the web page of Apache Ant at `http://ant.apache.org`)
- Java SDK 5 or higher

If your local machine fulfills these requirements, the build is very simple. We need to set an environment variable for Ant. Go to the **Control Panel**, click on the **System** to open the **System Properties**. Select the **Advanced** tab and click on the **Environment Variables** which will open the **Environment Variables** window. Click on **New** to create a new environment variable. Set the **Variable name** to **ANT_HOME** and the **Variable value** to the folder path pointing to your Ant root folder. Similarly, modify the **PATH** environment variable to include the **%ANT_HOME%\bin** folder. Now, go to the `projects/build-spring-webflow` folder from the command line and execute the `ant` command. Now, the projects start to build. If you have downloaded the distribution without dependencies, the essential libraries are downloaded with the dependency manager, Apache Ivy, which is included in the distribution. In these projects, the Amazon S3 protocol is used for the download. If you are having problems with the download of the dependencies, it could be a proxy problem. You can change the configuration in the `projects/spring-build/lib/ivy/jets3t.properties` file. If you need more information about the configuration, please read the document at `http://jets3t.s3.amazonaws.com/toolkit/configuration.html#jets3t`.

> **The examples are provided as binary file too**
>
> In case you have problems in building the examples, or that you do not want to build it on your own, the examples have also been provided as binary files. For that, you can download the examples as WAR archive from `http://www.springsource.org/webflow-samples`. On that page, all the examples are provided, except the `jsf-booking` example application.

After a successful build, the binaries of the samples are located inside the `target` folder of each example application. The `artifacts` subdirectory contains the WAR file of the application. The `war-expanded` subfolder contains the complete web application in a folder variant.

The following figure shows the folder layout of the example application, `booking-faces`. The other examples look similar to this:

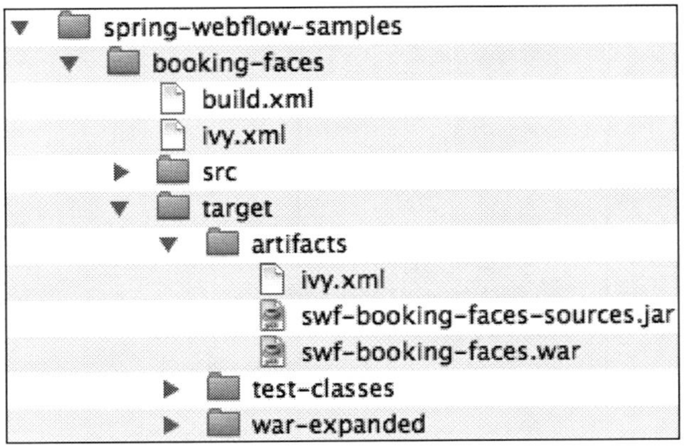

Installing the examples on your local machine

After you have the binaries, the installation is as simple as with the other applications on your preferred application server. In our case, we have used the latest version of Apache Tomcat, which you can download from `http://tomcat.apache.org`. For Apache Tomcat, you just have to drop the WAR file, and build into the `webapps` folder of the installation. Now, you can access the web application on your local machine.

> If you are new to Spring Web Flow 2, installing an example (such as `booking-faces`) on your local machine is highly recommended. With these examples, you can include your own steps by changing some files in the examples. It helps you get a quick overview of the functionality of Spring Web Flow 2.

> **Importing projects to Eclipse**
>
> In Eclipse, you can import an existing project by clicking on **File | Import...**. This should display the **Import** window. Click on **Existing Projects into Workspace** under **General** folder. Click on **Next**, enter the folder path of the target project in the **Select root directory** field and click on **Finish**.

Support for developers

To help developers build web applications using Spring Web Flow, we want to introduce these tools: build systems and IDEs. We will show you more about the Ant and the Maven build systems. We will also see how we can add support for the Spring Framework in the Eclipse IDE and include Spring NetBeans modules in the NetBeans IDE.

Build systems

Build systems are not necessary for building web applications with Spring Web Flow, but they greatly assist a developer by resolving dependencies between packages and automating the build process. In this chapter, we will show you how to build your projects with Apache Ant and Apache Maven.

Ant

Ant is a powerful and very flexible build tool. You can write **Extensible Markup Language** (**XML**) files, which tell Ant how to build your application, where to find your dependencies, and where to copy the compiled files. Often, you won't find the need to download Ant, as it is already built-in into popular IDEs such as Eclipse and NetBeans. Ant does not provide you with an automatic dependency resolving mechanism. So you will have to manually download all the libraries your application needs. Alternatively, you can use a third-party dependency resolving system such as Apache Ivy, which we will describe later in this chapter. When you have obtained a copy of Ant, you can write a `build.xml` file as shown in the following code. This file can be used to build the example application we will create later in this chapter:

```
<?xml version="1.0" encoding="UTF-8"?>
<project name="login.flow" default="compile">
   <description>
      login.flow
   </description>
   <property file="loginflow.properties"/>

   <path id="classpath">
      <fileset dir="lib/">
         <include name="*.jar" />
      </fileset>
   </path>

   <target name="init">
      <mkdir dir="${build}" />
      <mkdir dir="${build}/WEB-INF/classes" />
```

```
    </target>

    <target name="assemble-webapp" depends="init">
       <copy todir="${build}" overwrite="y">
          <fileset dir="${webapp-src}">
             <include name="**/*/" />
          </fileset>
       </copy>
    </target>

    <target name="compile" depends="assemble-webapp">
       <javac srcdir="${src}" destdir="${build}/WEB-INF/classes">
          <classpath refid="classpath" />
       </javac>

       <echo>Copying resources</echo>

       <copy todir="${build}/WEB-INF/classes" overwrite="y">
          <fileset dir="${resources}">
             <include name="**/*/" />
          </fileset>
       </copy>

       <echo>Copying libs</echo>

       <copy todir="${build}/WEB-INF/lib" overwrite="y">
          <fileset dir="lib/">
             <include name="*.jar" />
          </fileset>
       </copy>
    </target>
</project>
```

First of all, we will specify that we have defined a few required folders in an external PROPERTIES file. The `loginflow.properties`, stored in your project's root folder, looks like this:

```
src = src/main/java
webapp-src = src/main/webapp
resources = src/main/resources
build = target/chapter02
```

These define the folders where your source code lies, where your libraries are located, and where to copy the compiled files and your resources. You do not have to declare them in a PROPERTIES file, but it makes re-using easier. Otherwise, you will have to write the folder names everywhere. This would make the build script hard to maintain if the folder layout changes.

In the `init` target, we create the folders for the finished web application. The next is the `assemble-webapp` target, which depends on the `init` target. This means that if you execute the `assemble-webapp` target, the `init` target gets executed as well. This target will copy all the files belonging to your web application (such as the flow definition file and your JSP files) to the output folder.

If you want to build your application, you will have to execute the compile target. It will initialize the output folder, copy everything your application needs to it, compile your Java source code, and copy the compiled files, along with the dependent libraries.

If you want to use Apache Ivy for automatic dependency resolution, first, you have to download the distribution from `http://ant.apache.org/ivy`. While writing this book, Version 2.0.0 Release Candidate 1 was the most up-to-date version of Ivy. Unpack the ZIP file and put the `ivy-2.0.0-rc1.jar` file in your `%ANT_HOME%\lib` folder. If you are using the Eclipse IDE, Ant is already built into the IDE. You can add the JAR file to its **classpath** by right-clicking on the task you want to execute and choosing **Run As | Ant Build...**

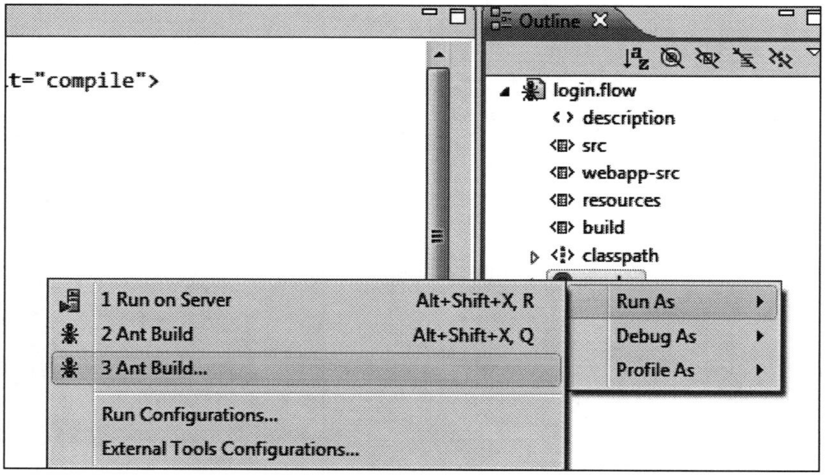

In the appearing dialog, you can add the JAR file on the **Classpath** tab, either by clicking on **Add JARs...** and selecting a file from your workspace, or by selecting **Add External JARs...**, and looking for the file in your file system.

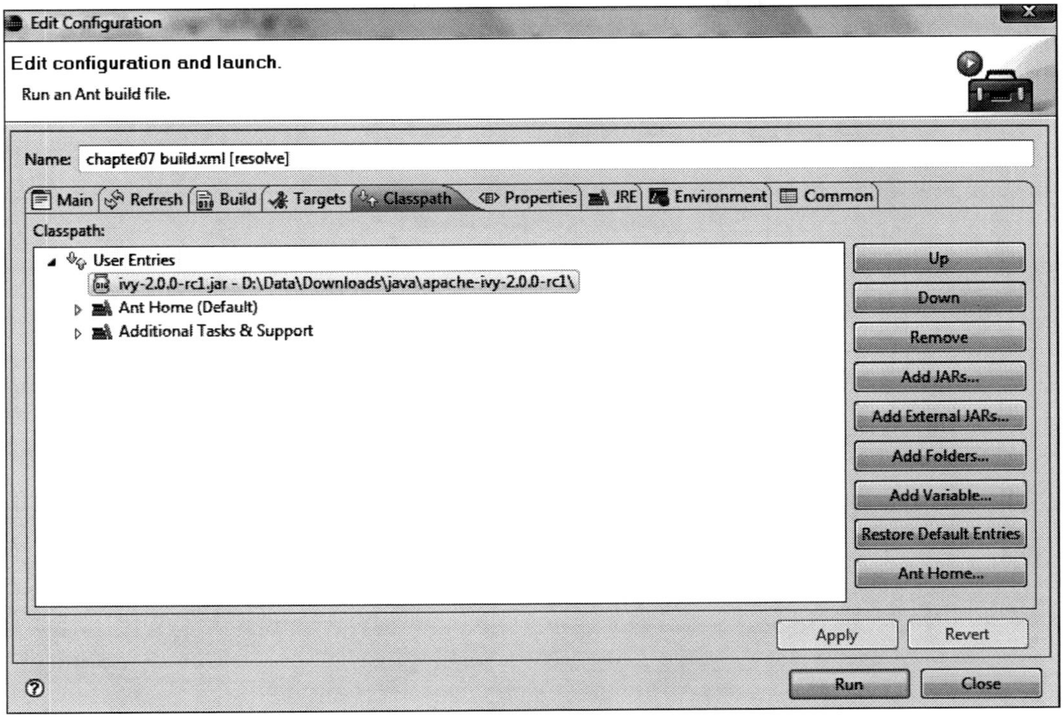

Afterwards, you just have to tell Ant to load the required libraries automatically by modifying your build script. We have highlighted the important changes (to be made in the XML file) in the following source code:

```
<project
   xmlns:ivy="antlib:org.apache.ivy.ant"
   name="login.flow"
   default="compile">

   ...

   <target name="resolve"
    description="--> retrieve dependencies with ivy">
      <ivy:retrieve />
   </target>

...
</project>
```

The last step, before we can actually build the project, involves specifying which libraries you want Ivy to download automatically. Therefore, we will now have to compose an `ivy.xml` file, stored in your project's root folder, which looks like this:

```
<ivy-module version="2.0">
   <info organisation="com.webflow2book" module="login.flow"/>

   <dependencies>
      <dependency org="org.springframework.webflow"
         name="org.springframework.binding" rev="2.0.5.RELEASE" />
      <dependency org="org.springframework.webflow"
         name="org.springframework.js" rev="2.0.5.RELEASE" />
      <dependency org="org.springframework.webflow"
         name="org.springframework.webflow" rev="2.0.5.RELEASE" />
   </dependencies>

   ...

</ivy-module>
```

To keep the example simple, we only showed the Spring Web Flow entries of the file we just mentioned. In order to be able to build your whole project with Apache Ivy, you will have to add all other required libraries to the file. The `org` attribute corresponds to the `groupId` tag from Maven, as does the `name` attribute with the `artifactId` tag. The `rev` attribute matches the `version` tag in your `pom.xml`.

Maven

Maven is a popular application build system published by the Apache Software Foundation. You can get a binary distribution and plenty of information from the project's web site at `http://maven.apache.org`. After you have downloaded and unpacked the binary distribution, you have to set the **M2_HOME** environment variable to point to the folder where you unpacked the files. Additionally, we recommend adding the folder **%M2_HOME%\bin** (on Microsoft® Windows system) or **$M2_HOME/bin** (on Unix or Linux systems) to your `PATH` variable.

Maven has a configuration file called `settings.xml`, which lies in the `M2_HOME\conf` folder. Usually, you do not edit this file, unless you want to define proxy settings (for example, when you are in a corporate network where you have to specify a proxy server to access the Internet), or want to add additional package repositories.

There are several plug-ins for the most popular IDEs around, which make working with Maven a lot easier than just using the command line. If you do not want to use a plug-in, you have to at least know that Maven requires your projects to have a specific folder layout. The default folder layout looks like this:

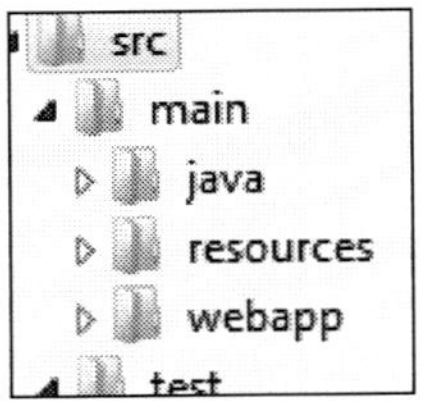

The root folder, directly below your projects folder, is the `src` folder. In the `main` folder, you have all your source files (`src/main/java`), additional configuration files, and other resources you need (`src/main/resources`), and all JSP and other files you need for your web application (`src/main/webapp`). The `test` folder can have the same layout, but is used for all your test cases. Please see the project's website for more information on the folder layout.

To actually build a project with Maven, you need a configuration file for your project. This file is always saved as `pom.xml`, and lies in the root folder of your project. The `pom.xml` for our example in this chapter is too long to be included in this book. Nevertheless, we want to show you the basic layout. You can get the complete file from the code bundle uploaded on `http://www.packtpub.com/files/code/5425_Code.zip`.

```
<project xmlns="http://maven.apache.org/POM/4.0.0" xmlns:xsi="http://
www.w3.org/2001/XMLSchema-instance"
  xsi:schemaLocation="http://maven.apache.org/POM/4.0.0 http://maven.
apache.org/maven-v4_0_0.xsd">
  <modelVersion>4.0.0</modelVersion>
  <groupId>com.webflow2book</groupId>
  <artifactId>chapter02</artifactId>
  <packaging>war</packaging>
  <version>0.0.1-SNAPSHOT</version>
  <name>chapter02 Maven Webapp</name>
  <url>http://maven.apache.org</url>
```

This is a standard file header where you can define the name and version of your project. Further, you can also specify how your project is supposed to be packaged. As we wanted to build a web application, we used the `war` option. Next, we can define all the dependencies our project has to the external libraries:

```
<dependencies>
    <dependency>
       <groupId>org.springframework.webflow</groupId>
       <artifactId>org.springframework.binding</artifactId>
       <version>2.0.5.RELEASE</version>
    </dependency>
    <dependency>
```

```
            <groupId>org.springframework.webflow</groupId>
            <artifactId>org.springframework.js</artifactId>
            <version>2.0.5.RELEASE</version>
        </dependency>
        <dependency>
            <groupId>org.springframework.webflow</groupId>
            <artifactId>org.springframework.webflow</artifactId>
            <version>2.0.5.RELEASE</version>
        </dependency>
    ...
    </dependencies>
```

As you can see, defining a dependency is pretty straightforward. If you are using an IDE plug-in, the IDE can do most of this for you.

To build the application, you can either use an IDE or open a command-line window and type commands that trigger the build. To build our example, we can enter the `projects` folder and type:

```
mvn clean compile war:exploded
```

This cleans up the `target` folder, compiles the source files, and compiles all necessary files for our web application in the `target` folder. If you use Tomcat, you can point your `context docBase` to the `target` folder. The application will be automatically deployed on the startup of Tomcat, and you can test your application.

IDE

There are several very good IDEs available for Java developers. For this book, we choose to explain two of the most popular ones: Eclipse and NetBeans.

Eclipse and Spring IDE

If your favorite IDE is Eclipse, you can use Spring IDE for adding support for the Spring Framework in general and, of course, for Spring Web Flow. Spring IDE is an open source project. You can get more information about the project, including a description of its features, on `http://springide.org`. Spring IDE uses the standard Eclipse update site mechanism to distribute the releases. In our examples, the IDE used is Eclipse, Ganymede (3.4). We will show you how to install the Spring IDE step-by-step:

1. First of all, you have to choose the **Software Updates...** entry from the **Help** menu.

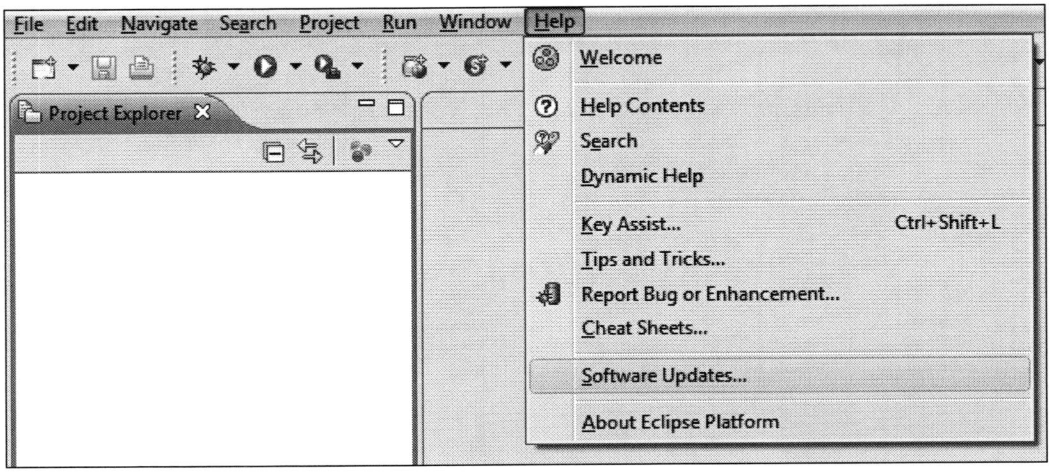

2. In the **Software Updates and Add-ons** dialog, choose the **Available Software** tab and click on the **Add Site...** button.

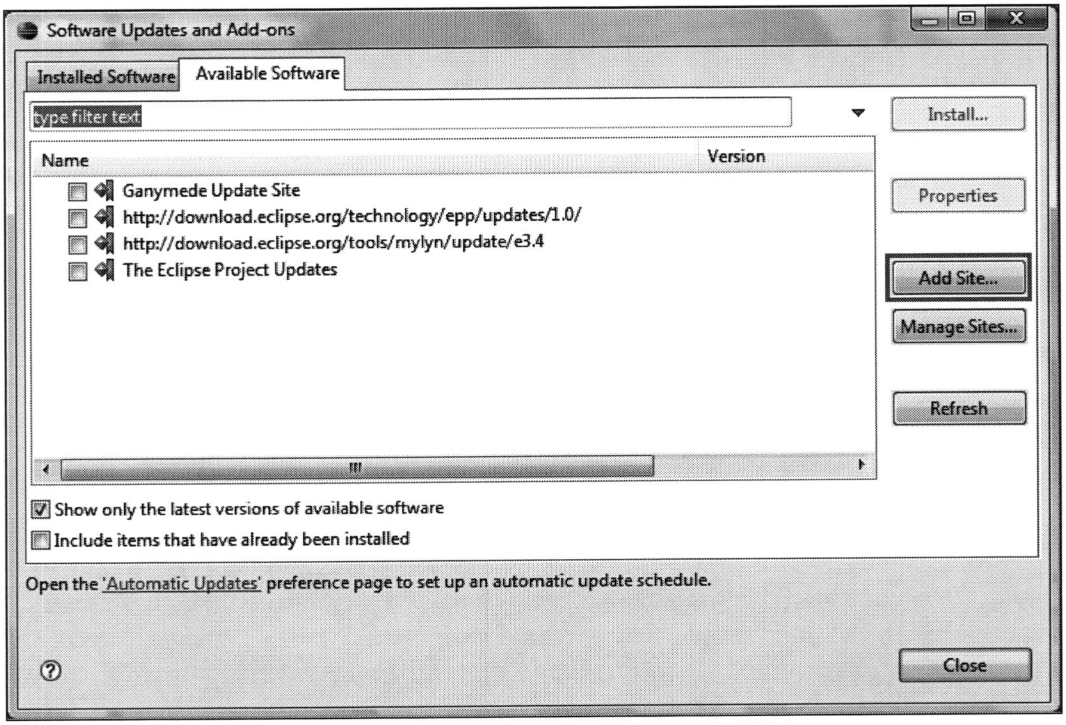

3. Enter the URL of the update site (**http://springide.org/updatesite**) in the **Add Site** dialog and click **OK**. The dialog closes, and you will see the **Software Updates and Add-ons** dialog again, this time with the new update site added. (This site is called **Spring IDE Update Site**.)
4. Make sure you check at least those checkboxes in front of the **required** update (**Spring IDE Core**) and the Web Flow support (**Spring IDE Web Flow Extension**), as shown in the following screenshot. Feel free to choose more features from the list.

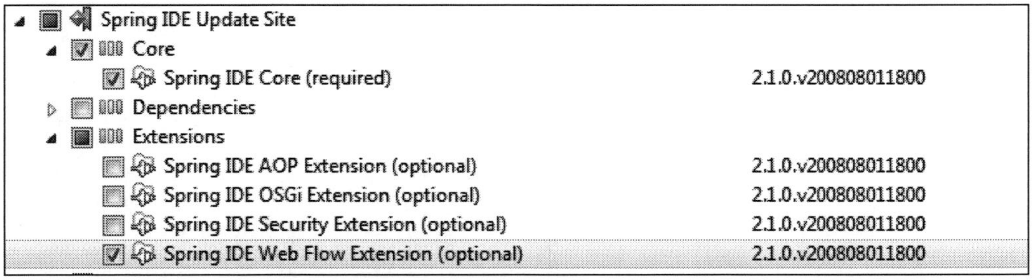

5. Click on the **Install...** button. Eclipse will start to resolve any dependencies on the Spring IDE packages you have chosen. You will be prompted again to confirm your choice, and you will have to accept the license text of the Spring IDE project. When you click the **Finish** button, Eclipse will download and install all the packages you have chosen.
6. Eclipse will prompt you afterwards as to whether you want to restart the IDE to apply the changes. We recommend choosing the **Yes** option. Eclipse will restart and you will be ready to use the features the Spring IDE add-on provides.

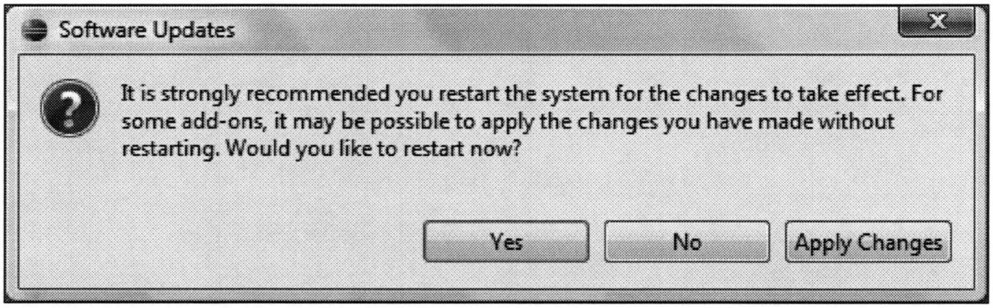

In case you cannot use the update site, or you want to use an older version of the plug-in, you can always use the archived update site. You just have to download the release you want to use directly from the web site `http://springide.org/updatesite`. Please note that you have to append the release you want to download to this URL. For example, the current release of Spring IDE can be downloaded by using the URL: `http://springide.org/updatesite/spring-ide_updatesite_2.2.1_v200811281800.zip`. Then you tell Eclipse to use this repository instead of the standard update site. You can do this by choosing the **Archive...** button in the **Add Site** dialog and selecting the downloaded archive file:

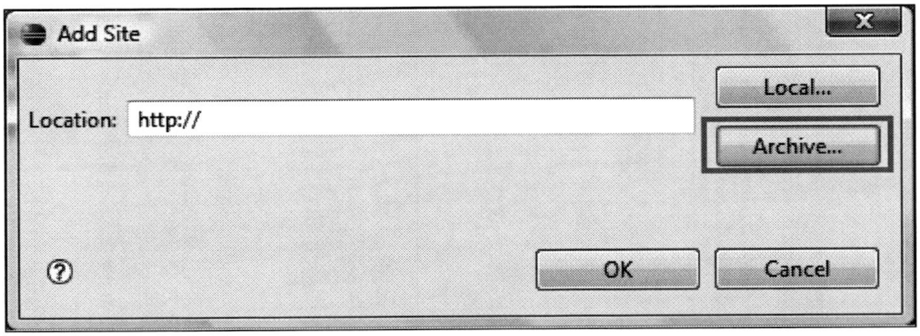

In order to test your new add-on, you can try to open up a new Spring project. If the plug-in is installed successfully, you should have a new entry in the **New Project** wizard, regardless of the type of installation you've chosen, from the update site or the archived version:

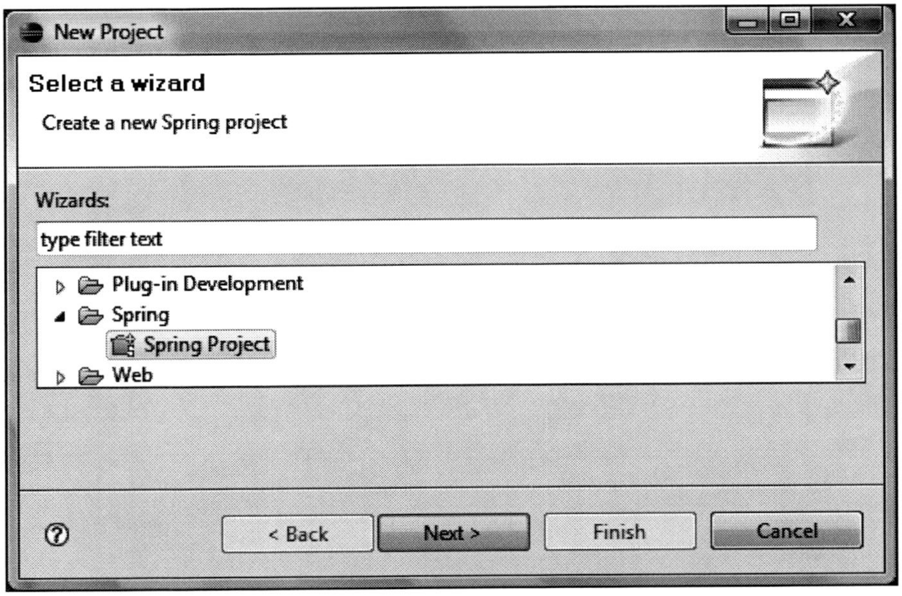

The project will already have the so-called *Spring Nature* enabled, which enables all the features of Spring IDE for the selected project. You can always add the *Spring Nature* to any project by right-clicking on the project name in the **Project Explorer** and selecting the **Spring Tools | Add Spring Project Nature** option in the pop-up menu. After you've added the Spring Nature to your project, you will have a new **Spring** entry in the projects' properties dialog. There are two sub-elements of the Spring entry:

1. **Beans Support**: You can add your Spring configuration files here. Later, they will be managed automatically by Spring IDE. For our example application, we would add the `firstexample-servlet.xml` file (which includes all our bean definitions) to this dialog:

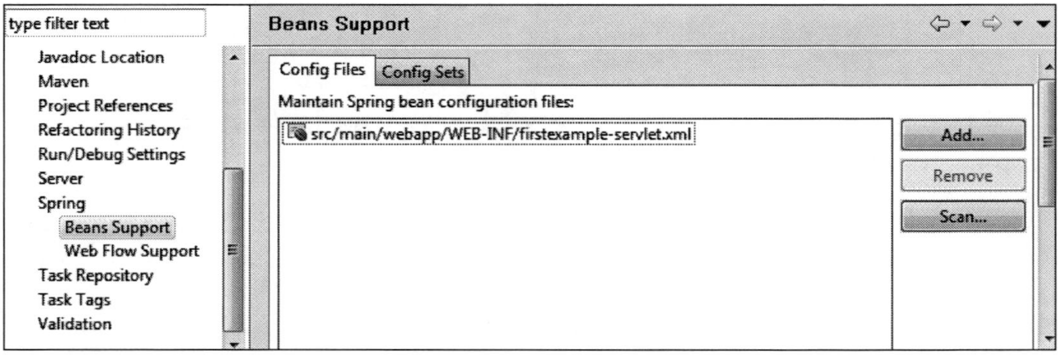

2. **Web Flow Support**: Here you can add your flow definition files. As with the Spring configuration files, your flow definition files will be automatically managed by Spring IDE afterwards:

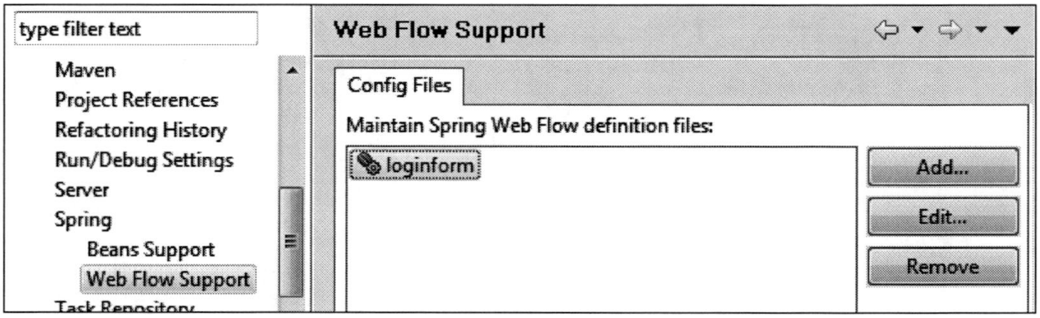

You get plenty of convenient features that make it much easier to develop your applications if you let Spring IDE handle your configuration files: for example, your references to beans are checked automatically. If you specify a reference to a bean which does not exist, Eclipse will warn you to check your configuration. Additionally, you will get auto-completion support for the Spring configuration files. For a full list of features that Spring IDE provides, please visit the project's web site under `http://springide.org`.

NetBeans

Starting with the 6.1 release of NetBeans, the application includes the Spring NetBeans module. To make sure it is present in your installation, open the **Plugins** dialog using **Tools | Plugins**. Then switch to the **Installed** tab. You should see an entry called **Spring Web MVC**.

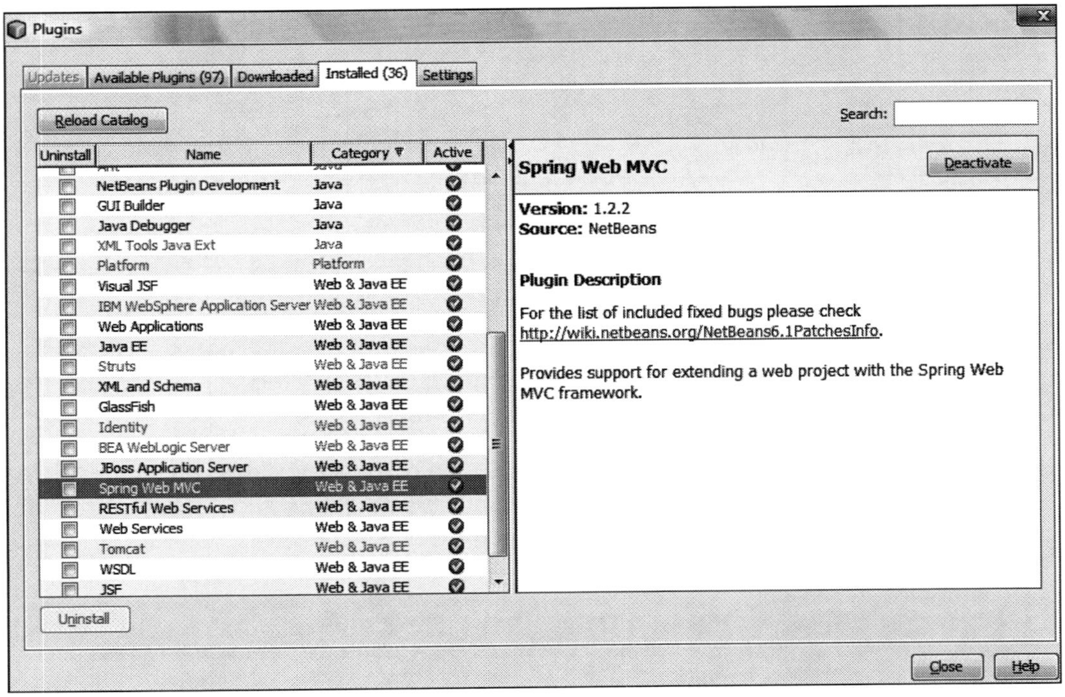

If it is not installed, it maybe because you've downloaded the Java SE version of NetBeans, which does not include any J2EE technologies; you can download the plug-in using the **Available Plugins** tab:

1. If you haven't done so already, open the Plugins dialog using **Tools | Plugins**
2. Switch to the **Available Plugins** tab and scroll down through the list until you find the entry **Spring Web MVC**. You will also need the **Java EE** module and the appropriate module for your application server. This means that you will need the **Tomcat** module if you want to use Apache Tomcat. Tick the checkboxes next to all the modules you want to install, and click on the **Install** button.

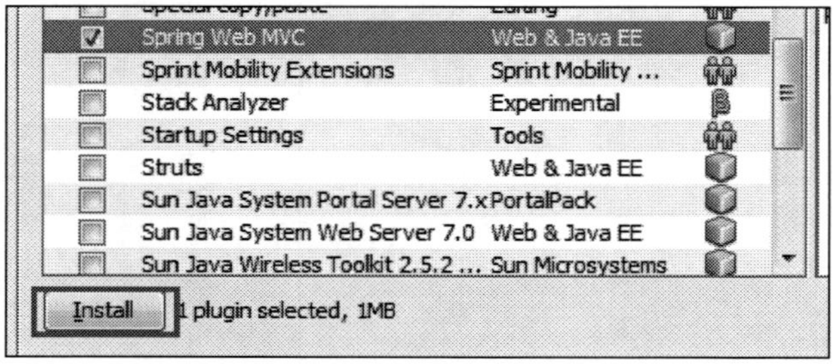

3. The **NetBeans IDE Installer** dialog opens up, which will show you the plug-ins that are going to be installed. When you click on the **Next** button, you will be presented with the license agreement.
4. When you accept them and click on the **Install** button, NetBeans will begin installing the add-ons. Afterwards you will be prompted to restart NetBeans, and we recommend you do it.

After you have successfully installed the Spring NetBeans module, you can create a new project using it. To do this, open the **New Project** wizard and click on the **Web Application** template, to be found under the **Web** category, and then click on the **Next** button.

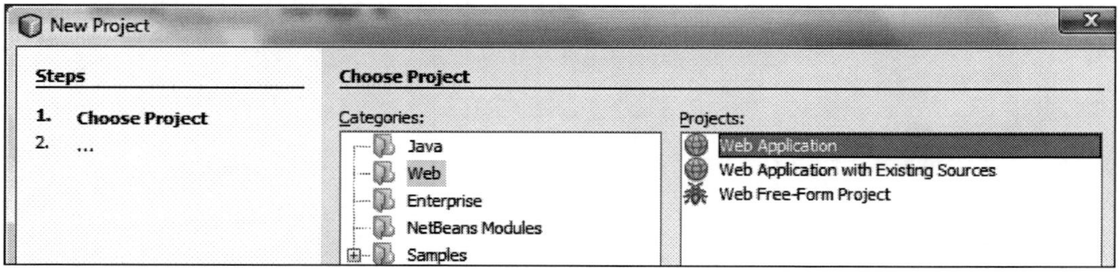

Now you have to enter a name for your project and the folder path where it should be saved. A further click on **Next**, and you will be presented with a dialog, where you can choose your application server. In case you have not already added one before, you can click on the **Add...** button to create one.

In the next dialog, you can select the frameworks you want to use in your web application. You'll find the option **Spring Web MVC 2.5** listed in the dialog. Select it and click on **Finish**.

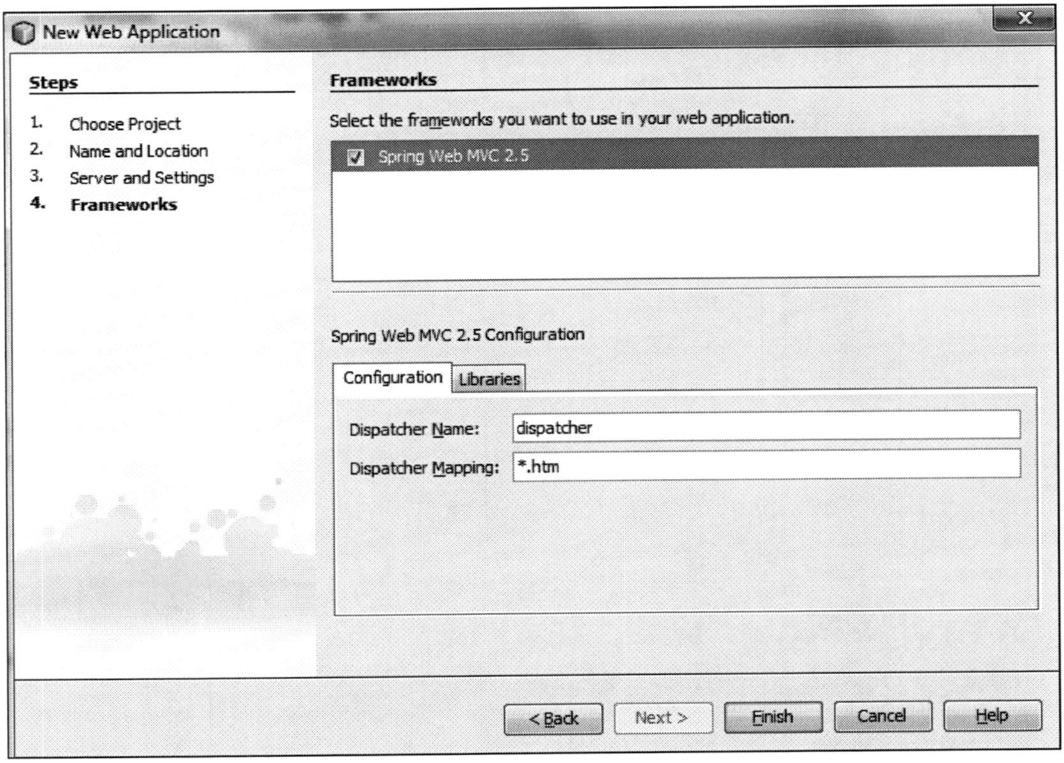

The Spring NetBeans module does not include explicit support for Spring Web Flow, but has several other very convenient features, which make the life of the developer much easier. Please see the project's web site for a full description of the various features. You can find information on the plug-in at `http://wiki.netbeans.org/SpringSupport`.

A sample for a quick start

First of all, we would like to show you how the folder layout of the finished web application looks:

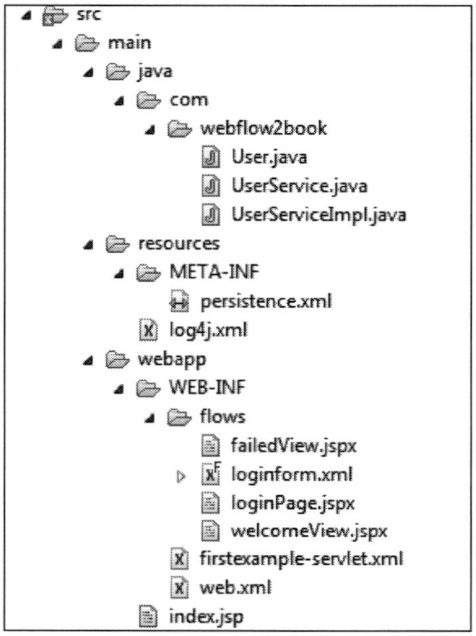

Next, we will show you how the finished web site looks and explain how the web site is created.

Overview over the example

First, let's look at the single web pages, and how to create them. When you open the web site created in this chapter in your favorite browser and enter your credentials, it appears as shown in the following screenshot:

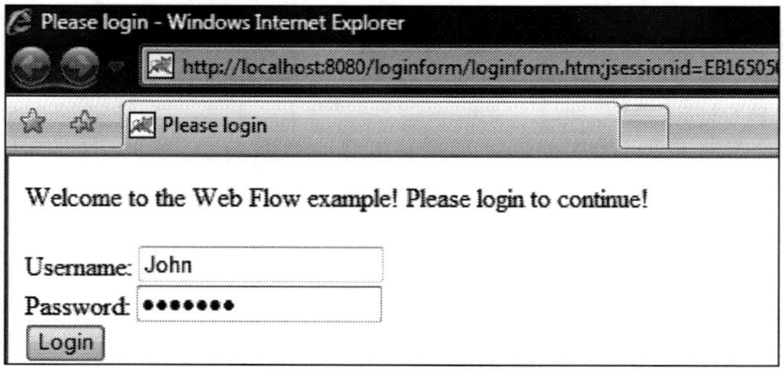

The JSP (`loginPage.jspx`) for this view has to be stored in the folder `src/main/webapp/WEB-INF/flows` and appears as shown in the following code:

```
<?xml version="1.0" encoding="ISO-8859-1" ?>
<jsp:root
   xmlns="http://www.w3.org/1999/xhtml"
   xmlns:jsp="http://java.sun.com/JSP/Page"
   xmlns:form="http://www.springframework.org/tags/form"
   version="2.1">
   <jsp:directive.page language="java"
      contentType="text/html; charset=ISO-8859-1"
      pageEncoding="ISO-8859-1" />

   <html>
      <head>
         <title>Please login</title>
      </head>
      <body>
         Welcome to the Web Flow example! Please login to continue!
         <form:form method="post" modelAttribute="user">
            Username: <form:input path="username" />
            <br />
            Password: <form:password path="password" />
            <br />
            <input type="submit"
                   name="_eventId_login"
                   value="Login" />
         </form:form>
      </body>
   </html>
</jsp:root>
```

In this file, we include a Spring `taglib`, which introduces the tags with the prefix `form`. They make it very straightforward to bind the form data to a bean. In this case, we bind the values of the `input` and the `password` fields to the `username` and the `password` properties of the `user` attribute. This is stated by the `modelAttribute` attribute in the `form` tag. There's a `submit` button on the web page, which has the `_eventId_login` value for the `name` attribute. This is a Spring Web Flow convention which says that an event will be triggered with the ID `login`.

When you enter the correct credentials, you will be forwarded to a very simple welcome page:

The source code of this JSP (`welcomeView.jspx`) is even easier than the code of the login page and has to be put alongside the `loginPage.jspx` file in the `src/main/webapp/WEB-INF/flows` folder:

```
<?xml version="1.0" encoding="ISO-8859-1" ?>
<jsp:root
   xmlns="http://www.w3.org/1999/xhtml"
   xmlns:jsp="http://java.sun.com/JSP/Page"
   version="2.1">
   <jsp:directive.page language="java"
      contentType="text/html; charset=ISO-8859-1"
      pageEncoding="ISO-8859-1" />
   <html>
      <head>
         <title>Welcome!</title>
      </head>
      <body>
         <h2>Login successful, thanks!</h2>
      </body>
   </html>
</jsp:root>
```

However, if you enter wrong credentials, the web application will notify that fact to you and will not give you access to the very exclusive parts of the web site, which is available only for valid users.

Here, we do not provide you with the source of this page. It is just a copy of the `welcomeView.jspx` file called `failedView.jspx` with different text.

Now that we have seen how to create the single JSP pages for our application, we will take a look at how the remaining parts of the web site are created.

The basics

We will start by defining our flow in the flow configuration file, `src/main/webapp/WEB-INF/flows/loginform.xml`:

```
<?xml version="1.0" encoding="UTF-8"?>
<flow xmlns="http://www.springframework.org/schema/webflow"
      xmlns:xsi="http://www.w3.org/2001/XMLSchema-instance"
      xsi:schemaLocation=
       "http://www.springframework.org/schema/webflow
        http://www.springframework.org/schema/webflow/
        spring-webflow-2.0.xsd">

   <persistence-context />

   <var name="user" class="com.webflow2book.User"/>

   <view-state id="loginPage" model="user" view="loginPage.jspx">
         <transition on="login" to="getUser" />
   </view-state>

   <action-state id="getUser">
      <evaluate
         expression="userservice.getUserByUsername(user.username)"
         result="flowScope.resultUser" />
      <transition to="checkCredentials" />
   </action-state>

   <decision-state id="checkCredentials">
      <if test="flowScope.resultUser == null" then="failedView" />
      <if test="flowScope.resultUser.password.equals(user.password)"
          then="updateUser"
          else="failedView" />
   </decision-state>

   <action-state id="updateUser">
      <evaluate expression="flowScope.resultUser
                          .setLastLogin(new java.util.Date())" />
      <transition to="welcomeView" />
   </action-state>

   <end-state id="welcomeView"
              view="welcomeView.jspx"
              commit="true" />
   <end-state id="failedView" view="failedView.jspx" />

</flow>
```

The `persistence-context` tag is used to open up a persistence context (using either the Java Persistence API or pure Hibernate) in our flow, which we can access using the special `persistenceContext` variable. In this case, we are using the Java Persistence API and in a way such that the interface behind the `persistenceContext` variable is the `EntityManager` interface. Refer to Chapter 3 for more information concerning persistent contexts.

Next, we define a variable called `user`, which represents the user we want to login. Our first state is a `view-state` that displays the login page. We are using the `model` attribute to bind the `user` variable to the login form on our welcome page. When the user clicks on the **Submit** button, the `action-state getUser` is executed. It calls the `getUserByUsername()` method on the `userService` bean we defined earlier. The method takes the `username` property of the `User` object bound to the form, now filled with the credentials of the user. Afterwards, the result of the method call is stored in the `flowScope`. The flow transitions to a `decision-state`, which checks if the `getUserByUsername()` method returned a null value. If it did, a web page with an error message is displayed to the user. Now the `decision-state` will check whether valid credentials have been entered by the user or not. If the credentials are valid, our flow transits to the next `action-state`, called `updateUser`. The state modifies the `lastLogin` member of the `User` object and saves it automatically to the database. The persistence context is not closed until the end of the flow, when the transaction is committed. Using the Spring IDE (explained earlier in this chapter) we can visualize this flow to make it easier to understand:

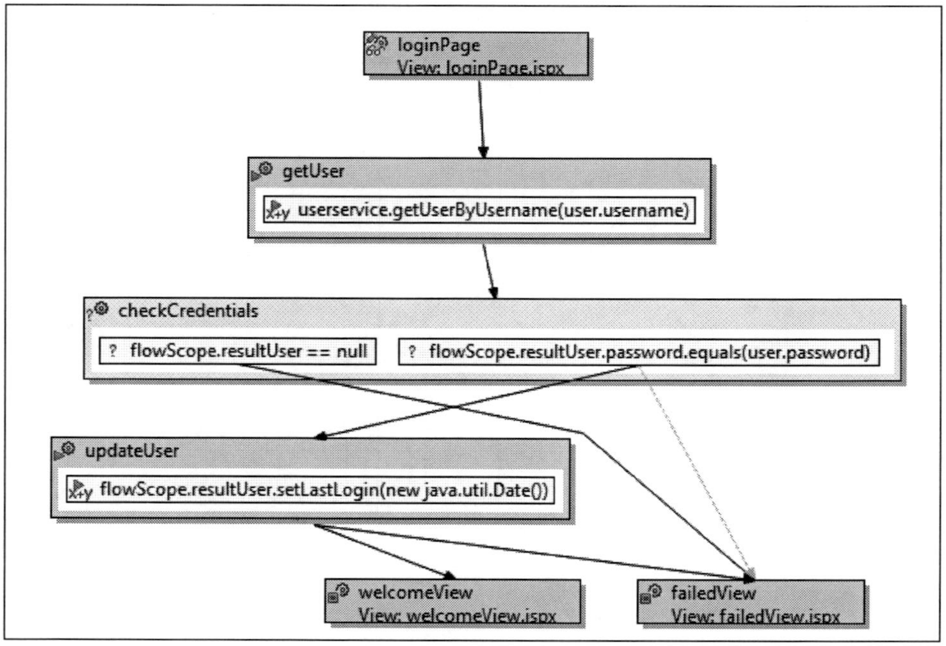

Now that we have written the flow configuration file, the most important ingredient of our example, we can proceed to the next file, the Spring context definition file (`firstexample-servlet.xml`). This has to be saved in the `src/main/webapp/WEB-INF/` folder.

For the `LoginForm` example, the `firstexample-servlet.xml` file could look like this:

```
<?xml version="1.0" encoding="UTF-8"?>
<beans xmlns="http://www.springframework.org/schema/beans" xmlns:
xsi="http://www.w3.org/2001/XMLSchema-instance" xmlns:webflow="http://
www.springframework.org/schema
                                            /webflow-config"
xmlns:tx="http://www.springframework.org/schema/tx" xsi:
schemaLocation="http://www.springframework.org/schema/beans
                    http://www.springframework.org/schema/
                                 beans/spring-beans-2.5.xsd
                           http://www.springframework.org/schema/tx
                           http://www.springframework.org/schema/tx
                                               /spring-tx-2.5.xsd
                           http://www.springframework.org/schema
                                                   /webflow-config
                           http://www.springframework.org/schema/
                                                 webflow-config/
                                spring-webflow-config-2.0.xsd">

   <!-- Data access -->
   <bean id="userservice" class="com.webflow2book.UserService" />
   </bean>

   <bean id="dataSource" destroy-method="close"
      class="org.springframework.jndi.JndiObjectFactoryBean">
      <property name="jndiName"
         value="java:comp/env/jdbc/chapter02db" />
      <property name="resourceRef" value="true" />
   </bean>

   <bean id="entityManagerFactory"
         class="org.springframework.orm.jpa
                .LocalContainerEntityManagerFactory    Bean">
      <property name="dataSource" ref="dataSource" />
      <property name="persistenceUnitName" value="default" />
      <property name="jpaVendorAdapter" ref="jpaVendorAdapter" />
   </bean>

   <bean id="jpaVendorAdapter"
         class="org.springframework.orm.jpa.vendor
                        .HibernateJpaVendorAdapter">
      <property name="showSql" value="true" />
```

```
    </bean>

    <bean id="transactionManager"
          class="org.springframework.orm.jpa.JpaTransactionManager">
       <property name="entityManagerFactory"
                 ref="entityManagerFactory"/>
    </bean>

    <bean class="org.springframework.orm.jpa.support.
                 PersistenceAnnotationBeanPostProcessor"/>

    <!-- Spring MVC -->
    <bean id="handlerMapping"
          class="org.springframework.web.servlet.handler
                                   .SimpleUrlHandlerMapping">
       <property name="mappings">
          <value>/loginform.htm=flowController</value>
       </property>
    </bean>

    <bean id="flowController"
          class="org.springframework.webflow.mvc
                            .servlet.FlowController">
       <property name="flowExecutor" ref="flowExecutor" />
    </bean>

    <!-- Spring Web Flow -->

    <webflow:flow-registry id="flowRegistry">
       <webflow:flow-location id="loginform"
                              path="/WEB-INF/flows/loginform.xml" />
    </webflow:flow-registry>

    <webflow:flow-executor id="flowExecutor"
                           flow-registry="flowRegistry">
       <webflow:flow-execution-listeners>
          <webflow:listener ref="jpaFlowExecutionListener" />
       </webflow:flow-execution-listeners>
    </webflow:flow-executor>

    <bean id="jpaFlowExecutionListener"
          class="org.springframework.webflow.persistence
                                   .JpaFlowExecutionListener">
       <constructor-arg ref="entityManagerFactory" />
       <constructor-arg ref="transactionManager" />
    </bean>
</beans>
```

This file contains everything you need for the first Spring Web Flow application.

First, we will create the basic beans that we need for our example: a `userservice` that will provide access to our persistence layer and a data source that we have externalized via the **Java Naming and Directory Interface** (**JNDI**). For this to work, we have to additionally define the data source in the application server or servlet container that we want to use. For our examples, we will use Apache Tomcat 6.0, so we first have to add a new data source to the `GlobalNamingResources` section of Tomcat's `server.xml` file. This XML file is located in the `conf` folder, which is within Tomcat's root folder.

```
<GlobalNamingResources>
   <Resource
      name="jdbc/chapter02db"
      type="javax.sql.DataSource"
      maxActive="4"
      maxIdle="2"
      maxWait="5000"
      driverClassName="com.microsoft.sqlserver.jdbc.SQLServerDriver"
      username="sqlserver"
      password="sqlserver"
      url="jdbc:sqlserver://localhost:1433;
           databaseName=chapter02;
           SelectMethod=cursor" />
</GlobalNamingResources>
```

We are using Microsoft® SQL Server 2008 database for our example. We have to specify the **Java Database Connectivity** (**JDBC**) connection string, along with the username and password for accessing the database. Of course, you do not have to use the Microsoft® database, feel free to use any other database you like. Finally, we have to add the resource to our Tomcat `context` file:

```
<Context docBase="D:\\Data\\Downloads\\java\\workspace\\chapter02
                              \\target\\chapter02" path="loginform">

   <ResourceLink name="jdbc/chapter02db"
                 type="javax.sql.DataSource"
                 global="jdbc/chapter02db"/>

</Context>
```

Afterwards, we declare an `entityManagerFactory` bean, which is responsible for providing us with the JPA `EntityManager`. We need the `EntityManager` interface to perform any operation on the database. We specify a `jpaVendorAdapter` to tell Spring that we are using Hibernate as the JPA implementation provider, and thus as the backend for our database layer.

> To learn more about the Hibernate project, you can visit `http://www.hibernate.org`. We are using Hibernate Core, Hibernate Annotations, and Hibernate EntityManager in our examples.

Last but not the least, we need a transaction manager for our example, which manages all database transactions. We also specify a `PersistenceAnnotationBeanPostProcessor`. This bean is required to make the JPA annotations visible to Spring.

This is all we need for our database layer. Now, we have to specify all the beans necessary for our web application.

We define a handler mapping using Spring MVCs `SimpleUrlHandlerMapping`, which forwards requests to a specific controller. In this case, every call to `/loginform.htm` is mapped to the `flowController` bean. The decision to use `*.htm` as suffix for the mapping target is up to the authors because after all, HTML content is generated and displayed to the user. Feel free to use other suffixes such as `*.do` if you like; just make sure to change the `web.xml`, which we will explain later. For a more thorough overview of Spring MVC, we recommend that you refer to Chapter 3 in this book or the book, "*Spring in Action*", written by *Craig Walls* and published by *Manning*.

Usually, in Spring Web Flow, you have to define `FlowHandlers` by extending the `AbstractFlowHandler` class and providing a sufficient implementation. `FlowHandlers` are used to handle a single flow. This means that you need an implementation for every flow your application uses. For our simple example this would be far too much work; so we are using a `FlowController` instead. `FlowController` is a Spring Web Flow class that you can use to map all your flow requests to a single controller. Its only attribute is a `flowExecutor` that we will define next.

A `flowExecutor` is required in every Spring Web Flow application because, as the name suggests, it is the attribute that is responsible for executing your flows. As you can see in the XML file, the `flowExecutor` needs an instance of a `flowRegistry`. You can think of the `flowRegistry` as a directory for all your flow definitions. If you have multiple flows, you can add the location of their flow definition files to the `flowRegistry`, so that the `flowExecutor` knows where to find them.

Building the service and database layer

As we want to develop a small login application, we need a Spring bean (`com.webflow2book.User`) that represents the user who wants to log in. Additionally, we need a persistence layer to access the database.

> There is an ongoing discussion on the Internet on whether to use the so-called **Data Access Object** (**DAO**) pattern or to inject the persistence context directly into the service layer. As this is not a book about persistence, we choose to let you decide and use the term *persistence layer* instead of a concrete implementation of a specific pattern.

The actual `User` class has four members: the username and password of the user, the date when the user had last logged into our application, and the ID of the user. To actually retrieve this data, we need a data source from where we can get the data. In this example, we will be using a database and access it with the persistence layer in our application. To do this, we will use the **Java Persistence API** (**JPA**), a standardized API to retrieve data from a database and map it to objects. This process of transforming relational data to plain Java objects is called **ORM** (**Object-relational mapping**). To learn more about the Java Persistence API, see the Java EE 5 Tutorial on Sun Microsystems' web site (`http://java.sun.com/javaee/5/docs/tutorial/doc/bnbpz.html`).

We have to add a couple of annotations in the `User` class. This `User.java` file is stored in your project's root folder in this folder path: `src/main/java/com/webflow2book`.

```
@Entity
@Table(name = "UserTable")
public class User implements Serializable {
   private static final long serialVersionUID = […];

   @Id
   @GeneratedValue(strategy = GenerationType.AUTO)
   private int id;

   private String username;
   private String password;

   @Temporal(TemporalType.DATE)
   private Date lastLogin;

   public int getId() {
      return this.id;
   }

   public void setId(int id) {
      this.id = id;
   }

   public String getUsername() {
      return this.username;
   }
```

```
    public void setUsername(String username) {
        this.username = username;
    }

    public String getPassword() {
        return this.password;
    }

    public void setPassword(String password) {
        this.password = password;
    }

     public Date getLastLogin() {
         if(lastLogin != null) {
             return new Date(lastLogin.getTime());
         }
         return null;
     }

     public void setLastLogin(Date lastLogin) {
         if(lastLogin != null) {
             this.lastLogin = new Date(lastLogin.getTime());
         }
     }
}
```

The `Entity` annotation marks this class as JPA entity, which can be loaded from and stored in a database table. As the database table does not share its name with the Java class, we have to use the `Table` annotation to specify which database table we want to use. The `id` member is mapped to the primary key of the database. Whenever we create a new `User` object and store it in the database, the JPA implementation provider (for example, Hibernate or TopLink) will take care of choosing the correct strategy for creating a new, unique ID for our object, depending on the capabilities and configurations of the underlying database system.

As we mentioned earlier, we want to use the Java Persistence API to access the database, so we created a JPA implementation, which is saved in the `UserServiceImpl.java` file and stored in your project's root folder in this folder path: `src/main/java/com/webflow2book`. You can see this JPA implementation in the following code listing:

```
...
    @PersistenceContext
    private EntityManager entityManager;

    public User getUserByUsername(String username) {
        Query query = this.getEntityManager().createQuery(
```

```
                    "select user from com.webflow2book.User user "
                    + "where user.username like :username");
        query.setParameter("username", username);
        return (User) query.getSingleResult();
    }

    public void setEntityManager(EntityManager entityManager) {
        this.entityManager = entityManager;
    }

    public EntityManager getEntityManager() {
        return entityManager;
    }
...
```

We implement the `getUserByUsername()` method in our persistence layer by creating a new `Query` object. In this example, we are creating the query on the fly. In this query, we use the **JPQL (Java Persistence Query Language)** to select all `User` objects with a given username. As seen earlier, we can set the parameter using the `setParameter()` method on the `Query` object:

```
query.setParameter("username", username).getSingleResult();
```

Finally, we need to create a `persistence.xml` file, to define the persistence unit we named `default` in our Spring configuration file. This file has to be saved in the `src/main/resources/META-INF` folder, as it must be present in your applications classpath to be found by the JPA implementation provider:

```
<persistence xmlns="http://java.sun.com/xml/ns/persistence"
             xmlns:xsi="http://www.w3.org/2001/XMLSchema-instance"
   xsi:schemaLocation="http://java.sun.com/xml/ns/persistence
                       http://java.sun.com/xml/ns/persistence
                                           /persistence_1_0.xsd"
             version="1.0">
   <persistence-unit name="default"
                     transaction-type="RESOURCE_LOCAL">
      <class>com.webflow2book.User</class>
      <properties>
         <property name="hibernate.dialect"
                   value="org.hibernate.dialect.SQLServerDialect" />
      </properties>
   </persistence-unit>
</persistence>
```

The web.xml file

Regardless of which technologies you choose to use together with Spring Web Flow (be it Spring MVC or JavaServer Faces), you will have to write a configuration file used in every web application, the `web.xml` file. A sample file is shown in the following code section; it has to be saved in the `src/main/webapp/WEB-INF` folder:

```
<?xml version="1.0" encoding="UTF-8"?>
<web-app id="LoginForm"
         version="2.4"
         xmlns="http://java.sun.com/xml/ns/j2ee"
         xmlns:xsi="http://www.w3.org/2001/XMLSchema-instance"
         xsi:schemaLocation="http://java.sun.com/xml/ns/j2ee
                             http://java.sun.com/xml/ns
                                      /j2ee/web-app_2_4.xsd">

      <servlet>
            <servlet-name>firstexample</servlet-name>
            <servlet-class>
                org.springframework.web.servlet.DispatcherServlet
            </servlet-class>
            <load-on-startup>1</load-on-startup>
      </servlet>

          <servlet-mapping>
            <servlet-name>firstexample</servlet-name>
            <url-pattern>*.htm</url-pattern>
      </servlet-mapping>

      <welcome-file-list>
            <welcome-file>index.jsp</welcome-file>
      </welcome-file-list>
</web-app>
```

There is nothing really special about this `web.xml`. You have to define at least one `servlet`, the Spring MVC `DispatcherServlet`. This servlet is, as the name suggests, responsible for dispatching requests to their destinations, typically a Spring MVC controller like our `flowController`. In this case, a mapping is declared that maps all requests that end with the suffix, `*.htm`, to the `DispatcherServlet`.

The last thing you need to try out the example, is to provide an entry point into your application. We've written a small JSP file that automatically redirects to our flow:

```
<%@ page session="false"%>
<%@ taglib prefix="c" uri="http://java.sun.com/jsp/jstl/core" %>

<c:redirect url="/loginform.htm" />
```

We called this file `index.jsp`, and put it into the `src/main/webapp` folder.

Dependencies

Please note that this example requires many third-party libraries to actually run. We list them here as Maven-style dependencies, so that you do not have to look for them. These dependencies are mentioned in the `pom.xml` file.

```
<dependency>
   <groupId>org.springframework.webflow</groupId>
   <artifactId>org.springframework.binding</artifactId>
   <version>2.0.5.RELEASE</version>
</dependency>
<dependency>
   <groupId>org.springframework.webflow</groupId>
   <artifactId>org.springframework.js</artifactId>
   <version>2.0.5.RELEASE</version>
</dependency>
<dependency>
   <groupId>org.springframework.webflow</groupId>
   <artifactId>org.springframework.webflow</artifactId>
   <version>2.0.5.RELEASE</version>
</dependency>
<dependency>
   <groupId>org.springframework</groupId>
   <artifactId>spring-jdbc</artifactId>
   <version>2.5.6</version>
</dependency>
<dependency>
   <groupId>org.springframework</groupId>
   <artifactId>spring-orm</artifactId>
   <version>2.5.6</version>
</dependency>
<dependency>
   <groupId>org.hibernate</groupId>
   <artifactId>hibernate-core</artifactId>
   <version>3.3.1.GA</version>
</dependency>
<dependency>
   <groupId>org.hibernate</groupId>
   <artifactId>hibernate-entitymanager</artifactId>
   <version>3.4.0.GA</version>
</dependency>
<dependency>
   <groupId>org.slf4j</groupId>
   <artifactId>slf4j-log4j12</artifactId>
   <version>1.5.2</version>
</dependency>
<dependency>
```

```
        <groupId>javax.servlet</groupId>
        <artifactId>jstl</artifactId>
        <version>1.2</version>
    </dependency>
    <dependency>
        <groupId>taglibs</groupId>
        <artifactId>standard</artifactId>
        <version>1.1.2</version>
    </dependency>
    <dependency>
        <groupId>ognl</groupId>
        <artifactId>ognl</artifactId>
        <version>2.7.3</version>
    </dependency>
```

Summary

In this chapter, we showed you how to install the distribution of Spring Web Flow, gave an overview of example applications provided within the distributions, and also discussed how you can install them on your local machine. Additionally, we explained which tools exist to support developers with their daily work with Spring Web Flow.

Finally, we showed you how to develop your first Spring Web Flow application. Usually this process includes the following steps:

1. Think about the flow you want to develop and write your flow definition file.
2. Define all the beans you need in your Spring context definition file.
3. Write your `web.xml` file. You will need to include at least the Spring MVC `DispatcherServlet`.
4. Design your views by writing your JSP files.

We guided you through all these steps in this chapter. Whenever you want to develop an application using Spring Web Flow, but do not exactly know what to do, just take a look at this chapter and you will find all the required steps.

This chapter explained how to get started with Spring Web Flow. In the next chapter, we will cover all the basics you have to know to create powerful applications with Spring Web Flow.

3
The Basics of Spring Web Flow 2

The central element of Spring Web Flow 2 (SWF2) is the flow. A flow is described inside a flow definition. There are two ways to describe a flow:

- The declarative definition: Usage of XML with XSD (XML Schema Definition) grammar (`http://www.springframework.org/schema/webflow/spring-webflow-2.0.xsd`).
- The programmatic definition: Usage of Java.

> In a standard Spring Web Flow 2 distribution, the `http://www.springframework.org/schema/webflow/spring-webflow-2.0.xsd` XSD is inside the `org.springframework.webflow-2.x.x.RELEASE.jar` library. The concrete location inside the mentioned library is the `org/springframework/webflow/engine/model/builder/xml` directory.

The usage of XML is more than recommended because the usage of Java for the flow definition has no direct support through a tool. Additionally, it is just not relevant for daily usage. If you want to use Java, you have to deal directly with the internal API of Spring Web Flow. We set our focus to show you the application development with Spring Web Flow and therefore we don't show the programmatic definition of a flow. In the case of the usage of the declarative approach, you can change the flow without changing your code for your application.

Continuations – Restore and Resume

A **continuation** represents the rest of the computation given a point in the computation. Another word for "rest of the computation" is control state, meaning the data structures and code needed to complete a computation. Most languages implement the data structure as a variant of the stack and the code as just a pointer to the current instructions. There are also programming languages that represent the control data as a heap-allocated object (see the reference: `http://en.wikipedia.org/wiki/Continuation`).

One of the important reasons for using the Spring Web Flow 2 framework is the fact that a use case mostly consists of more than one page. Therefore, there is a need for an interruption, maybe in case you need to wait for the input of the user. At the point of interruption, the system has to serialize the instances between the requests. Continuations are in order for the mechanism to restore and resume at a later point. Additionally, it helps to make interactions inside a web application easier. The Spring Web Flow framework does the work and therefore we have nothing to do with the infrastructure for continuations.

Elements of a flow

We mentioned before that the description of a flow is mostly done in an XML file. We named it the declarative definition. The concrete naming of that file is **flow definition file**.

Remark: For a better understanding of the internals, it could be helpful to check the source code from Spring Web Flow 2.

You can think of a flow definition as a state machine, because it consists of states and transitions between them. Besides these two concepts, there are actions which trigger the transitions between the states.

A flow definition file consists of the following main elements:

- Section head
- Section data (optional section)
- Section body
- Section footer (optional section)

We can visualize the central block of that flow definition file in the following figure:

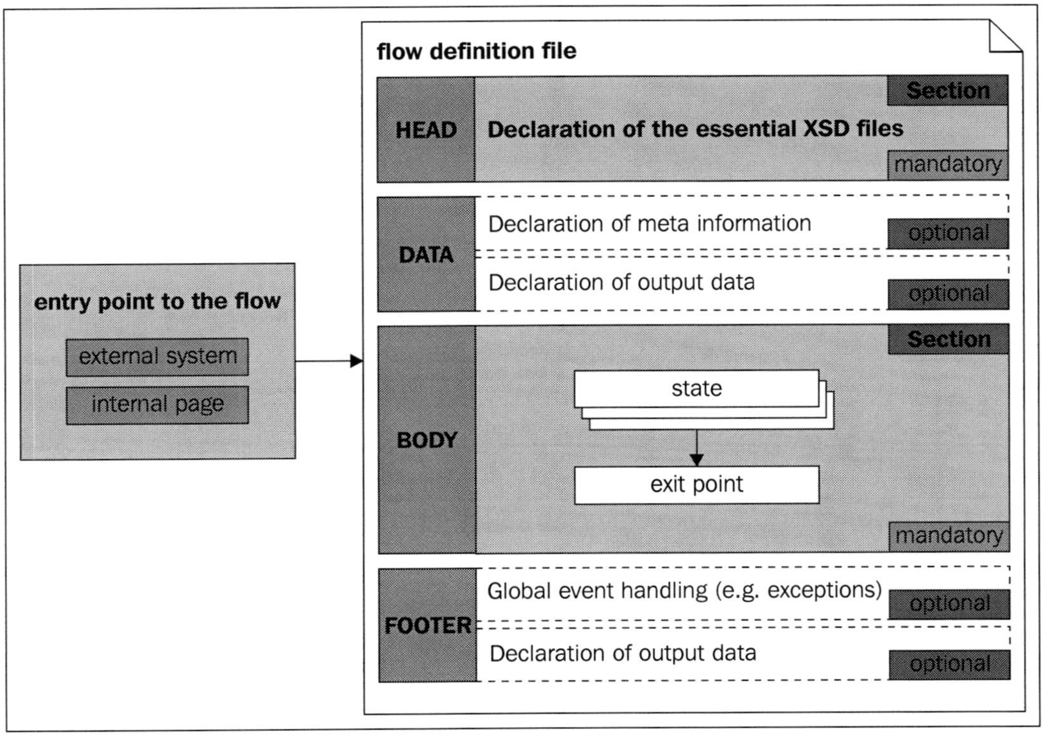

The entry point to the flow

In the previous figure, there is a section which is not directly described through the flow definition file, **the entry point to the flow**. There are two general types of entry points:

- Requests from an external system
- Requests from an internal page

A flow can have more than one entry point, because an entry point is just a request to the URI of the flow. In our example, the entry for the `add` flow is in the `view-issues.jsp` page.

Section head

The flow definition file is based on an XSD file. It is important to use the XSD file of version 2.0 because of the fact that the XSD has dramatically changed from version 1.0 to version 2.0.

> One of the significant changes from version 1.0 to version 2.0 of the Spring Web Flow framework is that the file size of a flow definition file is reduced to about 50%. For developers who come from the old version, there is an automatic tool for upgrading from the old to the new version. To use the automatic upgrade feature, just execute the following command in the command prompt:
>
> ```
> java org.springframework.webflow.upgrade.
> WebFlowUpgrader flow-to-upgrade.xml
> ```

The URLs for both the versions of the XSD files are shown in the following table.

Version	URL
1.0	`http://www.springframework.org/schema/webflow /spring-webflow-1.0.xsd`
2.0	`http://www.springframework.org/schema/webflow /spring-webflow-2.0.xsd`

The main element of the definition file is `flow`. To use the `webflow` elements, you have to declare the namespace (with the help of the mentioned XSD file). See the line below for a short example of the namespace definition.

```
<flow xmlns="http://www.springframework.org/schema/webflow"
        xmlns:xsi="http://www.w3.org/2001/XMLSchema-instance" xsi:
schemaLocation="http://www.springframework.org/schema/webflow
        http://www.springframework.org/schema/webflow/spring-webflow-
2.0.xsd">
```

> If you are using an editor (e.g. Eclipse) with an integrated validation for the syntax of the XML file, you will need access to the Internet to validate against the declared XSD schema in the header of the flow definition file.

Section data

There are two types of data that could be provided or handled inside a flow. There is some metadata for a flow. Additionally, there is a way of providing a flow with some input data from outside.

The metadata of a flow

The metadata of a flow is the section where you can specify attributes for configuring your flow, for example you configure whether the data inside the flow is persisted or not. The metadata is not directly related to the concrete use case which is described through the specific flow.

Persistence context

Most of the applications today are a variation of the classical CRUD (Create - Read - Update - Delete) pattern. That means each application has to handle information (or data) in a specialized way. For that issue, Spring Web Flow provides the persistence context which helps you to simplify the database access.

> If you are interested in more information about ORM (Object-relational mapping), start with the article at `http://en.wikipedia.org/wiki/Object-relational_mapping`.

The nature of web programming is to manage concurrency in a multi-user environment. Therefore, there is often the necessity to manage more than one user and therefore we are confronted with more than one read/write process on the underlying data layer. One cornerstone in the management of concurrency is the usage of transactions. The new Spring Web Flow release offers possibilities to handle the mentioned transactions for the developer.

> The transactions may be demarcated in presentation layer or service and DAO layers, even inside a database in the form of stored procedure.

In the latest release of Spring Web Flow 2, there is one implementation of the Persistence Context—the so-called *FlowScoped Persistence Context*.

> More implementations for the Persistence Context are scheduled for the next major release of Spring Web Flow. There is one issue for view state persistence context, which can be tracked with the `http://jira.springframework.org/browse/SWF-577` URL. Another issue is for the conversation-scoped persistence context, which can be traced with the `http://jira.springframework.org/browse/SWF-567` URL.

FlowScoped Persistence Context

> The concept of flow-managed persistence is inspired by the Hibernate Long Session. The changes are only committed at the end of the flow. This pattern is often used in conjunction with an **optimistic locking strategy** to protect the integrity of data modified in parallel by multiple users.

Before we can start working with FlowScoped persistence, we have to mark the flow description (see the following listing which shows the flow configuration) with `persistence-context`, or you can set the `persistence-context` attribute to `true`. It doesn't matter which of the two ways you choose. The authors think that the first one is more intuitive.

Direct usage of persistence-context

```
<?xml version="1.0" encoding="UTF-8"?>
<flow xmlns="http://www.springframework.org/schema/webflow"
      xmlns:xsi="http://www.w3.org/2001/XMLSchema-instance"
  xsi:schemaLocation="http://www.springframework.org/schema/webflow
                          http://www.springframework.org/schema/
webflow/spring-webflow-2.0.xsd">
    <persistence-context />
</flow>
```

Usage of the persistence-context attribute

```
<?xml version="1.0" encoding="UTF-8"?>
<flow xmlns="http://www.springframework.org/schema/webflow"
      xmlns:xsi="http://www.w3.org/2001/XMLSchema-instance"
  xsi:schemaLocation="http://www.springframework.org/schema/webflow
                          http://www.springframework.org/schema/
webflow/spring-webflow-2.0.xsd">
    <attribute name="persistence-context" value="true" />
</flow>
```

Additionally, we have to write the configuration of the beans to the configuration of the flow (often done in the `applicationContext.xml` file). In that mentioned configuration file, we have to define a listener for the underlying persistence technology. If you want to use the JPA (Java Persistence API), you have to define a `JpaFlowExcecutionListener` (see the listing below), or for Hibernate you have to define `HibernateFlowExecutionListener`.

```
<webflow:flow-executor id="flowExecutor" flow-registry="flowRegistry">
    <webflow:flow-execution-listeners>
```

```
        <webflow:listener ref="jpaFlowExecutionListener" />
    </webflow:flow-execution-listeners>
</webflow:flow-executor>

<bean id="jpaFlowExecutionListener"
     class="org.springframework.webflow.persistence.
JpaFlowExecutionListener">
    <constructor-arg ref="entityManagerFactory" />
    <constructor-arg ref="transactionManager" />
</bean>
```

Just for completion, we show the definitions for two beans, `entityManagerFactory` and `transactionsManager`.

```
   <!-- Drives transactions using local JPA APIs -->
   <bean id="transactionManager" class="org.springframework.orm.jpa.
JpaTransactionManager">
      <property name="entityManagerFactory" ref="entityManagerFactory"
/>
   </bean>

   <!-- Creates a EntityManagerFactory for use with the Hibernate JPA
provider and a simple in-memory data source populated with test data
-->
   <bean id="entityManagerFactory" class="org.springframework.orm.jpa.
LocalContainerEntityManagerFactoryBean">
      <property name="dataSource" ref="dataSource" />
      <property name="jpaVendorAdapter">
         <bean class="org.springframework.orm.jpa.vendor.
HibernateJpaVendorAdapter" />
      </property>
   </bean>
   <!-- Deploys a in-memory "booking" datasource populated -->
   <bean id="dataSource" class="org.springframework.jdbc.datasource.
DriverManagerDataSource">
      <property name="driverClassName" value="org.hsqldb.jdbcDriver"
/>
      <property name="url" value="jdbc:hsqldb:mem:flowtrac" />
      <property name="username" value="sa" />
      <property name="password" value="" />
   </bean>
```

It is worth mentioning that HSQLDB (`http://hsqldb.org/`) is more than simply a memory DataSource. It is a relational database which is completely compatible with Java.

At the end of the flow, we have to trigger the commit of the data changes. For that, we have the `commit` attribute, which can be set to `true`.

```
<end-state id="transactionConfirmed" commit="true" />
```

Those who are familiar with the JPA might now ask about the EntityManager (see the reference to `entityManagerFactory` in `applicationContext.xml`). Its instance will be created at the start of the flow with a listener. That EntityManager can be referenced in the flow configuration (use the `persistenceContext` variable). Additionally, each access on data, which is managed through the Spring framework, is using that EntityManager.

> The internal realization of the concept of Persistence Context is done through `FlowExecutionListener` (package: `org.springframework.webflow.execution`).

Section input

It is possible to provide a flow with some data. The data can be categorized into two sections:

- Variables which are created when the flow starts. These types of variables are called flow instance variables. These variables are changed typically in a programmatic way.
- Inputs which are provided from the caller of the flow. These variables are set through the request of the flow.

There is a difference between the definition of the flow (in XML or Java) and the programming of the flow. You can use XML or Java for the flow definition but with both of them you describe (or program) the flow with a specific DSL (**Domain Specific Language**). The name of that specific language is flow definition language. For the access of data in the different scopes (see the following section for the description of the different scopes), a special syntax is necessary.

> If you want to read more about the concept of Domain Specific Language, start with the article at `http://en.wikipedia.org/wiki/Domain-specific_programming_language`.

Programming in a flow

There are four places where you need more than simple XML in a flow. These are:

- access of the data provided from the client (see the *Input* section)
- access to data structures in the different scopes (see the *The scopes* section)
- invoking actions, especially methods on declared beans
- creating some control structures (for example, for defining a decision)

Spring Web Flow 2 uses an EL (Expression Language) for the programming logic inside the flow. The framework supports two different types of expression languages. These variants are described in the subsequent table:

Name	Description
Unified EL	The Unified EL is used by default in Spring Web Flow. As implementation library, the JBoss EL (download it from: `http://www.springsource.com/repository/app/bundle/detail? nme=com.springsource.org.jboss.el`) is used. For more information on Unified EL, visit `http://java.sun.com/products/jsp/reference/techart/unifiedEL.html`.
OGNL	OGNL is the acronym for Object-Graph Navigation Language. It is used as the default EL in version 1 of Spring Web Flow. For more information about OGNL, visit `http://www.ognl.org`.

Most of the syntax of both the implementations is the same. It is recommended to use the standard and not the proprietary syntax of OGNL (only if you need some special things from that). Inside the DSL of the flow definition, there can be two types of expressions. The difference is whether the expression has a delimiter (e.g. `${}` or `#{}`) or not. The expressions without a delimiter are called **standard eval expressions**. An example is `action.execute()`. If you use a delimiter, a run-time exception from type `java.lang.IllegalArgumentException` is thrown. The second type of expression is the template expression. For that, you have to use a delimiter. For example, `my-${name.locale}.xml`. The result of the template is text. Most of the attributes in the latest Spring Web Flow 2 schema accept expressions. Check the schema at `http://www.springframework.org/schema/webflow/spring-webflow-2.0.xsd` to see whether an attribute accepts it or not. The following implicit variables are available inside the EL expressions:

- `currentEvent`
- `currentUser`
- `externalContext`

- `flowExecutionContext`
- `flowExecutionUrl`
- `flowRequestContext`
- `messageContext`
- `resourceBundle`
- `requestParameters`

The internal implementation of these variables is done with the help of the `ImplicitFlowVariableElResolver` class inside the `org.springframework.webflow.expression.el` package. Dependent on the variable, there are specific implementations of the internal `PropertyResolver` class (see the class diagram below).

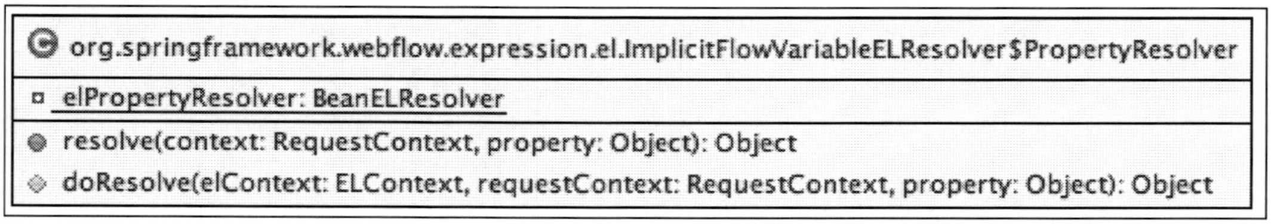

Now we will describe the variables and their usage:

Variable currentEvent:

With the `currentEvent` variable, you can access data of the current event, which is last processed by the active flow. The instance of the event is from the `Event` class (package `org.springframework.webflow.execution`).

Variable currentUser:

With the `currentUser` variable, you have access to `Principal` (the principal is the authenticated user) who is authenticated through the web container. For example, with `principal.name`, you access the name of the principal.

Variable externalContext:

Sometimes it is necessary to interact with the environment (e.g. the session object). For that case, you can use the `externalContext` variable.The instance is from type `ExternalContext` (package `org.springframework.webflow.context`). For a complete overview, see the following class diagram. You can understand that the ExternalContext is a façade which provides access to an external system that has called the Spring Web Flow system.

In case a servlet calls the Spring Web Flow system, you get an instance from the `ServletExternalContext` type (package `org.springframework.webflow.context.servlet`). It is worth mentioning that there is a subclass for `ServletExternalContext` which is used in the case of Spring MVC. Its name is `MvcExternalContext` (package: `org.springframework.webflow.context.mvc.servlet`). In the case of a portlet environment, the concrete class is `PortletExternalContext` (package: `org.springframework.webflow.context.portlet`).

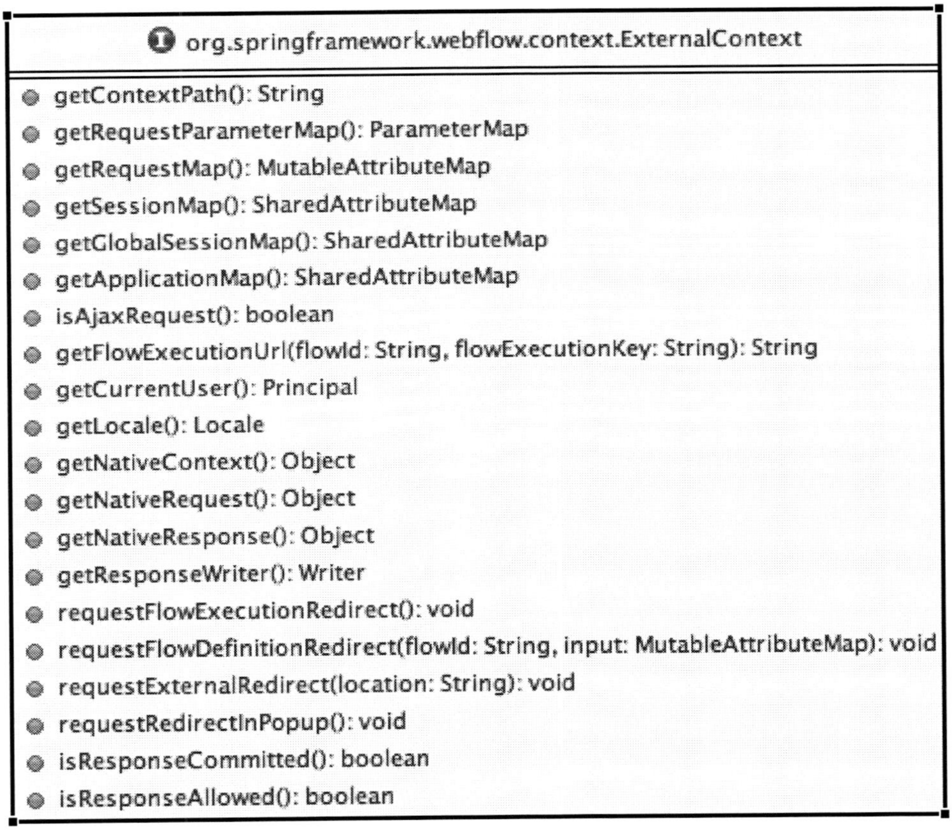

Variable flowExecutionContext:

The `flowExecutionContext` variable allows you to get access to an instance of the underlying `FlowExecutionContext` (package `org.springframework.webflow.execution`). See the following diagram for the methods:

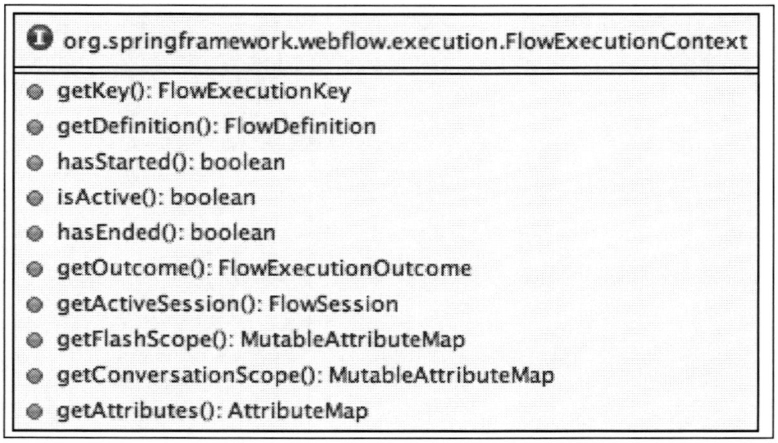

Variable flowExecutionUrl:

The developer has access to the context-relative URL of the flow with the help of the `flowExecutionUrl` variable. In the default implementation, the URL is created inside the `createFlowExecutionUrl` method of the `DefaultFlowUrlHandler` class (package `org.springframework.webflow.context.servlet`). In the default implementation, the flow execution key will be attached to the URI of the request as a parameter (name: `execution`).

Variable flowRequestContext:

With the `flowRequestContext` variable, the developer gets access to the actual instance of the `RequestContext` inside the `org.springframework.webflow.execution` package. The methods are shown in the following diagram:

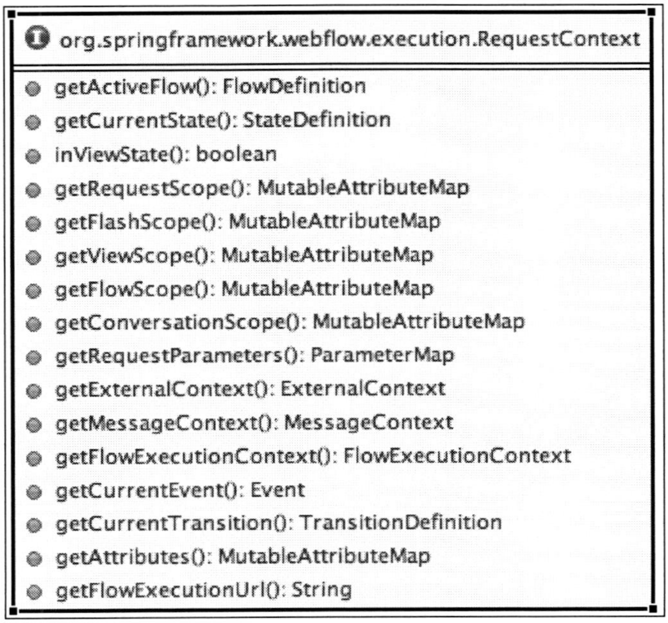

Variable messageContext:

The `messageContext` variable gives us the privilege to create and retrieve messages from the flow execution (e.g. error and success messages). The instance is from the `MessageContext` type in the `org.springframework.binding.message` package. For the methods, view the following diagram:

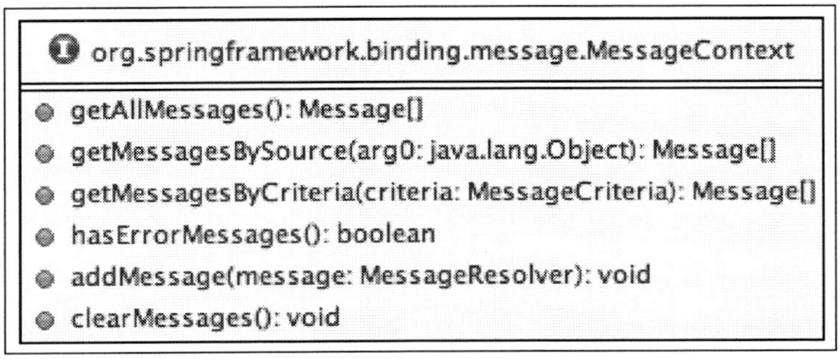

Variable resourceBundle:

To access a message inside the `messages.properties` file inside the `flow` directory, use the `resourceBundle` EL variable, for example `resourceBundle.name`. The following line shows a small example for the usage:

```
<set name="flashScope.ErrorMessage" value="resourceBundle.
myErrorMessage" />
```

It's possible to use that EL variable inside the views, too. See the example below for a demonstration:

```
<h:outputText value="#{resourceBundle.myErrorMessage}" />
```

Variable requestParameters:

The `requestParameters` variable offers the possibility to access the parameters of the incoming request, for example `requestParameters.issueId`.

The scopes

The data inside a flow can occur in different scopes. In short, a scope describes the duration for which the data is valid. Now, we introduce the different scopes for a better understanding.

Name	Description
`flow`	On the start of a flow, the `flow` scope is allocated and it is destroyed after the flow ends. Therefore, the `flow` scope lives as long as the flow and is the right place if you want to store data that should be accessible during the complete flow execution. The objects in the flow scope have to implement `java.io.Serializable`. To access the flow scope in the flow definition, use the EL variable `flowScope`. It's not possible to access the data in the subflow.
`view`	On the start of a `view-state` (states are explained later in the chapter; for understanding it is important to know that the lifecycle of a flow is fragmented into different states), the `view` scope is created. That scope is destroyed after the `view-state` ends. It is important to know that the view scope is only accessible inside a `view-state`. The objects in the `view` scope have to implement `java.io.Serializable`. To access the `view` scope in the flow definition, use the EL variable viewScope.
`request`	Variables which come in a request are stored inside the `request` scope. That scope is created when the flow is called and destroyed after the flow returns. To access the `request` scope in the flow definition, use the EL variable `requestScope`.

Name	Description
`flash`	The `flash` scope itself is created on the start of the flow. The cleanup is done after every view rendering. The destruction is done at the end of the flow. The objects in the `flash` scope have to implement `java.io.Serializable.` To access the `flash` scope in the flow definition, use the EL variable `flashScope`.
`conversation`	A conversation (and therefore the flow) spans a complete flow. It is created on the flow start and destroyed at the end of the flow. The `conversation` scope is valid inside the subflows too. That is the only difference between the `conversation` and `flow` scope. To access the `conversation` scope in the flow definition, use the EL variable `conversationScope`.

For a fast overview of the duration of the scopes, have a look at the following table:

Scope	Created	Cleaned	Destroyed
request scope	call of a flow	-	flow returns
view scope	enter view state	-	exit the view
flash scope	flow start	after a view render	end of flow
flow scope	flow start	-	flow end
conversation scope	(top-level) flow start	-	flow end

[In some situations, you often need an instance from a class in a clean state. Therefore, if the cleanup of the instance is as fast as the creation of a new instance, it could be preferable to clean the instance. In that case, you lower the memory footprint of your application.]

The scopes are sections to store the data. How to access these data is described in the following section.

Resolving variables

There are two ways to access the variables. You can address a variable with `Scope` as its prefix (e.g. `flashScope.name`) or without a prefix (e.g. `name`). If you use a prefix, the specified scope is searched for the variable. If no scope prefix is specified, a scope search algorithm (implemented in `org.springframework.webflow.expression.el.ScopeSearchingElResolver`) is used. In simple words, a scope (base interface is `org.springframework.beans.factory.config.scope.Scope`) is just a special `java.util.Map`. All scopes extend the abstract class named `org.springframework.webflow.scope.AbstractWebFlowScope`.

For a complete overview, we illustrated this in the class diagram below:

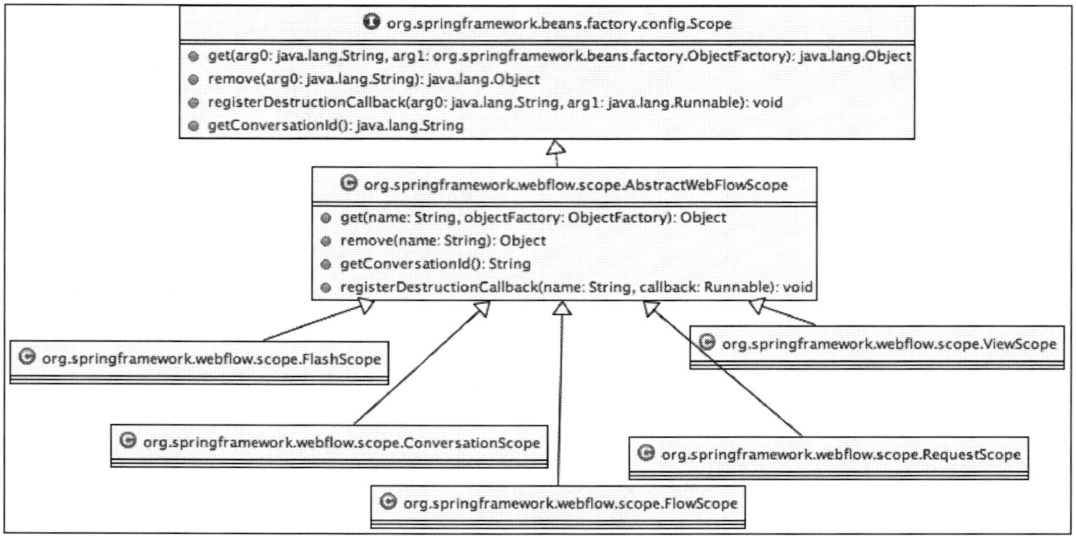

The scope searching algorithm is visualized in the figure below:

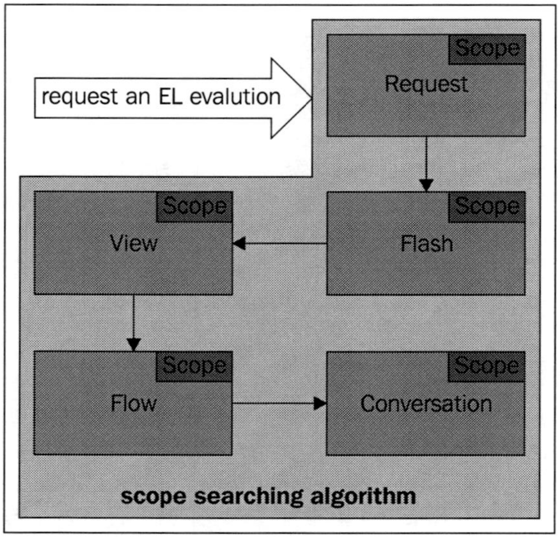

> **Request is not HttpServletRequest**
>
> If we talk about a request inside a flow, we talk about a single call (inside a thread) by an external actor. The representation for a request is the `RequestContext` class inside the `org.springframework.webflow.execution` package. If you work with Spring MVC, don't confuse it with the `RequestContext` class inside the `org.springframework.web.servlet.support` package. The actual instance (request specific) of `RequestContext` can be accessed through the `RequestContextHolder` class in the `org.springframework.webflow.execution` package. The call is `RequestContext context = RequestContextHolder.getRequestContext()`.

The flow instance variables

To handle data inside the flow, it is necessary to have a variable. Such a variable is defined in the data section of the flow. The name of the XML tag is `var`. You can define as many flow instance variables as you want. The limitation is only the memory of your machine.

Name	**Description**
`Name`	The name of the instance variable. Please take care that the name is unique, otherwise you can get unpredictable errors.
`Class`	The class which should be used for the variable. It is important that the class implements the `java.io.Serializable` marker interface because it is saved between the requests of a flow and therefore the instances are serialized. Additionally, it is important that the class should have a public default constructor, because the default implementation uses it to instantiate `SimpleInstantiationStrategy` (package: `org.springframework.beans.factory.support`) and that strategy searches for a public default constructor with the `clazz.getDeclaredConstructor((Class[]) null)` call.

In the following example, a flow instance variable with the name `issue` and the `flowtrac.core.model.issue.IssueImpl` class is shown.

```
<var name="issue" class="flowtrac.core.model.issue.IssueImpl" />
```

> It is important to know that if you use a complex object which has some transient member variables which are annotated with `@Autowired`, these variables are rewired after the flow resumes.

The variables are created on the start of the flow. It is not mandatory to define flow instance variables.

Assign a value to a scope variable

Instead of defining the flow instance variables with the `var` tag, there is an option to set a specific value inside the scope. For that, you can use `set`.

```
<set name="requestScope.issueId" value="requestParameters.id"
type="long" />
```

To advise Spring Web Flow that a conversion is essential, you have to specify the `type` attribute. The framework checks the value and does a type conversion if it is necessary.

Access the value of a scope

If you want to access the value of a scope inside the code, you have to use the `ScopeType` class inside the `org.springframework.webflow.execution` package. That class contains enumerations for each type of scope (see the following figure). To access the attributes of a scope, there is a method called `getScope` with the `RequestContext` parameter.

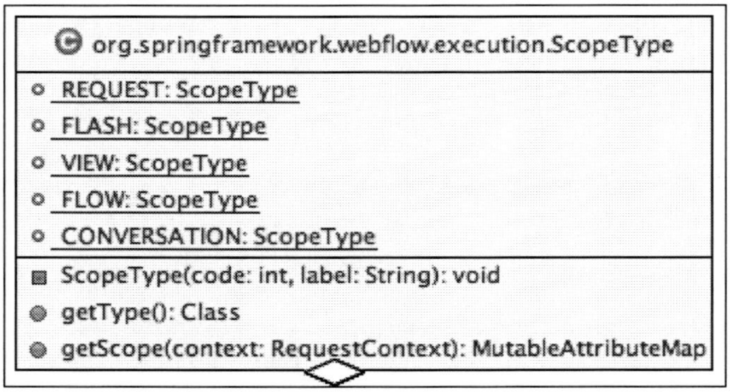

For convenience, we implemented a static method called `getFromScope` which can be placed in the helper class (in our example, we named it `ScopeValueHelper`). With that method, it is easy to obtain a value of the specific scope. You have to provide the name of the value, the type of the value, and the scope.

```
    public static <T> T getFromScope(final String name, final T
typeToConvert, final ScopeType scope)   {
        if (scope == null)  {
            throw new ScopeValueHelperException("A scope must be set.");
        }
        RequestContext context = RequestContextHolder.
getRequestContext();
        if (context == null)  {
            throw new ScopeValueHelperException("Could not retrieve the
```

```
context of the actual request. Please take care that you use that
class inside a flow.");
        }
        T value = null;
        MutableAttributeMap map = null;
        map = scope.getScope(context);
        if (map == null)   {
           throw new ScopeValueHelperException("The scope " + scope + "
has no value map.");
        }
        try  {
           value = (T) map.get(name);
        } catch (ClassCastException cce) {
           throw new ScopeValueHelperException("The value in the scope
is not from the correct type.",cce);
        }
        return value;
    }
```

An example for the usage of that method is shown in the following line:

```
boolean create = ScopeValueHelper.getFromScope("create", create =
false, ScopeType.REQUEST);
```

Additionally, we added a method which searches in all scopes (using the same scope searching algorithm like Spring Web Flow). The name of the method is also `getFromScope`; however you only have to provide the name of the value and the type. The implementation of the algorithm is very easy. We just have a list with the scopes inside (see below).

```
static List<ScopeType> scopeSequence;
static  {
   scopeSequence = new LinkedList<ScopeType>();
   scopeSequence.add(ScopeType.REQUEST);
   scopeSequence.add(ScopeType.FLASH);
   scopeSequence.add(ScopeType.VIEW);
   scopeSequence.add(ScopeType.FLOW);
   scopeSequence.add(ScopeType.CONVERSATION);
}
```

The list is used for searching like the scope searching algorithm does. The implementation of the method is shown below.

```
   public static <T> T getFromScope(final String name, T
typeToConvert)  {
      RequestContext context = RequestContextHolder.
getRequestContext();
```

```
        if (context == null)  {
            throw new ScopeValueHelperException("Could not retrieve the 
context of the actual request. Please take care that you use that 
class inside a flow.");
        }
        T value = null;
        MutableAttributeMap map = null;
        for (ScopeType type: scopeSequence)    {
            map = type.getScope(context);
            if (map == null)    {
                throw new ScopeValueHelperException("The scope " + type + 
" has no value map.");
            }
            try  {
                value = (T) map.get(name);
            } catch (ClassCastException cce) {
                throw new ScopeValueHelperException("The value in the 
scope is not from the correct type.",cce);
            }
            if (value != null)    {
                return value;
            }
        }
        return null;
    }
```

The usage is similar to the usage of the other `getFromScope` method. For completeness, we show it now:

```
boolean create = ScopeValueHelper.getFromScope("create", create = 
false);
```

Inputs

It is possible to provide a flow with some external data. For example, you specify the parameter in a GET or POST request. For that case, you have to use the `input` tag. Besides the name, you have to specify the `id`. That `id` is the name of the provided variable.

For example, we have a link for editing the issues:

```
<a href="/flowtrac-web/flowtrac/issue/add?id=${issue.id}" />
```

As you can see, the flow is started with the `id` parameter. To use that parameter, we define an `input` parameter with the name `id`.

```
<input name="id" />
```

Additionally, it is possible to specify the type of the input parameter. The name of the attribute is `type`. For example:

```
<input name="id" type="long" />
```

If an input value does match the specified type, a type conversion will be attempted. The conversion is done in `org.springframework.webflow.engine.builder.model.FlowModelBuilder`. If the conversion could not be done, the `org.springframework.binding.convert.ConversionExecutionException` run-time exception is thrown. The last possible (and optional too) attribute is `value`. With this parameter, you can map the input parameter to a value in a specific scope, as shown below.

```
<input name="id" value="flowScope.issue.id" />
```

The following table sums up the information.

Name	Description
`Id`	The name of the input variable.
`Type`	The type of the input variable. If you specify this, an automatic type conversion is attempted. The attribute is optional.
`Value`	With that optional attribute, you can map an input parameter to a flow variable.

The states

There are six states that can occur inside a flow definition. The states are:

- `start-state`
- `action-state`
- `view-state`
- `decision-state`
- `subflow-state`
- `end-state`

It is possible for a state to inherit configuration information from another state. For that, use the `parent` attribute. For more information about inheritance in the flow definition, see the section about inheritance.

The start-state

When the flow starts, there must be a state which should be executed first. For that, you have a choice between an explicit `start-state` and an implicit `start-state`. In our example, the first state which occurs is the `add` view-state.

```
<view-state id="add" model="issue">
```

In the above case, we choose the implicit way. That means that if you do not specify the `start-state`, the first state which occurs in the flow definition file is the `start-state`. The other way is the explicit way. For that, you have to specify on the `flow` tag the `start-state` attribute. An example for that is shown below:

```
<flow start-state="add" />
```

As you can see above, the `start-state` is no concrete state, it is only a contract. And therefore, there is no explicit state. If you have developed applications with Spring Web Flow 1, you might remember that there was a tag called `start-state`.

The action-state and execution of business logic

If you want to do more than navigate, you have to execute some business logic. For that, in many frameworks the concept of actions exists, like in Spring Web Flow 2. There are two ways to express the evaluation of an action. There is the `action-state` tag. With that, you have an extra state for executing an action. To minimize your flow definition, it is recommended to use the `evaluate` element inside your `view-state`.

The tag for executing an action is `evaluate`. The attributes for the tag are described in the following table.

Attribute	Description
`expression`	The expression to evaluate. Here, you can execute an action on each bean which is accessible inside the flow. You have to use the expression language for expressing what to execute. That attribute is mandatory.
`result`	With that optional attribute, you have the possibility to assign the result to a variable in a specific scope.
`resultType`	The type of the result.

Additionally, it is possible to provide the `evaluate` tag with attributes. That can be done with the `attribute` child tag . But first, an example for the usage of `evaluate` without `attribute`.

```
<evaluate expression="issueService.findById(id, true)"
result="flowScope.issue" />
```

For an example of the usage of the `attribute` child element for `evaluate`, we provide the second parameter for the `findById` method as `attribute`.

```
<evaluate expression="issueService.findById(id)" result="flowScope.
issue">
  <attribute name="create" value="true" type="boolean"></attribute>
</evaluate>
```

The attributes are provided inside `RequestContext`. That means we need access to the actual instance of `RequestContext` inside the code. For convenience, we wrapped the `ScopeValueHelper` helper class inside the `flowtrac.swf.extension.scope` package.

```
public static <T> T getFromRequestContext(final String name, T
typeToConvert) {
   //Get the attributes from the actual request
   MutableAttributeMap map = RequestContextHolder.getRequestContext().
getAttributes();
   if (map == null) {
      throw new AttributeHelperException("Could not retrieve the
attributes from the actual request.");
   }
   T value = null;
   try  {
      value = (T) map.get(name);
   } catch (ClassCastException cce) {
      throw new AttributeHelperException("The value in the request is
not from the correct type.",cce);
   }
   return value;
}
```

With this method, we can now easily access the attributes in the action methods of the code. For an example, we show the following lines of the implementation of the `findById` method.

```
public Issue findById(Long id) {
      boolean create = ActionAttributeHelper.get("create", create =
false);
      return findById(id, create);
   }
```

The previous example uses the `create` attribute which is provided through the flow definition file. In the following table, we want to give an overview of the points where you could execute an action.

<table>
<tr><th>Point of Execution</th><th>Usage</th></tr>
<tr><td>At the start of the flow</td><td>There is a tag with the name `on-start`.
In the case of our demo application, we used that way to search an issue. The following line shows an example for that:
<on-start>
<evaluate expression="issueService.findById(id, true)" result="flowScope.issue" />
</on-start></td></tr>
<tr><td>At the entry of a state</td><td>Inside a state, there is the `on-entry` tag.
If you use that element, the code inside the `on-entry` tag is executed first.
A small example:
<view-state ...>
<on-entry>
<evaluate ...>
</on-entry>
</view-state></td></tr>
<tr><td>At the time of rendering a view</td><td>Inside a state, there is the `on-render` tag.
If you use that element, the code inside the `on-render` tag is executed just before the view of the concerned.
A small example:
<view-state ...>
<on-render>
<evaluate ...>
</on-render>
</view-state>
The difference between the `on-entry` tag and the `on-render` tag is that the latter one is executed every time the view is rendered. A use case could be that every time you render a view you want to create a new instance from the database.</td></tr>
<tr><td>At the time a transition is executed</td><td>It is possible to execute an action on time when a transition is executed. We just show a small example for that:
<transition on="store" to="issueStore">
<evaluate expression="persistenceContext.persist(issue)" />
</transition>
If the method returns `false`, the transition is not executed and the old view is presented again.</td></tr>
</table>

Point of Execution	Usage

On the exit of a state	Inside a state, there is the `on-exit` tag.
	If you use that element, the code inside the `on-exit` tag is executed when the state exits.
	A small example:
	`<view-state ...>`
	`  <on-exit>`
	`<evaluate ...>`
	`  </on-exit>`
	`</view-state>`

At the end of a flow	There is a tag with the name `on-end`.
	In the case of our demo application, we used that way to add some data to the issue. The following line shows an example for that:
	`<on-end>`
	`  <evaluate expression="itemInformationService.`
	`enrich(issue)" />`
	`</on-end>`

Details of a transition

A transition is the process of transfer from one state to another. Transitions are triggered through events. There are two types of transitions internally:

- Transitions inside an `action-state`
- Transitions inside a `view-state`

Transitions inside an action state and a view state are both equally relevant for you as a developer.

> You can understand a transition as a glue for the views, because to navigate from one view to another a transition is needed.

We describe all parameters in the following table. We also mention if a parameter can only occur in one state.

Attribute name	Description	Available in
`bind`	Indicates whether model binding should occur before the state is transferred or not. The value is optional and is of type `boolean` (`bind="true"`). Without model binding, the validation is prevented, but you have to bind the values manually if you want to use the values further in your use case. The default value is `true`.	`view-state`
`history`	This attribute's value (optional) sets the history policy for this transition. That means that this setting decides whether you can use the back button of the browser or not. The following values are possible: • `preserve` (default value) • `discard` • `invalidate` The `preserve` value means that back-tracking to the current state (after the transition) is possible. The `discard` value prevents back-tracking to the actual state and `invalidate` prevents back-tracking to that state and any previously entered `view-state`.	`view-state`
`on`	The name of the outcome on which the transition is triggered. It is simple text.	Both
`on-exception`	The name of the exception (fully qualified, for example `java.lang.NumberFormatException`) on which the transition is triggered. It is not possible to mix `on` and `on-exception`.	Both
`to`	The name of the destination state.	Both

The view-state

The following table shows the attributes of a `view-state`:

Attribute	Description
`id` **(mandatory)**	The identifier for the state. This identifier must be unique inside the flow.
`parent` **(optional)**	The name of the parent of the state (see the *Inheritance for states* subsection for more information about this feature).

Attribute	Description
view **(optional)**	The name of the view. If you do not specify the name, the id of the view-state is used as the basename for the view file. That file has to be in the same directory as the flow definition file. If you define a view, the view has to be in the same directory as the flow definition file. A simple example is shown in the line below: <view-state id="add" view="addIssue.jsp" /> If you want to show a view outside your application, there is the externalRedirect prefix. It is possible to use expressions with ${} format. The supported formats for externalRedirect are: externalRedirect:<servlet relative path> externalRedirect:contextRelative:<context relative path> externalRedirect:serverRelative:<server relative path> externalRedirect:<fully qualified http:// or https:// URL> For example: • externalRedirect:contextRelative:/flowtrac /issue/all • externalRedirect:contextRelative:/flowtrac/issue/ all?id=${issue.id} The flowRedirect: prefix may be used to redirect to another flow: flowRedirect:myOtherFlow?someData=${flowScope.data} When this attribute is not specified, the view to render will be determined by convention. The default convention is to treat the id of this view-state as the view identifier. For exotic usages, you may plug in a custom ViewFactory bean.
redirect **(optional)**	With this attribute (the value is of type Boolean), the view-state sends a flow execution redirect before the view is rendered. This feature is essential if you need a refresh after event processing. Internally, it is done from FlowHandlerAdapter (package org.springframework.webflow.mvc.servlet) in the sendFlowExecutionRedirect method. The steps to do that redirection are first to elaborate the URL for the redirection and then to redirect to the flow in the actual state.
popup **(optional)**	With this attribute (the value is of type Boolean), the view is displayed in a pop-up dialog. For example: <view-state id="test" popup="true" />
model **(optional)**	With this attribute, it is possible to specify a model that can be bound to the properties of that view. <view-state id="add" model="issue" > The model can be in any accessible scope, for example in the flow scope. In our sample application, we add to the flow scope (<evaluate expression="issueService.findById(id)" result="flowScope.issue">)

> The current release of Spring Web Flow 2 (2.0.4 at the time of writing) supports two technologies for the view. On the one hand, there is the possibility to use plain JSP, and on the other, JSF facelets (check `https://facelets.dev.java.net/`). The technology for the view does not relate to the controller you use. This means you do not have to use Spring MVC as a controller framework. But the integration with Spring MVC is highly recommended because it is very seamless.

Validation inside the view-state

We have shown that the `view-state` has the optional `model` attribute, which is responsible for binding the data of a form to an internal model class. If we talk about the input of user data, there is often the need for a validation. Spring Web Flow offers us two ways for server-side validation. These two are:

- Implement a validate method inside the `model` class
- Implement an encapsulated Validator

The first way of validation is the mentioned implementation of a validate method inside the `model` class. The name of the method begins with the name `validate` appended with the state which should be validated (`validate${state}`). For example, if we have the following state:

```
<view-state id="add" model="issue">
```

we have to implement a method `validateAdd`. Additionally, we have to provide that method with a `MessageContext` (package `org.springframework.binding.message`).

The mentioned `MessageContext` is the central class for recording and retrieving messages for the case of display. See the class diagram below to get an overview about the methods.

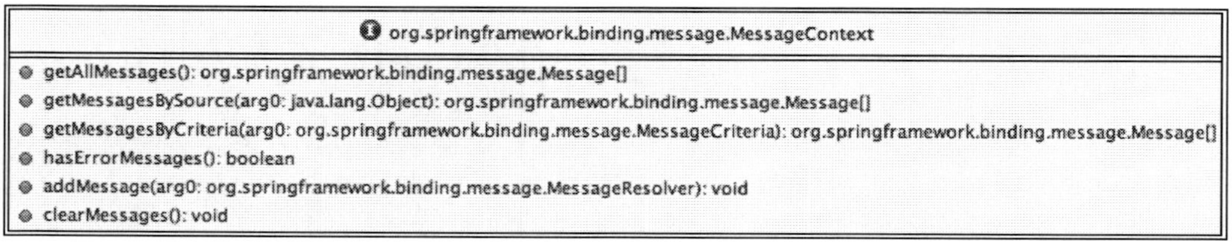

An example implementation for this method (in our sample, we added it to the used model class `Issue`) is shown below.

```
public void validateAdd(MessageContext context)  {
   if (this.name == null || this.name.trim().length() == 0) {
      context.addMessage(new MessageBuilder().error().source("name").
defaultText("the name is required").build());
   }
}
```

> To add messages to `MessageContext`, you have to provide an instance of a `MessageResolver` (package `org.springframework.binding.message`). To create such an instance, there is a class named `MessageBuilder` in the same package. This class has a fluent interface (the return values of the methods are the `MessageBuilder` instance). See the example above.

The second way for programmatic validation on the server side is to implement an own Validator class. The name of the method is the same as before. See the example implementation below.

```
@Component
public class IssueValidator {
   public void validateAdd(Issue issue, MessageContext context)  {
      if (issue.getName() == null || issue.getName().trim().length()
== 0) {
         context.addMessage(new MessageBuilder().error().
source("name").defaultText("validator: the name is required").
build());
      }
   }
}
```

If you use the `@Component` annotation (available in Spring 2.5 or above), the classpath-scanning registers the bean with the name `issueValidator`.

> **Which way should I take?**
>
> We have looked at the two ways which offer you the same functionality. The problem with the first way is that you mix the concerns. But the `model` class should only encapsulate the data and nothing else. Additionally, if you implement the method in your value object class, you get a dependency to the Spring Binding (library `org.springframework.binding-x.x.x.RELEASE.jar`). The implemention of an own validator class should be prefered to follow the concept of loose coupling.

More details about validation

To complete the validation, we want to provide a complete overview as to how the validation methods are called from the framework. The method which does the validation is a private method called `validate` (internally, the method calls the `validate` method of the `ValidationHelper` helper class inside the `org.springframework.webflow.validation` package) inside the `AbstractMvcView` class (package `org.springframework.webflow.mvc.view`).

Step 1: Create the name of the `validate` method. Append the name of the state to `validate` (capitalized, that means `add` becomes `Add`). The method name for the state `add` is `validateAdd`.

Step 2: Search for the method with the `MessageContext` parameter (package `org.springframework.binding.message`). If the method is found, it is called.

Step 3a: If a bean factory is available, a validator class is searched. This is done by appending the value of the model to `Validator`, for example `issueValidator`. If the bean is found, the next steps are executed.

Step 3b: A method with the same naming principle as in the above Step 3a is searched (additionally there is a parameter for the model first). If the method is found, it is executed.

Step 3c: If no method is found, there is a search for a method with a parameter called `Errors` (package `org.springframework.validation`). If the method is found, it is executed.

As you can see, it is possible to have two validator classes. First, the validate method inside the model class is executed (if available). Next, the method inside the validator (if available) is executed.

> It is not possible to have more than one Validator class. If you have more than one, a run-time exception from the `java.lang.IllegalStateException` type on starting the application context is thrown.

> **Externalize your messages**
>
> Inside the validator, we have used `MessageBuilder` to create an instance of `MessageResolver`. We have used the `defaultText` method to express your error message. Additionally, there is a method callled `code` to provide an error key. This key is resolved by looking into the `messages.properties` file inside the directory of the flow. The `messages.properties` file is available inside the flow and also inside the views for that flow. Therefore, you can use it for internationalization too. By the way, it is possible to mix the `defaultText` and `code` methods (fluent interface). If no error key is found, the value of `defaultText` is used.

The decision-state

There are often cases when you want to know whether a view is rendered or not. For that case, there is a concept of `decision-state`. In the following example, we select a specific state inside the flow depending on whether the `simpleValue` variable (it comes from a request) is set or not.

```
<input name="simpleValue" value="flashScope.simpleValue" />
<decision-state id="check">
  <if test=" simpleValue != null" then="${simpleValue}" else="init" />
</decision-state>
```

The subflow-state

A subflow is a flow inside a flow. With this concept, it is possible to have a hierarchy of flows. You have one main (parent) flow and can execute some subflows.

A small example of a subflow:

```
<subflow-state id="addGuest" subflow="createGuest">
    <transition on="guestCreated" to="reviewBooking">
        <evaluate expression="booking.guests.add(currentEvent.
attributes.guest)" />
    </transition>
    <transition on="creationCancelled" to="reviewBooking" />
</subfow-state>
```

More details about subflows are provided in Chapter 5 of this book. Besides subflows, there is a concept of flow hierarchy which is explained at the end of this chapter.

The end-state

To close a flow, you have to define an `end-state`. Just a small example from our sample application:

```
<end-state id="issueStore" commit="true" />
```

Additionally, it is possible to define an output for this flow.

```
<end-state id="issueStore" commit="true">
  <output name="name" value="issue.name" />
</end-state>
```

One important question is what to show after the flow ends. For that, you have the `view` attribute. With that, you can define the view which should be shown after the flow exits. One example from our example application:

```
<end-state id="issueStore" commit="true" view="externalRedirect:
contextRelative:/flowtrac/issue/all" />
```

The exit point

This is the page to go when the flow ends. Normally, it is defined in the `end-state`.

Section footer

The footer of a flow definition file can have the following elements:

- `global-transitions`
- `on-end`
- `output`
- `exception-handler`
- `bean-import`

The `on-end` event handler is described earlier in this chapter (in the *The action-state and execution of the business logic* section). The other elements are described below.

global-transitions: global handling of events

With the `global-transitions` element, you have the opportunity to define state transfers. Often applications have a global menu and the events can be handled globally. The child element of `global-transitions` is the `transition` element. Additionally, it is possible to use `global-transitions` in conjunction with the transitions as mechanism for global exception handling (see the *exception-handler: Exceptions between the execution of a flow* section below). An example for declaring `global-transitions` is shown below.

```
<global-transitions>
    <transition on="login" to="login">
    <transition on="logout" to="logout">
</global-transitions>
```

on-end: execution of actions at the end of the flow

Before the exit from a flow, it is possible to execute an action inside the `on-end` element. The following lines show an example for the usage of the `on-end` element.

```
<on-end>
  <evaluate expression="itemInformationService.enrich(issue)" />
</on-end>
```

output: output of the flow

Besides the option to declare the output for each `end-state`, it is possible to declare an output (the `output` element) for the flow. For example:

```
<output name="id" />
```

exception-handler: exceptions between the execution of a flow

Between the execution of a flow (or the states inside the flow), exceptions can occur. The default implementation throws the exception and the user is confronted with that exception. To prevent the situation of an unhandled exception which occurs inside a flow (or state), it is possible to register an own handler for exceptions.

The following elements can have an own exception handler:

- `action-state`
- `decision-state`
- `end-state`
- `view-state`
- `flow`

The exception handler has to be from the `FlowExecutionExceptionHandler` type. The package of that interface is `org.springframework.webflow.engine`. The methods for that handler are shown in the following class diagram:

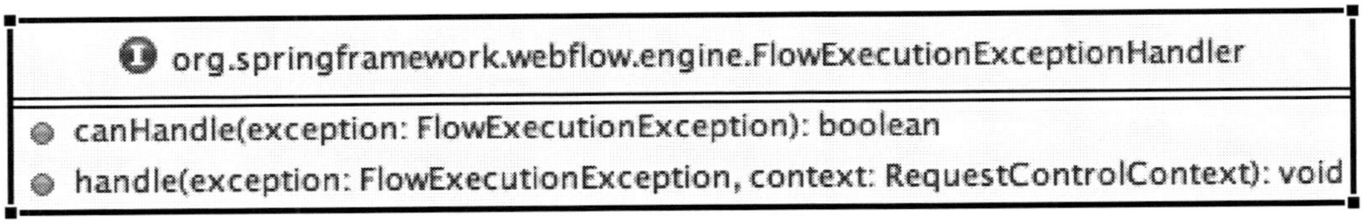

As you can see in the interface of `FlowExecutionExceptionHandler`, the general exception is `FlowExcecutionException` in the `org.springframework.webflow.execution` package. The class hierarchy of that exception is shown in the diagram below:

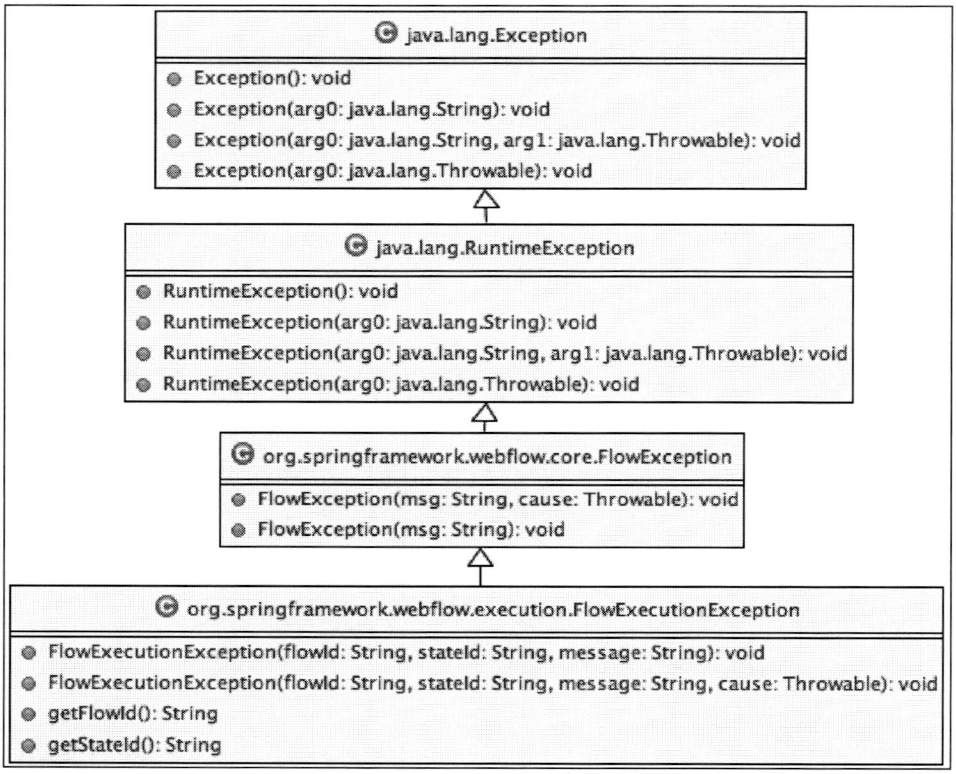

As you can see, the exception is from the `java.lang.RuntimeException` type and therefore it is an unchecked exception (that means you don't have to catch the exception). If an exception occurs, you can use the `getFlowId` method to get the `id` of the flow which has thrown the exception. Additionally, the `getStateId` method can be used for retrieving the `id` of the state in which the exception occurred. For handling a specific exception, you have to implement two methods of the interface.

First, there is a method called `canHandle`. If this method returns `true`, the handler tells the system that it is ready to handle the exception. For example, the following method returns `true` if `java.lang.NumberFormatException` occurs.

```
public boolean canHandle(FlowExecutionException exception) {
   return (exception.getCause() instanceof NumberFormatException);
}
```

The second method that needs to be implemented is the `handle` method with a parameter of the occurred exception (from the `FlowExecutionException` type) and an instance of `RequestControlContext`. The interface is shown in the diagram below:

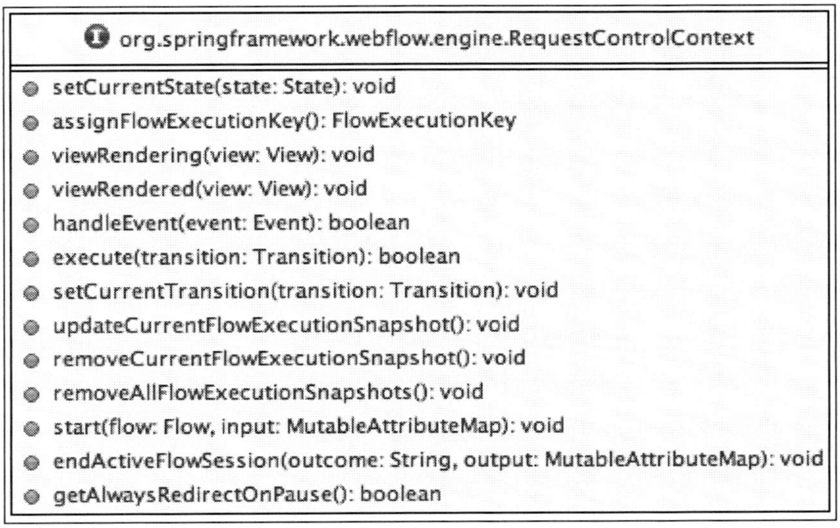

The instance of `RequestControlContext` is the central interface to manipulate an ongoing flow execution. It is used from various artifacts inside the context of a running flow. One important point to mention if we talk about handling exceptions is how to continue the flow with a specific transition. The method we need for this is the `execute(Transition transition)` method in `RequestControlContext`. As a parameter, we need an instance of the `Transition` class in the `org.springframework.webflow.engine` package. To create this class, we have to provide an instance of `TargetStateResolver` in the same package. There is a default implementation which should fit in most cases. The name of that implementation class is `DefaultTargetStateResolver` in the `org.springframework.webflow.engine.support` package. It has a constructor to provide only the `id` of the state to transfer. The following line shows an example of the usage:

```
context.execute(new Transition(new DefaultTargetStateResolver("target
StateId")));
```

> A `TargetStateResolver` has only the `resolveTargetState` method with a state as the return value. It is interesting to know that the return value `null` indicates that there is no state transfer. The task of that class is to resolve the target state of the transition from the source state (it comes as a parameter, but it could be `null`) in the current request context.

To use an own exception handler, you have to register (inside the flow definition file) the handler with the `exception-handler` tag. An example for a `view-state` is shown in the lines below:

```
<view-state id="add" model="issue" >
   <exception-handler bean="myExceptionHandler" />
</view-state>
```

The `exception-handler` tag has only the `bean` attribute, which is a required attribute. The value of the attribute is the name of a bean which has to be registered inside an application context that is reachable from the flow. The bean has to implement the mentioned handler interface (`FlowExecutionExceptionHandler`). The declaration of that bean inside an application context file is not different from the other definition. For completeness, a sample definition is shown below:

```
<bean id="myExceptionHandler" class="flowtrac.service.
MyExceptionHandler" />
```

The algorithm for handling exceptions is implemented inside the `FlowExecutionImpl` internal class (package `org.springframework.webflow.engine.impl`). The following diagram visualizes how exceptions are handled if they occur while the flow executes:

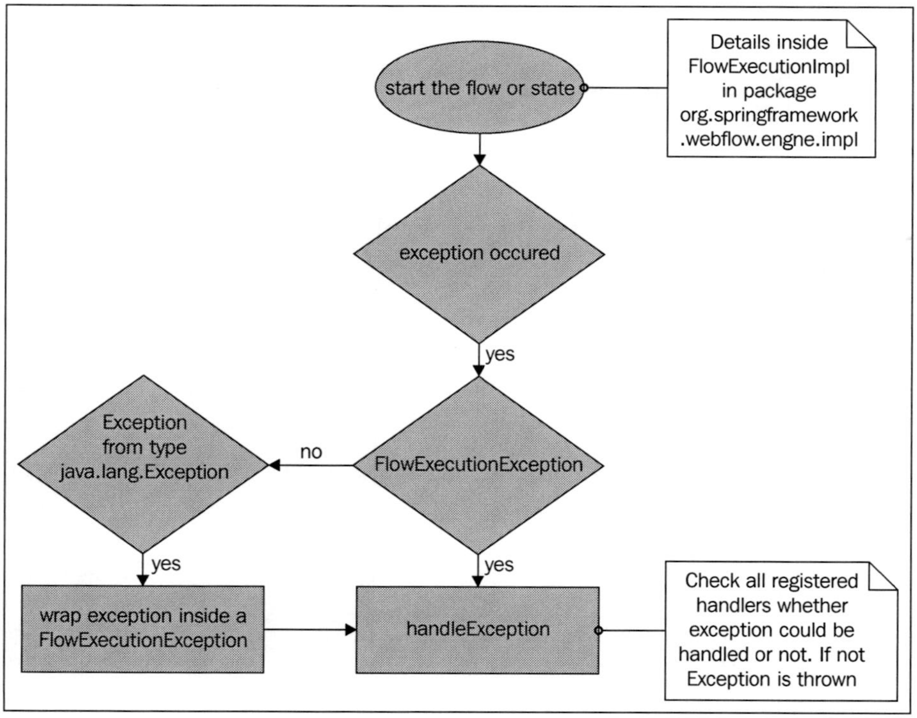

For starting and resuming a flow, there is a central interface called FlowExecution (inside the org.springframework.webflow.execution package). The methods of this interface are shown in the diagram below:

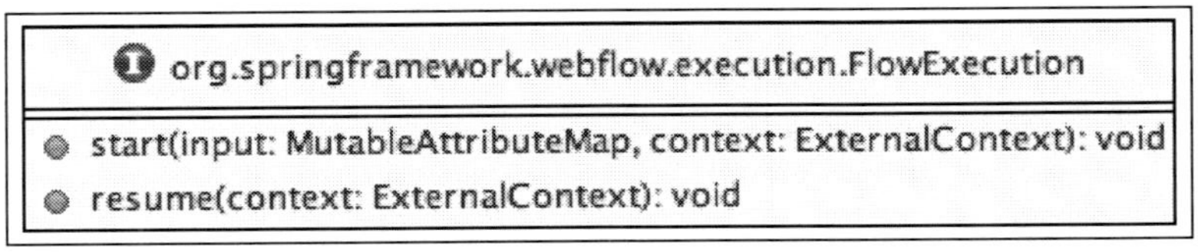

Additionally, there is one more place where you can deal with exceptions. It is on a transition. Here, you have an additional attribute called on-exception. The value of this attribute is the fully qualified exception (e.g. java.lang.NumberFormatException) which you want to handle. If the mentioned exception occurs, the transition is triggered and the flow is transferred to the specified state in the to attribute. An example for that is shown below:

```
<transition on-exception="java.lang.NumberFormatException" to="add" />
```

> Take care that you do not use the on and on-exception attributes together. If you mix these attributes in one transition, an exception of the NoMatchingTransitionException type (package org.springframework.webflow.engine) is thrown, because the transition cannot be found. The on-exception attribute cannot be used in conjunction with a secured element (see more about security in Chapter 7).

The internal implementation of the on-exception attribute is done with an exception handler from type of the already mentioned interface FlowExecutionExceptionHandler. The name of the class is TransitionExecutingFlowExecutionExceptionHandler. This handler is automatically registered from FlowModelFlowBuilder if an on-exception attribute occurred. If the handler handles an exception, the exception and the root cause are stored inside the flash scope (remember: the el variable name is flashScope). See the following table for the names:

Attribute	**Description**
flowExecutionException	The attribute name where the handled exception is stored inside the flash scope.
rootCauseException	The attribute name where the root cause of the handled exception is stored inside the flash scope.

> With the combination of the `on-exception` and the `global-transitions` attributes, you have the opportunity to define global exception handlers. An idea is to create an abstract flow with just such global exception handlers and define the flow as abstract. With the possiblity of the inheritance of the flows, you can isolate the exception handling from your flows (seperation of concerns).

bean-import: declaring beans for a flow

With the `bean-import` element, it is possible to import beans which become part of the bean factory for the flow that imports the beans. The beans must be defined inside a Spring configuration file. To define that file, there is a mandatory attribute called `resource`. Here, you specify the file relative to the location of the flow definition file. In the example below, the `addIssue-beans.xml` resource file is imported and the beans inside are added to the bean factory of the flow. The mentioned resource file in our example must be in the same directory as the flow definition file:

```
<bean-import resource="addIssue-beans.xml" />
```

If you want to import more than one file, you can add just another `bean-import` tag to the flow definition file.

Internals of building a flow

To have a complete overview of building a flow, we describe the building also from the Java view.

> Building a flow is a synonym for the transformation of the DSL (Domain Specific Language) which is used to describe the flow in the flow definition file and is needed for the internal representation with instances of Java classes.

Step 1: The initialization

The first step is the initialization of `FlowBuilder` (implementation of `org.springframework.webflow.engine.builder.FlowBuilder`). Create the initial flow definition by calling the `init` method with an instance of `org.springframework.webflow.engine.builder.FlowBuilderContext`. This class is an internal helper to access the elements of a flow definition. For a complete overview, see the class diagram below.

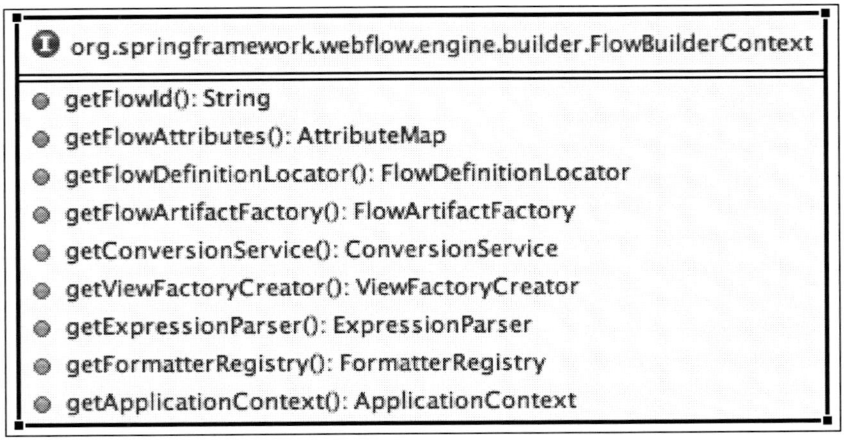

The flow itself is created by an internal call of the `create` method on the `org.springframework.webflow.engine.Flow` class.

Step 2: The variables

Now the `buildVariables` method of `FlowBuilder` is called in order to build any variables initialized by the flow when it starts.

Step 3: The inputs

The input mapper (from type `org.springframework.binding.mapping.Mapper`) is created and set for the flow. The method for that is `buildInputMapper`.

Step 4: The start actions

The `buildStartAction` method creates and adds each of the start actions to the flow.

Step 5: The states

Now the states of the flow in development are created and added to the internal representation of the flow. The method is called `buildStates`.

Step 6: The global transitions

The `buildGlobalTransitions` method creates the transitions which are shared between the states.

Step 7: The end actions

The end actions are created and added through the `buildEndActions` method.

Step 8: The outputs

Now the output mapper is created and set inside the called `buildOutputManager` method. The output mapper is from the `org.springframework.binding.mapping.Mapper` type. It is from the same type as the input mapper.

Step 9: The exceptions

Inside the `buildExceptionHandlers` method, the handlers of the flow are created and added to the internal flow representation.

Step 10: Get the full flow definition

From `org.springframework.webflow.engine.builder.FlowAssembler`, the `getFlow` method is called (inside the `assembleFlow` method). It is done to get a reference to the fully built flow definition (directly called from `org.springframework.webflow.config.FlowRegistryFactoryBean`).

The internal representation of the flow is from the `FlowDefinition` type in the `org.springframework.webflow.definition` package. See the class diagram below:

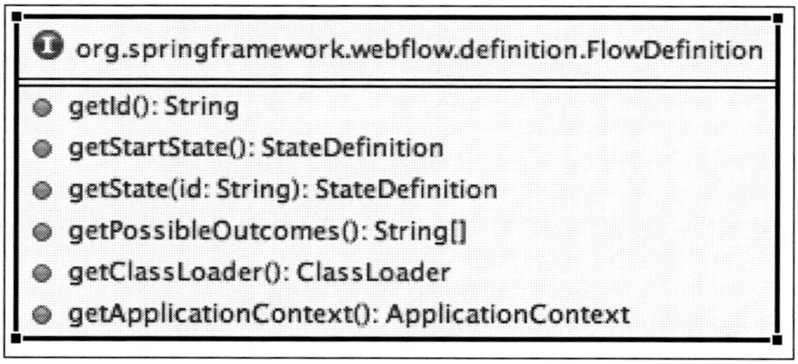

Step 11: Cleanup

The last step is a cleanup of resources which are allocated during the creation process. This is done with the help of the `dispose` method.

For completion, the eleven steps for creating an instance of the `FlowDefiniton` class (package `org.springframework.webflow.definition`) are shown below.

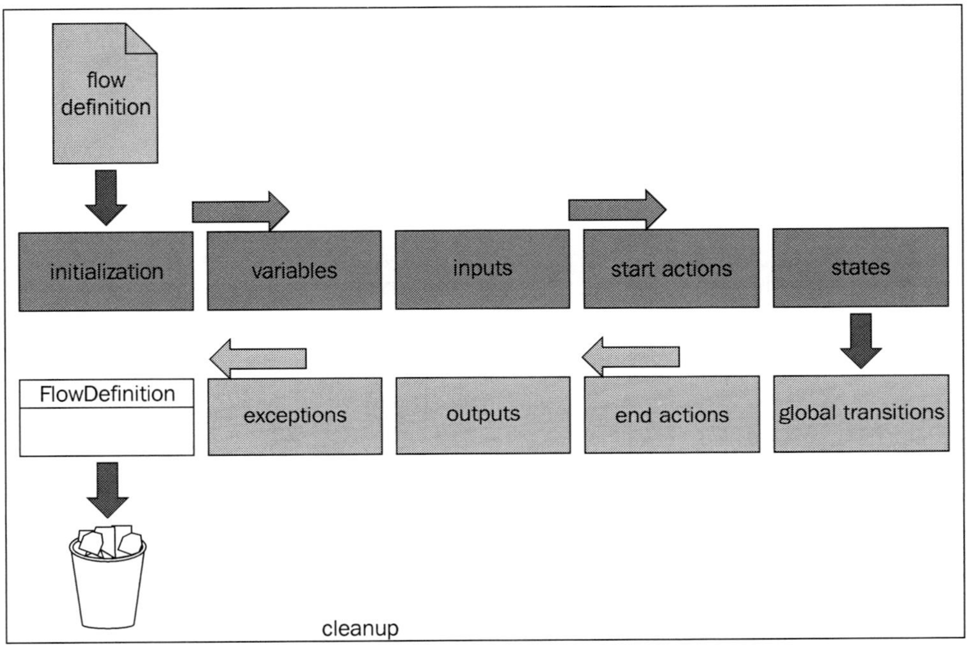

Configuration

Besides the flow definition file, there is a main configuration file for configuring the flow engine. That configuration file is an XML file, too. The grammar for the file is the XSD `http://www.springframework.org/schema/webflow-config/spring-webflow-config-2.0.xsd`. The XSD file is located inside the `org.springframework.webflow-2.X.X.RELEASE.jar` library in the `org/springframework/webflow/config folder`. The configuration is not only a Spring Web Flow configuration but a Spring configuration too. Therefore, you have to add an XSD for that, too. An example header for the configuration file is shown below.

This configuration file has to be loaded in order to bootstrap the Spring Web Flow subsystem. The process of loading this file is often done in the deployment descriptor file of a web application, which is named `web.xml`. For an example, see the quickstart example in Chapter 2 of this book.

```
<beans xmlns="http://www.springframework.org/schema/beans"
   xmlns:xsi="http://www.w3.org/2001/XMLSchema-instance"
   xmlns:webflow="http://www.springframework.org/schema/webflow-
config"
```

```
    xsi:schemaLocation="
              http://www.springframework.org/schema/beans
              http://www.springframework.org/schema/beans
/spring-beans-2.5.xsd
              http://www.springframework.org/schema/webflow-config
              http://www.springframework.org/schema/webflow-config/
spring-webflow-config-2.0.xsd">
```

There are two important elements in the configuration which you have to configure. These two elements are:

- FlowRegistry
- FlowExecutor

To use these elements in the XML configuration, you have to use the `webflow` namespace (e.g. `webflow:flow-registry`).

FlowRegistry

You have to provide the webflow system with the location of your flow definition files. These files are registered in the FlowRegistry. An example from the bug tracker application is shown below.

```
<webflow:flow-registry id="flowRegistry">
      <webflow:flow-location path="/WEB-INF/issue/add/add.xml"/>
</webflow:flow-registry>
```

As mentioned before, you have to use elements from the defined namespace for the webflow configuration. The name of the element is `flow-registry`. Additionally, it is essential to provide an `id` for `flow-registry`, which is done with the help of the `id` attribute. The line below shows an empty flow registry:

```
<webflow:flow-registry id="flowRegistry" />
```

The flow registry can be filled with the flow definition file. For that, there is the `flow-location` element. You can define more than one `flow-location` element inside the flow registry. With the `path` attribute, you can specify one single flow definition file (see the line below).

```
<webflow:flow-location path="/WEB-INF/issue/add/add.xml"/>
```

Additionally, it is possible to provide an `id` for the flow location.

```
<webflow:flow-location path="/WEB-INF/issue/add/add.xml" id="addIssue"
/>
```

The mentioned `id` is the unique identifier for the flow. With the `id`, you can call the flow. In the case of our example, we don't define an `id`. Therefore, the flow has the `id` added (see *Internals of the WebFlow Configuration* for more information about this). We call the flow with the `/flowtrac-web/flowtrac/issue/add` URL. If we set the `id` to `addIssue` (the last example), the URL changes to `/flowtrac-web/flowtrac/issue/addIssue`.

The shown possibilities are useful if you have just a few definition files. If you have more configuration files, it could be painful to insert each single flow definition file. For that case, it is possible to provide a directory (with subdirectory) as the location for the configuration files.

```
<webflow:flow-location-pattern value="/WEB-INF/issue/**/*-flow.xml" />
```

In the sample above, all files inside `issue` and below are searched for files which end with `flow.xml`. The notation is similar to the patterns which are known from the build system Apache ANT (see `http://ant.apache.org`).

The flow location can be enriched with meta attributes. For that case, you can specify these attributes inside the `flow-definition-attributes` element.

```
<webflow:flow-location path="/WEB-INF/flows/booking/booking.xml">
    <flow-definition-attributes>
        <attribute name="caption" value="Books a hotel" />
        <attribute name="persistence-context" value="true"
type="boolean" />
    </flow-definition-attributes>
</webflow:flow-location>
```

You can use the attributes in the flow definition file inside the context of the request.

FlowExecutor

A **FlowExecutor** acts as the central point of entrance into the Spring Web Flow system. The FlowExecutor is responsible for executing the flow definition. Internally, it is represented as an interface from the `FlowExecutor` type (package: `org.springframework.webflow.executor`). The implementation of this interface is done in the `FlowExecutorImpl` internal class (package: `org.springframework.webflow.executor`). The FlowExecutor's task is to launch new flow executions and resume flow executions which are paused. The paused flow executions are stored in a `FlowExecutionRepostory` between requests. It is worth mentioning that there is no coupling with the HTTP environment. This means that the implementation is just an execution engine for the flow definition file. The coupling to the HTTP protocol is done in the used controllers.

FlowExecutor Listeners

With the `flow-execution-listeners` element, it is possible to define one or more listeners which observe the lifecycle of flow executions.

```
<flow-execution-listeners>
    <listener ref="listener1"/>
    <listener ref="listener2"/>
</flow-execution-listeners>
```

Two use cases where listeners can be useful are:

- Security
- Persistence

In our example application, we use such a listener for the persistence.

```
    <webflow:flow-executor id="flowExecutor">
       <webflow:flow-execution-listeners>
          <webflow:listener ref="jpaFlowExecutionListener" />
       </webflow:flow-execution-listeners>
    </webflow:flow-executor>

    <bean id="jpaFlowExecutionListener" class="org.springframework.
webflow.persistence.JpaFlowExecutionListener">
       <constructor-arg ref="entityManagerFactory" />
       <constructor-arg ref="transactionManager" />
    </bean>
```

The listener class has to be from the `org.springframework.webflow.execution.FlowExecutionListener` type. Just to see what you have to implement, we show the class diagram for the listener:

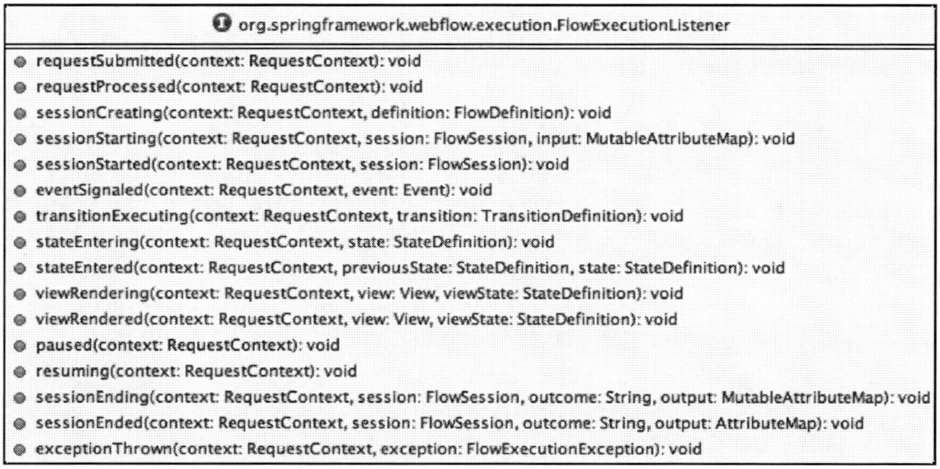

Implement your own FlowExecutionListener

The interface for `FlowExecutionListener` has many methods, but often you only need just a few of them. For this scenario, there is an abstract class which implements the methods with an empty body (the template method pattern which is known from GoF). The mentioned abstract class with the name `FlowExecutionListenerAdapter` is located in the same package as the `FlowExecutionListener` interface. The Spring Web Flow framework comes with many classes which work as listeners for a flow. But only the mentioned adapter class implements the `FlowExecutionListener` interface. All other classes are just subclasses from the adapter (for example, the `org.springframework.webflow.persistence.JpaFlowExecutionListener` class).

Internals of the Webflow Configuration

For the creation of the internal configuration of a class, there is a definition inside the `spring.handlers` properties file (inside the `META-INF` directory of the webflow JAR). Here is the class: `org.springframework.webflow.config.WebFlowConfigNamespaceHandler` (a mapping from XSD to handler class). It is worth mentioning that there is an additional `spring.schemas` file in the `META-INF` directory which sets the location of the XSD files. The namespace handler is defined for four elements (`flow-executor`, `flow-execution-listeners`, `flow-registry`, and `flow-builder-services`), which are the parsers for internal representation of the configuration. All parsers are located in the `org.springframework.webflow.config` package.

Name	Class
`flow-executor`	`FlowExecutionBeanDefintionParser`
`flow-execution-listeners`	`FlowExecutionListenerLoaderBeanDefintionParser`
`flow-registry`	`FlowRegistryBeanDefinitionParser`
`flow-builder-services`	`FlowBuilderServicesBeanDefintionParser`

The flow registry is an internal implementation of `org.springframework.webflow.engine.model.registry.FlowModelRegistry`. The name of the implementation class is `FlowModelRegistryImpl`. One interesting detail is the `getFlowId` method of the `FlowDefintionResourceFactory` class. This method creates the `id` of the flow if not specified.

```
protected String getFlowId(Resource flowResource) {
String fileName = flowResource.getFilename();
   int extensionIndex = fileName.lastIndexOf('.');
```

```
        if (extensionIndex != -1) {
            return fileName.substring(0, extensionIndex);
        } else {
            return fileName;
        }
    }
```

As you can see above, the method just uses the filename of the flow definition as the `id` (without extension). If you want to change the algorithm, you can do so with the help of the `id` attribute. The method is only called if the `id` is specified. See the following extract from `createResource` of the `FlowDefinitionResourceFactory` class.

```
if (flowId == null || flowId.length() == 0) {
        flowId = getFlowId(resource);
}
```

By the way, the mentioned factory is responsible for the creation of an instance of `FlowDefintionResource`.

A helpful configuration is the parameter development of the mentioned element— `flowBuilderServices`. With this parameter, the system goes into development mode and each change results in a reload. See the following line for an example:

```
<webflow:flow-builder-services id="flowBuilderServices"
development="true" />
```

Inheritance inside a flow definition

With Spring Web Flow 2, the principle of inheritance for a flow definition is introduced. That means one flow can inherit the configuration of another flow. It is possible to use inheritance for states and flows. If you want to use inheritance, it is important that the parent flow is an element of the `flow-registry`.

If we compare the Java inheritance model and the flow model, there are some important differences. The key elements of the flow (state) inheritance are:

- it is not possible for a child flow to override an element from the parent flow
- elements which are similar between the child and parent are merged
- elements from the parent flow which are unique will be added to the child flow

From Java, we know that we can only extend from one class. In terms of a flow, it is possible to extend from **more** than one flow. The attribute on the flow (and the state) for declaring inheritance is `parent`. It is important to say that a state can only extend from **one** other state and not more. Now, we just show two examples for a better understanding.

Inheritance for flows

The attribute for the inheritance for flows is `parent`. For a flow, it is possible to use more than one definition for `parent`. For that case, you have to use a comma as a delimiter. The merge process starts from the left to the right. See the line below for a simple definition of a flow inheritance with two parents:

```
<flow parent="base, common">
```

The diagram below helps to understand the direction of the merge process:

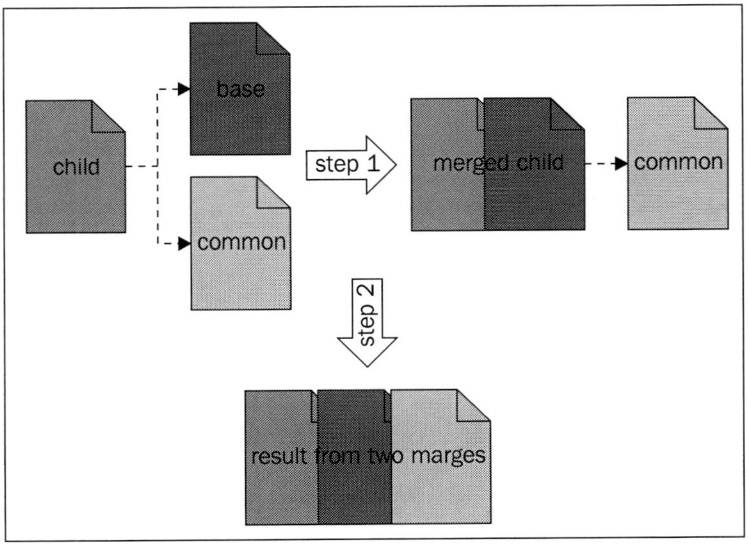

There is one additional feature in the case of inheritance. There is a possibility to declare a flow as abstract. This means that the flow cannot be instantiated. You can do so with the help of the `abstract` attribute for the `flow` element. An example is shown below:

```
<flow abstract="true" />
```

If you try to instantiate an abstract flow, a run-time exception from the `FlowBuilderException` type (package `org.springframework.webflow.engine.builder`) is thrown.

Inheritance for states

A state can only extend one state. For that, there is the `parent` attribute. Besides the name of the state (remember: you can only inherit from **one** state), you have to mention the flow. The name of the flow and the state are separated with the help of the # character.

Example:

```
<view-state id="child-state" parent="parent-flow#parent-view-state">
```

Merge or no merge

The inheritance of a flow or state is done by merging the elements. It depends on the element or attribute as to whether the merge process is started or not.

Name of element	Name of the attribute	M	NM
action-state	Id	X	
Attribute	Name	X	
bean-import	-		X
decision-state	Id	X	
Evaluate	-		X
end-state	Id	X	
exception-handler			X
end-state	Id	X	
Flow	-	X	
If	Test	X	
on-end	-	X	
on-entry	-	X	
on-exit	-	X	
on-render	-	X	
on-start	-	X	
Input	Name	X	
Output	Name	X	
persistence-context	-		X

Name of element	Name of the attribute	M	NM
Render	-		X
Secured	Attributes	X	
Set	-		X
subflow-state	-	X	
transition	On	X	
Var	-		X
view-state	Id	X	

The complete flow for the example

For your overview, we want to show you a complete flow file (`add.xml` from the `webapp/WEB-INF/issue/add` directory) from our example application:

```
<?xml version="1.0" encoding="UTF-8"?>
<flow xmlns="http://www.springframework.org/schema/webflow"
       xmlns:xsi="http://www.w3.org/2001/XMLSchema-instance"
     xsi:schemaLocation="http://www.springframework.org/schema/webflow
        http://www.springframework.org/schema/webflow/spring-webflow-
2.0.xsd" >

    <persistence-context/>

    <!-- The id of the issue which should be edited -->
    <input name="id" />

    <on-start>
      <evaluate expression="issueService.findById(id)"
result="flowScope.issue">
         <attribute name="create" value="true" type="boolean"></
attribute>
      </evaluate>
   </on-start>

      <!--
      If no view is specified a page with the same name
      as the id is searched in the directory of the flow definition.
      Additionally its possible to define a view with the attribute
view.
     -->
```

```
    <view-state id="add" model="issue">
        <transition on="store" to="issueStore" >
            <evaluate expression="persistenceContext.persist(issue)"/>
        </transition>
    </view-state>
    <end-state id="issueStore" commit="true" view="externalRedirect:
contextRelative:/flowtrac/issue/all" />
    <on-end>
        <evaluate expression="itemInformationService.enrich(issue)" />
    </on-end>
</flow>
```

Summary

In this chapter, we have shown you all the basics around the creation of a flow with the Spring Web Flow framework in version 2. With that knowledge, you should be ready to implement your own flows.

In the following chapters we are going to show you more concepts of Spring Web Flow 2. Especially, the integration with other frameworks will be a topic in the upcoming chapters.

4
Spring Faces

The main focus of the Spring Web Flow framework is to deliver the infrastructure to describe the page flow of a web application. The flow itself is a very important element of a web application, because it describes its structure, particularly the structure of the implemented business use cases. But besides the flow which is only in the background, the user of your application is interested in the graphical user interface (GUI). Therefore, we need a solution of how to provide a rich user interface to the users. One framework which offers components is JavaServer Faces (JSF). With the release of Spring Web Flow 2, an integration module to connect these two technologies has been introduced. The name of the module is **Spring Faces**. This chapter starts with the description of the configuration of the integration. Following this, the usage of the Spring Faces module is shown. This chapter is no introduction to the JavaServer Faces technology. It is only a description about the integration of Spring Web Flow 2 with JSF. If you have never previously worked with JSF, please refer to the JSF reference to gain knowledge about the essential concepts of JavaServer Faces.

> **JavaServer Faces (JSF)—a brief introduction**
>
> The JavaServer Faces (JSF) technology is a web application framework with the goal to make the development of user interfaces for a web application (based on Java EE) easier. JSF uses a component-based approach with an own lifecycle model, instead of a request-driven approach used by traditional MVC web frameworks. The version 1.0 of JSF is specified inside **JSR (Java Specification Request) 127** (`http://jcp.org/en/jsr/detail?id=127`).

Enabling Spring Faces support

To use the Spring Faces module, you have to add some configuration to your application. The diagram below depicts the single configuration blocks. These blocks are described in this chapter.

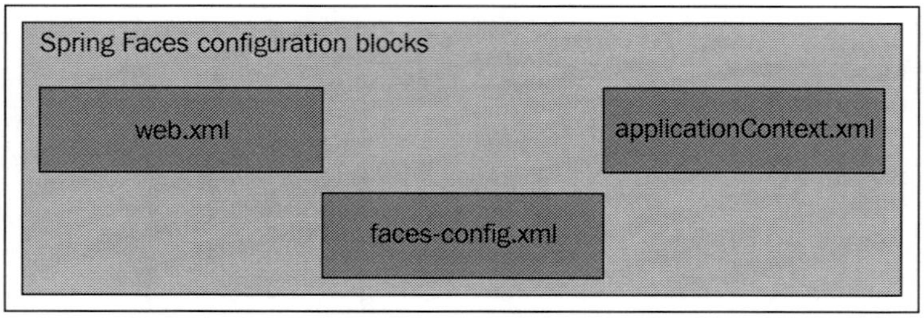

The first step in the configuration is to configure the JSF framework itself. That is done in the deployment descriptor of the web application—`web.xml`. The servlet has to be loaded at the startup of the application. This is done with the `<load-on-startup>1</load-on-startup>` element.

```
    <!-- Initialization of the JSF implementation. The Servlet is not
used at runtime -->
    <servlet>
        <servlet-name>Faces Servlet</servlet-name>
        <servlet-class>javax.faces.webapp.FacesServlet</servlet-class>
        <load-on-startup>1</load-on-startup>
    </servlet>
    <servlet-mapping>
        <servlet-name>Faces Servlet</servlet-name>
        <url-pattern>*.faces</url-pattern>
    </servlet-mapping>
```

> For the work with the JavaServer Faces, there are two important classes. These are the `javax.faces.webapp.FacesServlet` and the `javax.faces.context.FacesContext` classes.
>
> You can think of `FacesServlet` as the core base of each JSF application. Sometimes that servlet is called an **infrastructure servlet**. It is important to mention that each JSF application in one web container has its own instance of the `FacesServlet` class. This means that an infrastructure servlet cannot be shared between many web applications on the same JEE web container.
>
> `FacesContext` is the data container which encapsulates all information that is necessary around the current request.
>
> For the usage of **Spring Faces,** it is important to know that `FacesServlet` is only used to instantiate the framework. A further usage inside Spring Faces is not done.

To be able to use the components from Spring Faces library, it's required to use **Facelets** instead of JSP. Therefore, we have to configure that mechanism.

> If you are interested in reading more about the Facelets technology, visit the Facelets homepage from `java.net` with the following URL: `https://facelets.dev.java.net`. A good introduction inside the Facelets technology is the `http://www.ibm.com/developerworks/java/library/j-facelets/` article, too.

The configuration process is done inside the deployment descriptor of your web application—`web.xml`. The following sample shows the configuration inside the mentioned file.

```
<context-param>
    <param-name>javax.faces.DEFAULT_SUFFIX</param-name>
    <param-value>.xhtml</param-value>
</context-param>
```

As you can see in the above code, the configuration parameter is done with a context parameter. The name of the parameter is `javax.faces.DEFAULT_SUFFIX`. The value for that context parameter is `.xhtml`.

Inside the Facelets technology

To present the separate views inside a JSF context, you need a specific view handler technology. One of those technologies is the well-known JavaServer Pages (JSP) technology. Facelets are an alternative for the JSP inside the JSF context. Instead, to define the views in JSP syntax, you will use XML. The pages are created using XHTML.

The Facelets technology offers the following features:

- A template mechanism, similar to the mechanism which is known from the Tiles framework
- The composition of components based on other components.
- Custom logic tags
- Expression functions
- With the Facelets technology, it's possible to use HTML for your pages. Therefore, it's easy to create the pages and view them directly in a browser, because you don't need an application server between the processes of designing a page
- The possibility to create libraries of your components

The following sample shows a sample XHTML page which uses the **component aliasing** mechanism of the Facelets technology.

```
<!DOCTYPE html PUBLIC "-//W3C//DTD XHTML 1.0 Transitional//EN"
"http://www.w3.org/TR/xhtml1/DTD/xhtml1-transitional.dtd">
<html xmlns="http://www.w3.org/1999/xhtml" xmlns:h="http://java.sun.
com/jsf/html">
 <body>
  <form jsfc="h:form">
   <span jsfc="h:outputText" value="Welcome to our page: #{user.name}"
disabled="#{empty user}" />
   <input type="text" jsfc="h:inputText" value="#{bean.theProperty}"
/>
   <input type="submit" jsfc="h:commandButton" value="OK"
action="#{bean.doIt}" />
  </form>
 </body>
</html>
```

The sample code snippet above uses the mentioned expression language (for example, the `#{user.name}` expression accesses the `name` property from the `user` instance) of the JSF technology to access the data.

What is component aliasing

One of the mentioned features of the Facelets technology is that it is possible to view a page directly in a browser without that the page is running inside a JEE container environment. This is possible through the **component aliasing** feature. With this feature, you can use normal HTML elements, for example an input element. Additionally, you can refer to the component which is used behind the scenes with the `jsfc` attribute. An example for that is `<input type="text" jsfc="h:inputText" value="#{bean.theProperty}" />`. If you open this inside a browser, the normal `input` element is used. If you use it inside your application, the `h:inputText` element of the component library is used.

The ResourceServlet

One main part of the JSF framework are the components for the GUI. These components often consist of many files besides the class files. If you use many of these components, the problem of handling these files arises. To solve this problem, the files such as JavaScript and CSS (Cascading Style Sheets) can be delivered inside the JAR archive of the component.

> If you deliver the file inside the JAR file, you can organize the components in one file and therefore it is easier for the deployment and maintenance of your component library.

Regardless of the framework you use, the result is HTML. The resources inside the HTML pages are required as URL. For that, we need a way to access these resources inside the archive with the HTTP protocol. To solve that problem, there is a servlet with the name `ResourceServlet` (package `org.springframework.js.resource`).

The Servlet can deliver the following resources:

- resources which are available inside the web application (for example, CSS files)
- resources inside a JAR archive

The configuration of the Servlet inside `web.xml` is shown below.

```
<servlet>
    <servlet-name>Resource Servlet</servlet-name>
    <servlet-class>org.springframework.js.resource.ResourceServlet</
servlet-class>
    <load-on-startup>0</load-on-startup>
</servlet>

<servlet-mapping>
    <servlet-name>Resource Servlet</servlet-name>
    <url-pattern>/resources/*</url-pattern>
</servlet-mapping>
```

It is important that you use the correct `url-pattern` inside `servlet-mapping`. As you can see in the sample above, you have to use `/resources/*`. If a component does not work (from the Spring Faces components), first check if you have the correct mapping for the Servlet. All resources in the context of Spring Faces should be retrieved through this Servlet. The base URL is `/resources`.

Internals of the ResourceServlet

`ResourceServlet` can only be accessed via a GET request. The `ResourceServlet` servlet implements only the GET method. Therefore, it's not possible to serve POST requests. Before we describe the separate steps, we want to show you the complete process, illustrated in the diagram below.

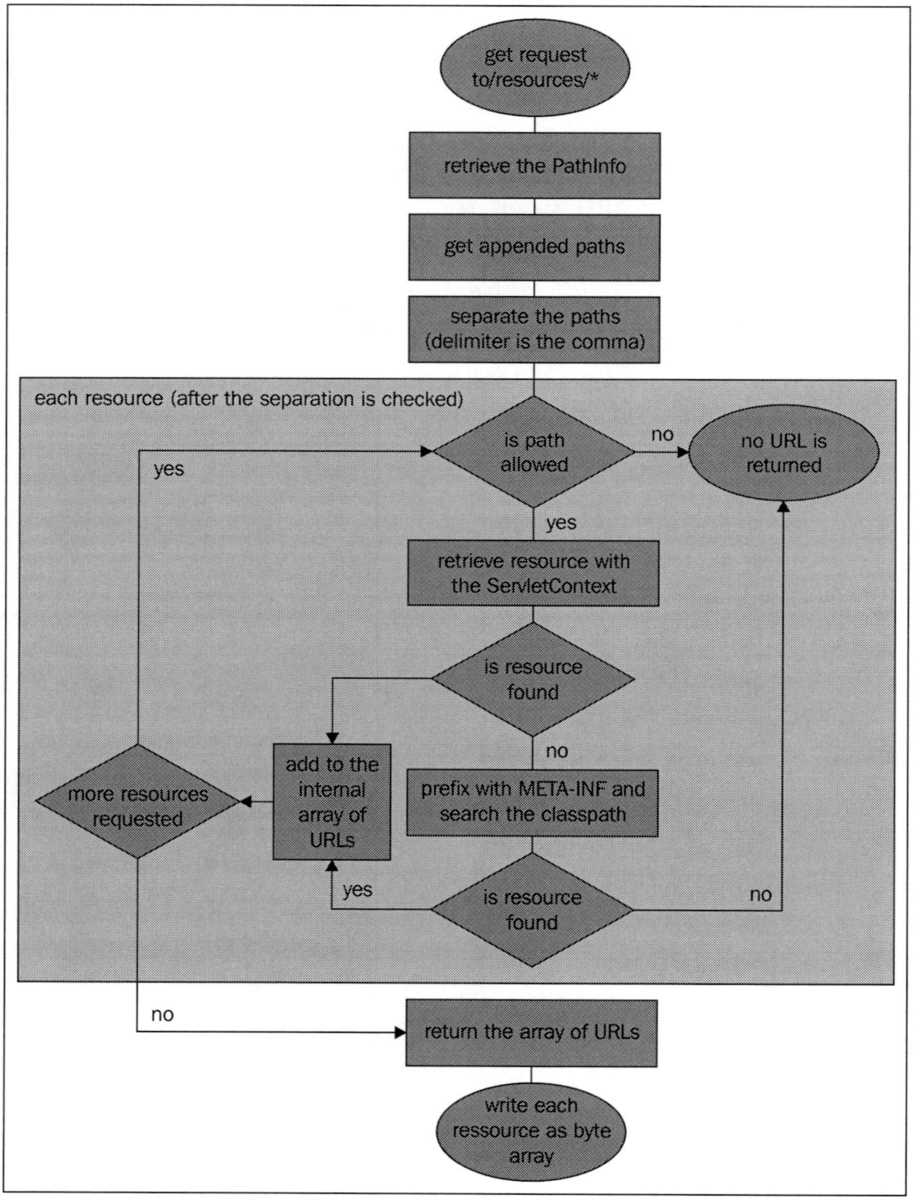

For a better understanding, we choose an example for the explanation of the mechanism which is shown in the previous diagram. Let us assume that we have registered the `ResourcesServlet` as mentioned before and we request a resource by the following sample URL: `http://localhost:8080/ flowtrac-web-jsf/resources/css/test1.css`..

> **How to request more than one resource with one request**
>
> First, you can specify the `appended` parameter. The value of the parameter is the path to the resource you want to retrieve. An example for that is the following URL: `http://localhost:8080/ flowtrac-web-jsf/resources/css/test1.css?appended=/css/test2.css`. If you want to specify more than one resource, you can use the delimiter comma inside the value for the `appended` parameter. A simple example for that mechanism is the following URL: `http://localhost:8080/ flowtrac-web-jsf/resources/css/test1.css?appended=/css/test2.css, http://localhost:8080/flowtrac-web-jsf/resources/css/test1.css?appended=/css/test3.css`. Additionally, it is possible to use the comma delimiter inside the PathInfo. For example: `http://localhost:8080/flowtrac-web-jsf/resources/css/test1.css,/css/test2.css`. It is important to mention that if one resource of the requested resources is not available, none of the requested resources is delivered. This mechanism can be used to deliver more than one CSS in one request. From the view of development, it can make sense to modularize your CSS files to get more maintainable CSS files. With that concept, the client gets one CSS, instead of many CSS files. From the view of performance optimization, it is better to have as few requests for rendering a page as possible. Therefore, it makes sense to combine the CSS files of a page. Internally, the files are written in the same sequence as they are requested.

To understand how a resource is addressed, we separate the sample URL into the specific parts. The example URL is a URL on a local servlet container which has an HTTP connector at port 8080. See the following diagram for the mentioned separation.

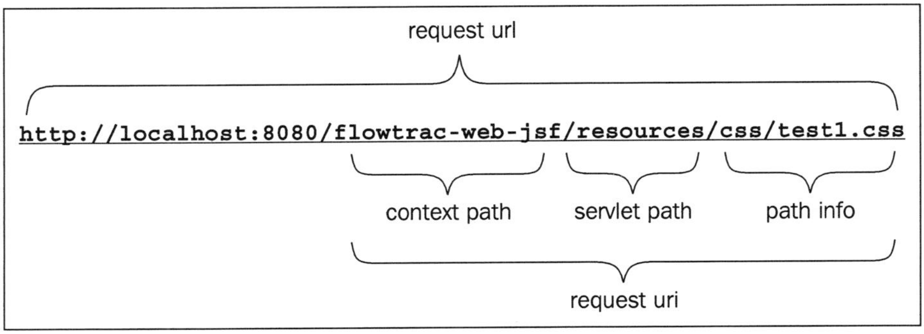

The table below describes the five sections of the URL that are shown in the previous diagram.

request url	**request url** is the complete URL. You can retrieve it with the help of the `getRequestURL` method from `HttpServletRequest`.
request uri	This is the URL without the server information. You can retrieve it with the help of the `getRequestURI` method from `HttpServletRequest`.
context path	The name of the servlet context. You can retrieve it with the help of the `getContextPath` method from `HttpServletRequest`.
servlet path	The name of the servlet. You can retrieve it with the help of the `getServletPath` method from `HttpServletRequest`.
path info	**path info** is the part of the URL after the name of the servlet and before the first parameter begins. In other words, before the query sign starts. The reason for that parameter type is to have the possibility to provide a servlet (or a CGI script) with a complete absolute filename. You can retrieve it with the help of the `getPathInfo` method from `HttpServletRequest`.

Step 1: Collect the requested resources

The GET method of `ResourceServlet` calls the internal `getRequestResourceURLs` method, which fetches the path info and appends the value from the `appended` parameter. As a delimiter, a comma is used. At the end, the complete string is separated to an array.

Step 2: Check whether the path is allowed or not

The first step for each resource is to check whether the specified path is allowed to be retrieved or not, because it is not appropriate to allow the deliverance of the class or library files inside the secured `WEB-INF` directory. That check is done through the internal method called `isAllowed` of `ResourceServlet`. At first, it is validated whether the path is a protected path or not. The protected path is `/?WEB-INF/.*`. That means everything inside the `/WEB-INF` directory can not be delivered with `ResourceServlet`. The protected path (stored inside private final variable `protectedPath`) can not be changed.

> With the protection of the `WEB-INF` directory, it's ensured that there will be a web application, which is compliant to the Servlet specification. In that specification, all content inside the `WEB-INF` directory cannot be accessed. With the `protectedPath` variable, it is ensured that there is no possibility to directly address a resource. If you want to change that, you have to write your own `ResourceServlet`, an extension of the existing servlet does not help in that case.

The next check is whether the specified path is inside the list of allowed paths (stored inside the `allowedResourcePaths` array. The array is implemented as a private instance variable of the `String[]` type). The following paths are allowed in the default implementation:

- `/**/*.css`
- `/**/*.gif`
- `/**/*.ico`
- `/**/*.jpeg`
- `/**/*.jpg`
- `/**/*.js`
- `/**/*.png`
- `META-INF/**/*.css`
- `META-INF/**/*.gif`
- `META-INF/**/*.ico,`
- `META-INF/**/*.jpeg`
- `META-INF/**/*.jpg`
- `META-INF/**/*.js`
- `META-INF/**/*.png`•

The paths are in Ant-style (`http://ant.apache.org`) path patterns. The paths are checked through an implementation of the `PathMatcher` class (package `org.springframework.util`).

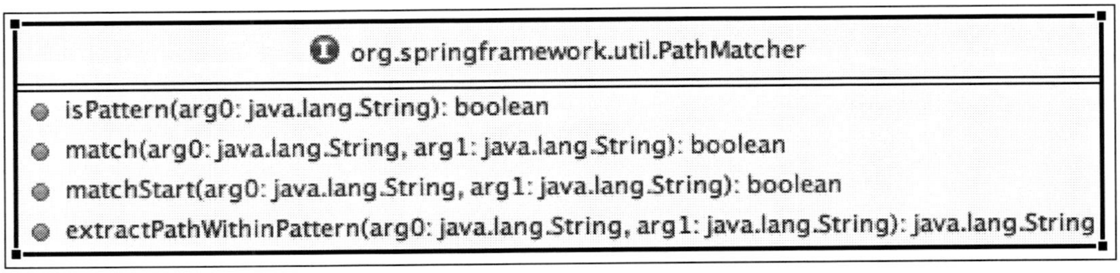

> The class which implements the Ant-Style is the `AntPathMatcher` class inside the same package as the interface. Both are inside the Spring Core framework. You can use it without the other parts of the Spring framework (maybe in your own classes to have an ant-like resource selecting, too). You only need a dependency to the `spring-core-x.x.x.jar` library (in the case of version 2.5.4, `spring-core-2.5.4.jar`).

If you want to allow other parameters, there is a public method called `setAllowedResourcePaths`. `ResourceServlet`, which extends from `HttpServletBean` (package `org.springframework.web.servlet`). This servlet implements the opportunity to configure a servlet in a Spring way. That means for each `init` parameter inside the `web.xml` file, a setter method on the servlet is called. In our case, if you have an `init` parameter `allowedPaths`, the `setAllowedPaths` method is called. See an example for the configuration below.

```
<servlet>
  <servlet-name>Resource Servlet</servlet-name>
  <servlet-class>org.springframework.js.resource.ResourceServlet</
servlet-class>
  <load-on-startup>0</load-on-startup>
  <init-param>
     <param-name>allowedResourcePaths</param-name>
     <param-value>/**/*.png,/**/*.css</param-value>
  </init-param>
</servlet>
```

In most of the cases, you want to specify more than one value for the `allowedResourcePaths` parameter. Therefore, the usage of a comma to separate the values is preferred. Unfortunately, the default implementation does not convert that value into an array. If you want to use a comma as a delimiter for the values, you have to manually register `StringArrayPropertyEditor` inside the `org.springframework.beans.propertyeditors` package. An easy way to implement this is to overwrite the `initBeanWrapper` method of `ResourceServlet`.

```
    @Override
    protected void initBeanWrapper(BeanWrapper bw) throws
BeansException {
        bw.registerCustomEditor(String[].class, new
StringArrayPropertyEditor());
    }
```

Finally, we want to show how to use such a servlet inside the web deployment descriptor of your web application. Just assume that the servlet has the name `ResourceServlet` and is inside the `flowtrac.swf.extension.resources` sample package. The configuration is done as shown below.

```
<servlet>
        <servlet-name>Resource Servlet</servlet-name>
        <servlet-class>flowtrac.swf.extension.resources.
ResourceServlet</servlet-class>
```

```
        <load-on-startup>0</load-on-startup>
        <init-param>
            <param-name>allowedResourcePaths</param-name>
            <param-value>/**/*.tss,/**/*.css</param-value>
        </init-param>
</servlet>
```

> Just remember: If the resource is not allowed, the `isAllowed` method returns `false` and the servlet delivers no resource for the actual request.

Step 3: Try to load from the servlet context

The next step after the positive check on allowance is to try to load the resource within the servlet context. This is done with the `getServletContext().getResource(resourcePath)` expression. Do not confuse the load from the servlet context with a load from the classpath. With that method, you only get resources which are reachable directly through a filesystem access. There is no search done. That means the specified `resourcePath` is relative to the base directory of the web application.

Step 4: Load from the classpath

If the resource cannot be found, the `META-INF` path (that prevents from delivering classes which are on the classpath) is prefixed to the path of the resource. The next step is to try to load the resource with the classloader. This is done with the `ClassUtils.getDefaultClassLoader().getResource(resourcePath)` helper method. The `ClassUtils` utility class is inside the `org.springframework.util` package of the `spring-core` library. If no resource is found, the method returns `null` and no resource is delivered by the actual request.

Step 5: Stream the resources

Each resource is now written as a separate byte stream.

> Remember if you request more than one resource, the resources are only delivered if all of the resources could be found from `ResourceServlet`. If one of the requested resources could not be found (or not allowed), none of the requested resources is delivered.

For the usage of `ResourceServlet`, dependency to the `org.springframework.js` library is necessary.

Configuration of the application context

The next step is to configure the application context which is used for the Spring Web Flow project. This is done in the deployment descriptor of the web application. We use the same technique as in the samples in the chapters before. For our example, we choose the name `web-application.config.xml` in the `/WEB-INF/config` directory.

```
<context-param>
   <param-name>contextConfigLocation</param-name>
   <param-value>
      /WEB-INF/config/web-application-config.xml
   </param-value>
</context-param>
<listener>
   <listener-class>org.springframework.web.context.
ContextLoaderListener</listener-class>
</listener>
```

The configuration of `web.xml` is now complete. For the simple purpose of an overview, we repeat the configuration steps below:

- Configure the Resources Servlet
- Configure `contextConfigLocation`
- Configure the Faces Servlet
- Configure `faces.DEFAULT_SUFFIX`

After we have configured the used file for the configuration of the application context, it is time to configure the application context itself. For that case, we have to add an additional XSD file (`http://www.springframework.org/schema/faces/spring-faces-2.0.xsd`). Therefore, the header of the file is extended with the definition of that grammar under the accessor faces.

```
<beans xmlns="http://www.springframework.org/schema/beans"
   xmlns:xsi="http://www.w3.org/2001/XMLSchema-instance"
   xmlns:webflow="http://www.springframework.org/schema/
    webflow-config"
   xmlns:faces="http://www.springframework.org/schema/faces"
   xsi:schemaLocation="
            http://www.springframework.org/schema/beans
            http://www.springframework.org/schema/beans/
             spring-beans-2.5.xsd
            http://www.springframework.org/schema/webflow-config
            http://www.springframework.org/schema/webflow-config/
             spring-webflow-config-2.0.xsd
             http://www.springframework.org/schema/faces
            http://www.springframework.org/schema/faces/
             spring-faces-2.0.xsd">
```

The integration of JSF into Spring Web Flow is done through the configuration of a special parser which creates builders for the integration. To register that parser, the following line is added to the application context configuration file:

```
<faces:flow-builder-services id="facesFlowBuilderServices" />
```

In the case of the usage of the `faces:` prefix in the XML configuration file, the `FacesNamespaceHandler` class (package: `org.springframework.faces.config`) is used to handle the tags. The class is extended from `NamespaceHandlerSupport` (package: `org.springframework.beans.factory.xml`) and implements only the `init` method. The implementation of the method is shown below.

```
public void init() {
   registerBeanDefinitionParser("flow-builder-services", new
FacesFlowBuilderServicesBeanDefinitionParser());
}
```

As you can see, the method creates an instance of `FacesFlowBuilderServicesBeanDefinitionParser`, which resides inside the `org.springframework.faces.config` package. Besides the definition of `facesFlowBuilderServices`, it is important to provide that instance to `flow-registry`. The instance can be provided with the help of the `flow-builder-services` attribute of the `flow-registry`.

```
<webflow:flow-registry id="flowRegistry" flow-builder-services="facesF
lowBuilderServices">
   <webflow:flow-location path="/WEB-INF/issue/add/add.xml" />
</webflow:flow-registry>
```

With the registration of `facesFlowBuilderServices`, some other default classes for the JSF integration are instantiated. It is possible to change the default behavior. To better understand what is customizable, we look at the `FacesFlowBuilderServicesBeanDefinitionParser` class. The class defines some internal constants which are used through the process of parsing the XML configuration file. The following diagram shows the class diagram of `FacesFlowBuilderServicesBeanDefinitionParser`.

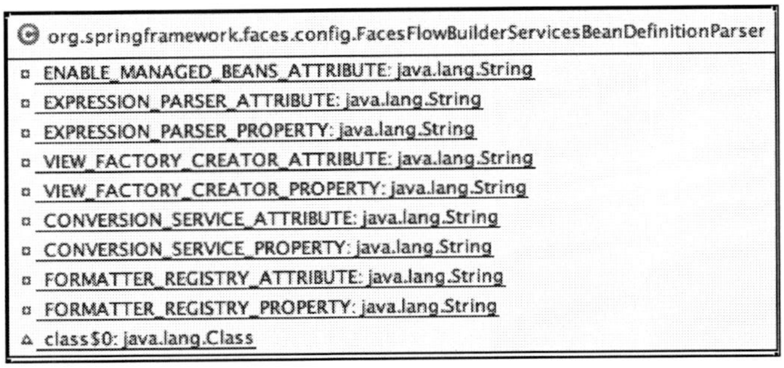

There are five important attributes that you can configure in the `faces:flow-builder-services` tag. These attributes influence the behavior of the application. Therefore, it is important to understand the meaning of the attributes. The attributes are evaluated through `FacesFlowBuilderServicesBeanDefinitionParser`. The diagram below shows the sequence of the evaluation of the attributes. The evaluation of the attributes is done in four or five steps. The number of steps depends on the value of the `enable-managed-beans` attribute. The value is of the `Boolean` type.

Step 1: Evaluation of the `enable-managed-beans` attribute.

Step 2: If the `enable-managed-beans` attribute is set to `false`, the `expression-parser` value is evaluated.

Step 3: Evaluate the `formatter-registry` attribute.

Step 4: Evaluate the `conversion-service` attribute.

Step 5: Evaluate the `view-factory-creator` attribute.

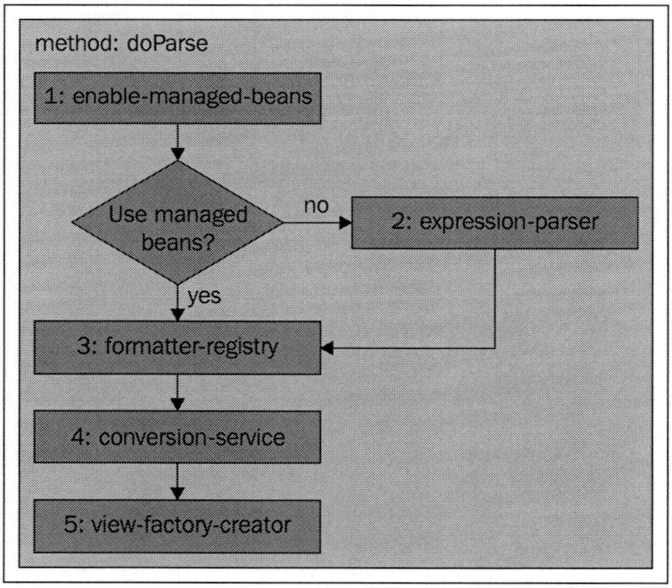

The `doParse` internal method is called from the `AbstractSingleBeanDefinitionParser` class. The `doParse` method has to be provided with an instance of the `BeanDefinitionBuilder` class inside the `org.springframework.beans.factory.support` package. That instance is created inside the `parseInternal` method of `AbstractSingleBeanDefinitionParser`. The instance is created with the `genericBeanDefinition` static method of the `BeanDefinitionBuilder` class.

After the evaluation sequence, we describe the meaning of the attributes.

Name of the attribute	Description
enable-managed-beans	JSF uses the concept of managed beans. In the context of the Spring framework, there is a concept of Spring beans. If you want to use the managed beans facility of JSF, you have to provide the `enable-managed-beans` attribute. The attribute is a `boolean` attribute. If you set that attribute to `true`, the `JsfManagedBeanAwareELExpressionParser` class (package: `org.springframework.faces.webflow`) is used for the evaluation of the referenced beans inside the flow. Otherwise, the `expression-parser` attribute is evaluated. The default value for that attribute is `false`.
expression-parser	If the `enable-managed-beans` attribute is not set or set to `false`, the `expression-parser` attribute is evaluated. With that attribute, you can provide a specific parser of the expression which is used inside the flow. If the value is not set, a new instance of the `WebFlowELExpressionParser` class (package: `org.springframework.webflow.expression.el`) is created. That instance is created with an `ExpressionFactory` by using the `createExpressionFactory` static method of the `DefaultExpressionFactoryUtils` class. The default expression factory is `org.jboss.el.ExpressionFactoryImpl`.
formatter-registry	A formatter registry is the class which creates or provides the formatter for a specific class. With a formatter from the `org.springframework.binding.format.Formatter` type, you can format a specific class for the output. Additionally, a formatter provides a method called `parse` to create the specific class. If you do not provide that attribute, a default formatter registry is created with the `getSharedInstance` method of the `DefaultFormatterRegistry` class. That registry has formatters for the following classes: `Integer (`for numbers, a `NumberFormatter` inside the `org.springframework.binding.format.formatters` package is used`), Long, Short, Float, Double, Byte, BigInteger, BigDecimal, Boolean (`for Boolean, a `BooleanFormatter` inside the `org.springframework.binding.format.formatters` package is registered`)` and `Date (`for Date, a `DateFormatter` inside the `org.springframework.binding.format.formatters` package is registered`).` `DefaultFormatterRegistry` extends the `GenericFormatterRegistry` class from the `org.springframework.binding.format.registry` package. If you want to implement your own formatter registry, it could be a choice to extend from that class.

Name of the attribute	Description
`conversion-service`	A conversion service is responsible to provide instances of `ConversionExecutor` (package: `org.springframework.binding.convert`) for a specific class. A conversion service is from type `ConversionService` (package: `org.springframework.binding.convert`). A conversion service converts a source object into a specific target object. If no value for the `conversion-service` attribute is provided, an instance of the `FacesConversionService` class (package: `org.springframework.faces.model.converter`) is registered. The class extends `DefaultConversionService`. If you implement your own conversion service, you could extend from `GenericConversionService` (package: `org.springframework.binding.convert.service`). This default implementation registers the following four converters: `TextToClass` (the `FacesConversionService` class registers on the `TextToClass` converter an alias for the `DataModel` class from the `javax.model.DataModel`. `TextToClass` package converts a piece of text to a class.), `TextToBoolean`, `TextToLabeledEnum` and `TextToNumber`.
`view-factory-creator`	A view factory creator is responsible to provide a view factory. A view factory creator is from type `ViewFactoryCreator` (package: `org.springframework.webflow.engine.builder`). Such a `ViewFactoryCreator` is responsible for creating instances from type `ViewFactory` (package: `org.springframework.webflow.execution`). If the value for the `view-factory-creator` attribute is not provided, an instance of the `JsfViewFactoryCreator` class (package: `org.springframework.faces.webflow`) is registered. That class creates instances of `JsfViewFactory` (package: `org.springframework.faces.webflow`).

The next step is the configuration of JSF itself. This is done in `faces-config.xml`, which can be located inside the `WEB-INF` directory.

```
<?xml version="1.0"?>
<!DOCTYPE faces-config PUBLIC
  "-//Sun Microsystems, Inc.//DTD JavaServer Faces Config 1.0//EN"
  "http://java.sun.com/dtd/web-facesconfig_1_0.dtd">

<faces-config>
   <application>
      <!-- Enables Facelets -->
      <view-handler>com.sun.facelets.FaceletViewHandler</view-handler>
   </application>
</faces-config>
```

Using Spring Faces

The following section shows you how to use the Spring Faces module.

Overview of all tags of the Spring Faces tag library

The Spring Faces module comes with a set of components, which are provided through a tag library. If you want more detailed information about the tag library, look at the following files inside the Spring Faces source distribution:

- `spring-faces/src/main/resources/META-INF/spring-faces.tld`
- `spring-faces/src/main/resources/META-INF/springfaces.taglib.xml`
- `spring-faces/src/main/resources/META-INF/faces-config.xml`

> If you want to see the source code of a specific tag, refer to `faces-config.xml` and `springfaces.taglib.xml` to get the name of the class of the component. The `spring-faces.tld` file can be used for documentation issues.

The following table should give you a short description about the available tags from the Spring Faces component library.

Name of the tag	Description
`includeStyles`	The `includeStyles` tag renders the necessary CSS stylesheets which are essential for the components from Spring Faces. The usage of this tag in the head section is recommended for performance optimization. If the tag isn't included, the necessary stylesheets are rendered on the first usage of the tag. If you are using a template for your pages, it's a good pattern to include the tag in the header of that template. For more information about performance optimization, refer to the Yahoo performance guidelines, which are available at the following URL: `http://developer.yahoo.com/performance`. Some tags (`includeStyles`, `resource`, and `resourceGroup`) of the Spring Faces tag library are implementing patterns to optimize the performance on client side.

Name of the tag	Description
`resource`	The `resource` tag loads and renders a resource with `ResourceServlet`. You should prefer this tag instead of directly including a CSS stylesheet or a JavaScript file because `ResourceServlet` sets the proper response headers for caching the resource file.
`resourceGroup`	With the `resourceGroup` tag, it is possible to combine all resources which are inside the tag. It is important that all resources are the same type. The tag uses `ResourceServlet` with the `appended` parameter to create one resource file which is sent to the client.
`clientTextValidator`	With the `clientTextValidator` tag, you can validate a child `inputText` element. For the validation, you have an attribute called `regExp` where you can provide a regular expression. The validation is done on client side.
`clientNumberValidator`	With the `clientNumberValidator` tag, you can validate a child `inputText` element. With the provided validation methods, you can check whether the text is a number and check some properties for the number, e.g. range. The validation is done on client side.
`clientCurrencyValidator`	With the `clientCurrencyValidator` tag, you can validate a child `inputText` element. This tag should be used if you want to validate a currency. The validation is done on client side.
`clientDateValidator`	With the `clientDateValidator` tag, you can validate a child `inputText` element. The tag should be used to validate a date. The field displays a pop-up calendar. The validation is done on client side.
`validateAllOnClick`	With the `validateAllOnClick` tag, you can execute all client-side validation on the click of a specific element. That can be useful for a **submit** button.
`commandButton`	With the `commandButton` tag, it is possible to execute an arbitrary method on an instance. The method itself has to be a public method with no parameters and a `java.lang.Object` instance as the return value.
`commandLink`	The `commandLink` tag renders an AJAX link. With the `processIds` attribute, you can provide the ids of components which should be processed through the process.
`ajaxEvent`	The `ajaxEvent` tag creates a JavaScript event listener. This tag should only be used if you can ensure that the client has JavaScript enabled.

A complete example

After we have shown the main configuration elements and described the Spring Faces components, the following section shows a complete example in order to get a good understanding about how to work with the Spring Faces module in your own web application.

The following diagram shows the screen of the sample application. With the shown screen, it is possible to create a new issue and save it to the bug database.

> It is not part of this example to describe the bug database or to describe how to work with databases in general. The sample uses the model classes which are described inside the Appendix of this book.

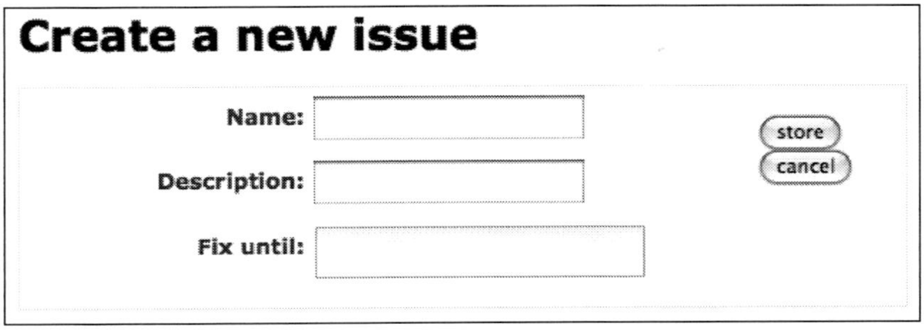

The diagram has three required fields. These fields are:

- **Name**: the name of the issue
- **Description**: a short description for the issue
- **Fix until**: the fixing date for the issue

Additionally, there are the following two buttons:

- **store**: With a click on the **store** button, the system tries to create a new issue that includes the provided information.
- **cancel**: With a click on the **cancel** button, the system ignores the data which is entered and navigates to the overview page.

Now, the first step is to create the implementation of that input page. That implementation and its description are shown in the section below.

Creating the input page

As we described above, we use Facelets as a view handler technology. Therefore, the pages have to be defined with XHTML, with `.xhtml` as the file extension. The name for the input page will be `add.xhtml`. In the example from Chapter 3, the name of the page was `add.jsp`. This is because in that example we had used JavaServer Pages as a view technology.

For the description, we separate the page into the following five parts:

- Header
- Name
- Description
- Fix until
- The Buttons

This separation is shown in the diagram below.

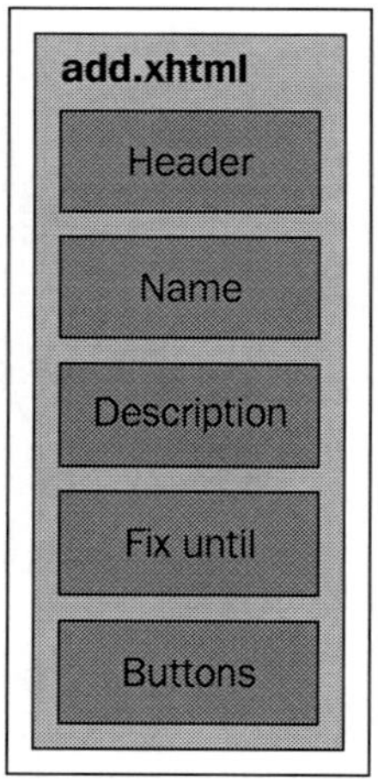

The Header part

The first step in the header is to define that we have an XHTML page. This is done through the definition of the correct doctype.

```
<!DOCTYPE composition PUBLIC "-//W3C//DTD XHTML 1.0 Transitional//EN"
"http://www.w3.org/TR/xhtml1/DTD/xhtml1-transitional.dtd">
```

An XHTML page is described as an XML page. If you want to use special tags inside the XML page, you have to define a namespace for that. For a page with Facelets and Spring Faces, we have to define more than one namespace. The following table describes those namespaces.

Namespace	Description
`http://www.w3.org/1999/xhtml`	The namespace for XHTML itself.
`http://java.sun.com/jsf/facelets`	The Facelet defines some components (tags). These components are available under this namespace.
`http://java.sun.com/jsf/html`	The user interface components of JSF are available under this namespace.
`http://java.sun.com/jsf/core`	The core tags of JSF, for example `converter`, can be accessed under this namespace.
`http://www.springframework.org/tags/faces`	The namespace for the Spring Faces component library.

For the header definition, we use the `composition` component of the Facelets components. With that component, it is possible to define a template for the layout. This is very similar to the previously mentioned Tiles framework. The following code snippet shows you the second part (after the `doctype`) of the header definition.

> A description and overview of the JSF tags is available at: `http://developers.sun.com/jscreator/archive/learning/bookshelf/pearson/corejsf/standard_jsf_tags.pdf`.

```
<ui:composition xmlns="http://www.w3.org/1999/xhtml"
            xmlns:ui="http://java.sun.com/jsf/facelets"
             xmlns:h="http://java.sun.com/jsf/html"
             xmlns:f="http://java.sun.com/jsf/core"
               xmlns:sf="http://www.springframework.org/tags/faces"
               template="/WEB-INF/layouts/standard.xhtml">
```

With the help of the `template` attribute, we refer to the used layout template. In our example, we refer to `/WEB-INF/layouts/standard.xhtml`.

The following code shows the complete layout file `standard.xhtml`. This layout file is also described with the Facelets technology. Therefore, it is possible to use Facelets components inside that page, too. Additionally, we use Spring Faces components inside that layout page.

```
<!DOCTYPE html PUBLIC "-//W3C//DTD XHTML 1.0 Transitional//EN"
"http://www.w3.org/TR/xhtml1/DTD/xhtml1-transitional.dtd">
<html xmlns="http://www.w3.org/1999/xhtml"
      xmlns:ui="http://java.sun.com/jsf/facelets"
```

```
        xmlns:f="http://java.sun.com/jsf/core"
        xmlns:c="http://java.sun.com/jstl/core"
        xmlns:sf="http://www.springframework.org/tags/faces">
<f:view contentType="text/html">
<head>
   <meta http-equiv="Content-Type" content="text/html; charset=UTF-8"
/>
   <title>flow.tracR</title>

   <sf:includeStyles/>
   <sf:resourceGroup>
      <sf:resource path="/css-framework/css/tools.css"/>
      <sf:resource path="/css-framework/css/typo.css"/>
      <sf:resource path="/css-framework/css/forms.css"/>
      <sf:resource path="/css-framework/css/layout-navtop-localleft.
css"/>
      <sf:resource path="/css-framework/css/layout.css"/>
   </sf:resourceGroup>
   <sf:resource path="/css/issue.css"/>
   <ui:insert name="headIncludes"/>
</head>
<body class="tundra spring">
<div id="page">

   <div id="content">
      <div id="main">
         <ui:insert name="content"/>
      </div>
   </div>
</div>

</body>
</f:view>
</html>
```

The Name part

The first element in the input page is the section for the input of the name. For the description of that section, we use elements from the JSF component library. We access this library with `h` as the prefix, which we have defined in the header section. For the general layout, we use standard HTML elements, such as the `div` element. The definition is shown below.

```
<div class="field">
   <div class="label">
      <h:outputLabel for="name">Name:</h:outputLabel>
   </div>
   <div class="input">
      <h:inputText id="name" value="#{issue.name}" />
   </div>
</div>
```

The Description part

The next element in the page is the `Description` element. The definition is very similar to the `Name` part. Instead of the definition of the `Name` part, we use the element description inside the `h:inputText` element—the `required` attribute with `true` as its value. This attribute tells the JSF system that the `issue.description` value is mandatory. If the user does not enter a value, the validation fails.

```
<div class="field">
   <div class="label">
      <h:outputLabel for="description">Description:</h:outputLabel>
   </div>
   <div class="input">
     <h:inputText id="description" value="#{issue.description}"
required="true"/>
   </div>
</div>
```

The Fix until part

The last input section is the `Fix until` part. This field is a very common field in web applications, because there is often the need to input a date. Internally, a date is often represented through an instance of the `java.util.Date` class. The text which is entered by the user has to be validated and converted in order to get a valid instance. To help the user with the input, a calendar for the input is often used. The Spring Faces library offers a component which shows a calendar and adds client-side validation. The complete definition of the **Fix until** part is shown below. The name of the component is `clientDateValidator`. The `clientDateValidator` component is used with `sf` as the prefix. This prefix is defined in the namespace definition in the shown header of the `add.xhtml` page.

```
<div class="field">
   <div class="label">
      <h:outputLabel for="checkinDate">Fix until:</h:outputLabel>
   </div>
   <div class="input">
      <sf:clientDateValidator required="true" invalidMessage="please
insert a correct fixing date. format: dd.MM.yyyy"
promptMessage="Format: dd.MM.yyyy, example: 01.01.2020">
      <h:inputText id="checkinDate" value="#{issue.fixingDate}"
required="true">
         <f:convertDateTime pattern="dd.MM.yyyy" timeZone="GMT"/>
      </h:inputText>
      </sf:clientDateValidator>
   </div>
</div>
```

In the example above, we use the `promptMessage` attribute to help the user with the format. The message is shown when the user sets the cursor on the input element.

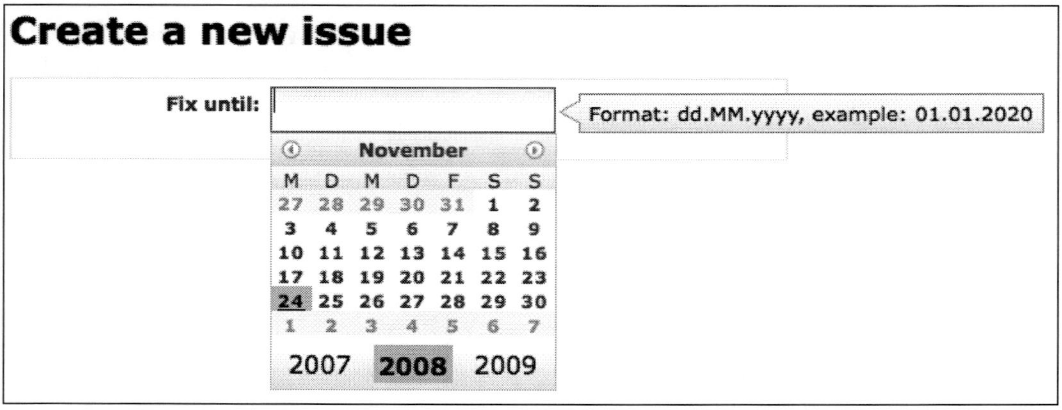

If the validation fails, the message of the `invalidMessage` attribute is used to show the user that a wrong formatted input has been entered.

The Buttons part

The last element in the page are the buttons. For these buttons, the `commandButton` component from Spring Faces is used. The definition is shown below:

```
<div class="buttonGroup">
   <sf:commandButton id="store" action="store" processIds="*"
value="store"/>
   <sf:commandButton id="cancel" action="cancel" processIds="*"
value="cancel"/>
</div>
```

> It is worth mentioning that JavaServer Faces binds an action to the `action` method of a backing bean. Spring Web Flow binds the action to events.

Handling of errors

It's possible to have validation on the client side or on the server side. For the `Fix until` element, we use the previously mentioned `clientDateValidator` component of the Spring Faces library. The following figure shows how this component shows the error message to the user.

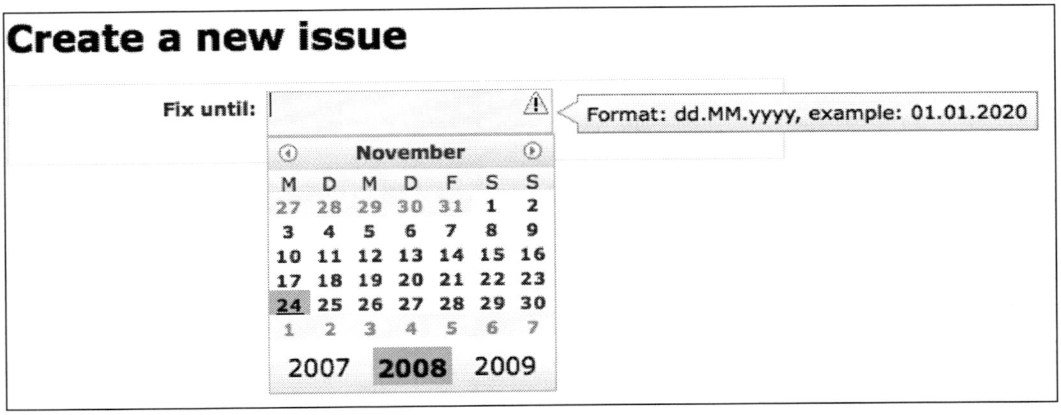

Reflecting the actions of the buttons into the flow definition file

Clicking the buttons executes an action that has a transition as the result. The name of the action is expressed in the `action` attribute of the button component which is implemented as `commandButton` from the Spring Faces component library. If you click on the **store** button, the validation is executed first. If you want to prevent that validation, you have to use the `bind` attribute and set it to `false`. This feature is used for the **cancel** button, because in this state it is necessary to ignore the inputs.

```
<view-state id="add" model="issue">
      <transition on="store" to="issueStore" >
         <evaluate expression="persistenceContext.persist(issue)"/>
      </transition>
      <transition on="cancel" to="cancelInput" bind="false">
</transition>
</view-state>
```

Showing the results

To test the implemented feature, we implement an overview page. We have the choice to implement the page as a flow with one view state or implement it as a simple JSF view. Independent from that choice, we will use Facelets to implement that overview page, because Facelets does not depend on the Spring Web Flow framework as it is a feature of JSF.

The example uses a table to show the entered issues. If no issue is entered, a message is shown to the user. The figure below shows this table with one row of data. The **Id** is a URL. If you click on this link, the input page is shown with the data of that issue. It is the same mechanism we saw in Chapter 3. With data, we execute an update. The indicator for that is the valid ID of the issue.

Id	Name	fix until	creation date	last modified
1	test	2008-11-29 06:00:00.0	2008-11-25 17:26:31.334	2008-11-25 17:26:31.334

create a new issue

If your data is available, the **No issues in database** message is shown to the user. This is done with a condition on the `outputText` component. See the code snippet below:

```
<h:outputText id="noIssuesText" value="No Issues in the database"
rendered="#{empty issueList}"/>
```

For the table, we use the `dataTable` component.

```
<h:dataTable id="issues" value="#{issueList}" var="issue"
rendered="#{not empty issueList}" border="1">
   <h:column>
      <f:facet name="header">Id</f:facet>
      <a href="add?id=#{issue.id}">#{issue.id}</a>
   </h:column>
   <h:column>
      <f:facet name="header">Name</f:facet>
      #{issue.name}
   </h:column>
   <h:column>
      <f:facet name="header">fix until</f:facet>
      #{issue.fixingDate}
   </h:column>
   <h:column>
      <f:facet name="header">creation date</f:facet>
      #{issue.creationDate}
   </h:column>
   <h:column>
      <f:facet name="header">last modified</f:facet>
      #{issue.lastModified}
   </h:column>
</h:dataTable>
```

Integration with other JavaServer Faces component libraries

One of the basic concepts of JavaServer Faces is the components. The idea is to have one implementation of the JavaServer Faces infrastructure and use the components which are appropriate for your web application. It should be possible to use any third-party JSF component library with Spring Faces.

> It is important to say that the configuration in the web deployment descriptor `web.xml` is different if you are using Spring Faces, because the requests are not routed through the standard FacesServlet. FacesServlet is used only to establish the infrastructure for the JavaServer Faces subsystem.

Many JSF component libraries are available in the market. Some libraries are open-source, other libraries are commercial. In this section, we will have a look at the following two open-source JSF component libraries:

- JBoss RichFaces, available at: `http://www.jboss.org/jbossrichfaces`.
- Apache MyFaces Trinidad, available at: `http://myfaces.apache.org/trinidad`.

Integration with JBoss RichFaces

One open-source JavaServer Faces component library is **JBoss RichFaces**. The web site of that framework is available at the following URL: `http://www.jboss.org/jbossrichfaces`. This component library offers many components which are based on **AJAX** (Asynchronous JavaScript and XML). If you want to use that component library in conjunction with Spring Faces, you **first** have to download the latest release from the download section of the web page of JBoss RichFaces at the `http://www.jboss.org/jbossrichfaces/downloads/` URL. We have used Version 3.2.2 in our example. After the download of the `richfaces-ui-3.2.2.GA-bin.zip` archive (the size is about 25 MB), extract the archive into an arbitrary folder. Other formats (`tar.gz`) and the source files are also available from the mentioned download page. The directory layout of the extracted archive looks like the figure which is shown below.

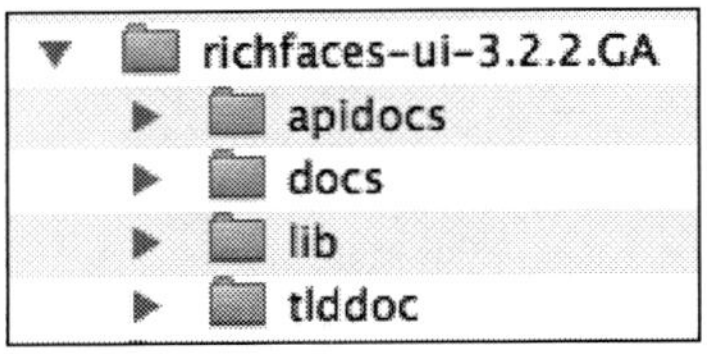

The binary libraries are located inside the `lib` folder. The `apidocs`, `docs`, and `tlddoc` folders contain the documentation for the component library. If you need more information, it is highly recommended to read the documentation inside the `docs` folder. To use the RichFaces component library inside your web application, copy the `richfaces-api-3.2.2.GA.jar`, `richfaces-impl-3.2.2.GA.jar`, and `richfaces-ui-3.2.2.GA.jar` files into the `WEB-INF/lib` folder of your web application.

The next step is the configuration inside the web deployment descriptor file `web.xml`. RichFaces comes with a servlet filter which has to be configured as shown in the example below:

```
<filter>
    <display-name>RichFaces Filter</display-name>
    <filter-name>richfaces</filter-name>
    <filter-class>org.ajax4jsf.Filter</filter-class>
</filter>
```

After the configuration of the filter, the mapping of the filter has to be done. The important parameter for the integration with Spring Faces is the `servlet-name` parameter. Here, you have to mention the name of your used dispatch servlet.

```
<filter-mapping>
    <filter-name>richfaces</filter-name>
    <servlet-name>flowtrac</servlet-name>
    <dispatcher>REQUEST</dispatcher>
    <dispatcher>FORWARD</dispatcher>
    <dispatcher>INCLUDE</dispatcher>
</filter-mapping>
```

After this configuration, you can use the components inside your views. The namespace for the components is available at `http://richfaces.org/rich`. The example page header below shows the usage of the namespace.

```
<ui:composition xmlns="http://www.w3.org/1999/xhtml"
             xmlns:ui="http://java.sun.com/jsf/facelets"
              xmlns:h="http://java.sun.com/jsf/html"
              xmlns:f="http://java.sun.com/jsf/core"
              xmlns:rich="http://richfaces.org/rich"
                xmlns:sf="http://www.springframework.org/tags/faces"
                template="/WEB-INF/layouts/standard.xhtml">
```

After the configuration in the page header, you can use the components with the configured prefix `rich`. The following example uses the component for uploading a file.

```
<rich:fileUpload maxFilesQuantity="3" />
```

The figure below shows the sample component in action:

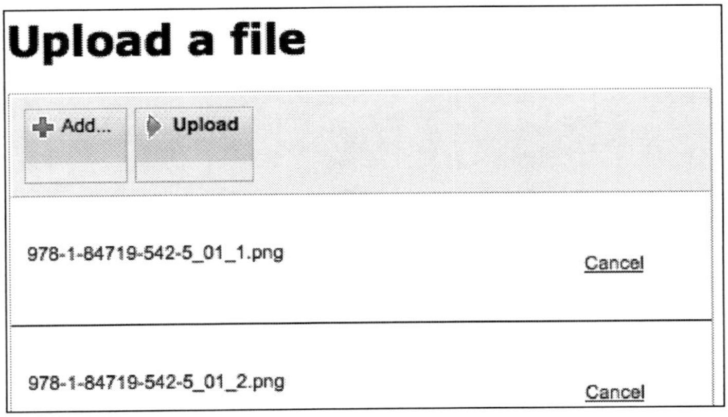

> The number of components inside the RichFaces library is quite comprehensive. We recommend reading chapter 6 of the documentation of RichFaces to learn more about the possibilities which are offered through these components.

Integration with Apache MyFaces Trinidad

Apache MyFaces Trinidad is an open-source JSF framework which offers many components that you can use in conjunction with your own web application. The web page of the framework is at `http://myfaces.apache.org/trinidad`. The first step is to download the distribution of Apache MyFaces Trinidad from the download section from the following URL: `http://myfaces.apache.org/trinidad/download.html`. For our example, we have used the version 1.0.10 of Apache MyFaces Trinidad. After the download of the `trinidad-1.0.10-dist.zip` file (the size of the compressed archive is about 11.9 MB), extract it into an arbitrary folder. The layout of the folder is shown in the figure below.

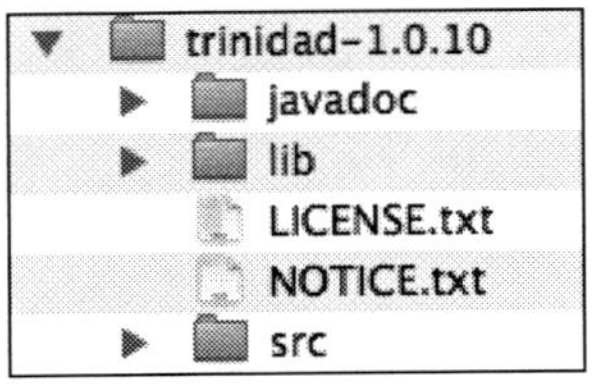

The `lib` folder contains the binary libraries. The library as the source archive is included in the `src` folder. The `javadoc` folder comprehends the API documentation of the library. After the download, you have to copy two libraries, `trinidad-api-1.0.10.jar` and `trindad-impl-1.0.10.jar`, into the `WEB-INF/lib` folder of your web application. The libraries themselves are located inside the `lib` folder. Apache MyFaces Trindad comes with two component libraries which can be used inside your web application. The namespace of these libraries is shown in the table below:

Recommended Shortcut for the library	Namespace
Tr	`http://myfaces.apache.org/trinidad`
Trh	`http://myfaces.apache.org/trinidad/html`

The first step in the configuration process is the configuration inside the web deployment descriptor (`web.xml`) of your web application. You have to configure some context parameters, the **Trinidad filter,** and the **Trinidad Resource Servlet**. If you use Facelets to describe your views, do not forget to set the `org.apache.myfaces.trinidad.ALTERNATE_VIEW_HANDLER` parameter.

```
    <context-param>
       <param-name>org.apache.myfaces.trinidad.ALTERNATE_VIEW_
HANDLER</param-name>
       <param-value>com.sun.facelets.FaceletViewHandler</param-value>
     </context-param>
<context-param>
    <param-name>javax.faces.STATE_SAVING_METHOD</param-name>
    <param-value>server</param-value>
</context-param>

<context-param>
    <param-name>
        org.apache.myfaces.trinidad.CHANGE_PERSISTENCE
    </param-name>
    <param-value>session</param-value>
</context-param>

<context-param>
    <param-name>
        org.apache.myfaces.trinidad.ENABLE_QUIRKS_MODE
    </param-name>
    <param-value>false</param-value>
</context-param>

<filter>
```

```
    <filter-name>Trinidad Filter</filter-name>
    <filter-class>
        org.apache.myfaces.trinidad.webapp.TrinidadFilter
    </filter-class>
</filter>

<filter-mapping>
    <filter-name>Trinidad Filter</filter-name>
    <servlet-name>Faces Servlet</servlet-name>
</filter-mapping>

<servlet>
    <servlet-name>Trinidad Resource Servlet</servlet-name>
    <servlet-class>
        org.apache.myfaces.trinidad.webapp.ResourceServlet
    </servlet-class>
</servlet>

<servlet-mapping>
    <servlet-name>Trinidad Resource Servlet</servlet-name>
    <url-pattern>/adf/*</url-pattern>
</servlet-mapping>
```

The next step is the configuration of `faces-config.xml`.

```
<?xml version="1.0"?>
<!DOCTYPE faces-config PUBLIC
  "-//Sun Microsystems, Inc.//DTD JavaServer Faces Config 1.0//EN"
  "http://java.sun.com/dtd/web-facesconfig_1_0.dtd">

<faces-config>
   <application>
       <default-render-kit-id>org.apache.myfaces.trinidad.core</
default-render-kit-id>
        <property-resolver>org.springframework.faces.webflow.
FlowPropertyResolver</property-resolver>
        <variable-resolver>org.springframework.faces.webflow.
FlowVariableResolver</variable-resolver>
        <variable-resolver>org.springframework.web.jsf.
DelegatingVariableResolver</variable-resolver>
   </application>
</faces-config>
```

After the configuration inside `faces-config.xml`, we can use the mentioned namespaces inside the header of our views.

```
<ui:composition xmlns="http://www.w3.org/1999/xhtml"
             xmlns:ui="http://java.sun.com/jsf/facelets"
              xmlns:h="http://java.sun.com/jsf/html"
              xmlns:f="http://java.sun.com/jsf/core"
              xmlns:tr="http://myfaces.apache.org/trinidad"
                xmlns:sf="http://www.springframework.org/tags/faces"
                template="/WEB-INF/layouts/standard.xhtml">
```

For our example, we use a color chooser for selecting a color.

```
<div class="section">
   <h1>Choose color</h1>
   <h:messages errorClass="errors" />
   <h:form id="issueForm">
      <tr:inputColor id="sic1" chooseId="cc2"/>
      <tr:chooseColor id="cc2" width="18" />
   </h:form>
</div>
```

The component in action is shown in the figure below.

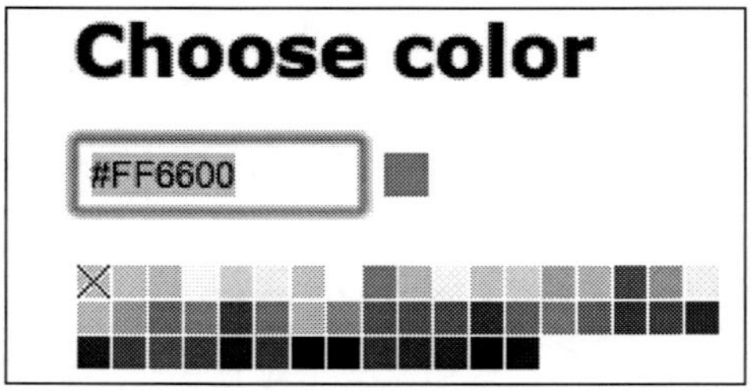

> As you have seen in the two examples, the integration of component libraries needs some additional work. Therefore, it is not recommended to use more than one or two component libraries. Our recommendation is to select one rich component library and take care that the integration is working in a maintainable way.

Summary

In this chapter, we have shown you how to use the Spring Faces module in your web applications which are based on the Spring Web Flow 2 Framework.

In the beginning of this chapter, we have described `ResourceServlet`, which you can use as a central mechanism to serve the resource files, for example, a CSS file. With this servlet, it is possible to serve more than one CSS file with one request. This improves the performance on the client side because with this technique you reduce the number of requests. Do not forget that you can override the servlet to add more functionality to it. This was explained with an example.

The later pages of this chapter shows a complete example of using Spring Faces in your own project. The last section in this chapter shows the integration with JSF component libraries. You have seen explicitly the integration with RichFaces and Apache MyFaces Trinidad. If you want to integrate with other component libraries, just remember not to configure it with FacesServlet.

If you need more information about Spring Faces that is not shown in this chapter, refer to the reference documentation from SpringSource, which is available online at `http://static.springframework.org/spring-webflow/docs/2.0.x/reference/html/index.html`. Additionally, the documentation is contained inside the distribution of Spring Web Flow 2.

5

Mastering Spring Web Flow

In this chapter, we will delve into the depth of Spring Web Flow and show you all the new features in Spring Web Flow 2 in more detail than in the previous chapters. First of all, we would like to show you what *subflows* are, and how to use them in your applications. Afterwards, we will cover how to use Spring JavaScript to enhance your Web Flow applications with AJAX functionality and additionally give you a very detailed look into the web flow configuration file.

Subflows

We have already mentioned in the early chapters of this book that Spring Web Flow is all about *re-usability*. Remember the *loginform* application from Chapter 2? Wouldn't it be nice if we could re-use this application in all our other web applications that need authentication? But, first of all, what is a subflow? A **subflow** is simply a flow, which is called from another flow using the `subflow-state` element in your flow definition file. As you can imagine, that makes subflows in Spring Web Flow 2 very easy to use.

Here is the flow definition from Chapter 2, again as a basis for comparison:

```
<?xml version="1.0" encoding="UTF-8"?>
<flow xmlns="http://www.springframework.org/schema/webflow"
      xmlns:xsi="http://www.w3.org/2001/XMLSchema-instance"

      xsi:schemaLocation=
        "http://www.springframework.org/schema/webflow
         http://www.springframework.org/schema/webflow
                                /spring-webflow-2.0.xsd">

   <persistence-context />

   <var name="user" class="com.webflow2book.User"/>

   <view-state id="loginPage" model="user" view="loginPage.jspx">
   <transition on="login" to="getUser" />
```

```
    </view-state>

    <action-state id="getUser">
       <evaluate
          expression="userservice.getUserByUsername(user.username)"
          result="flowScope.resultUser" />
       <transition to="checkCredentials" />
    </action-state>

    <decision-state id="checkCredentials">
       <if test="flowScope.resultUser == null" then="failedView" />
       <if test="flowScope.resultUser.password.equals(user.password)"
          then="updateUser" else="failedView" />
    </decision-state>

    <action-state id="updateUser">
       <evaluate expression="flowScope.resultUser.setLastLogin(
                                     new java.util.Date())" />
       <transition to="welcomeView" />
    </action-state>

    <end-state id="welcomeView"
               view="welcomeView.jspx"
               commit="true" />
    <end-state id="failedView" view="failedView.jspx" />

</flow>
```

We will change this flow definition slightly to make it more appropriate for usage in a subflow. We will change the last few lines from:

```
<end-state id="welcomeView" view="welcomeView.jspx"
   commit="true" />
<end-state id="failedView" view="failedView.jspx" />
```

to:

```
    <end-state id="success" commit="true" />
    <end-state id="failedView" view="failedView.jspx" />
```

We can react to the `success` `end-state` in our calling flow, which looks like this:

```
<?xml version="1.0" encoding="UTF-8"?>
<flow xmlns="http://www.springframework.org/schema/webflow"
      xmlns:xsi="http://www.w3.org/2001/XMLSchema-instance"
      xsi:schemaLocation=
             "http://www.springframework.org/schema/webflow
              http://www.springframework.org/schema/webflow
                                   /spring-webflow-2.0.xsd">
```

```
    <var name="user" class="com.webflow2book.User"/>

    <view-state id="testPage" view="testPage.jspx">
       <transition on="login" to="getUser" />
    </view-state>

    <subflow-state id="getUser" subflow="loginform">
       <input name="user" />
       <transition on="success" to="welcomeView" />
    </subflow-state>

    <end-state id="welcomeView" view="welcomeView.jspx" />
</flow>
```

This flow shows a small web site that has only one `submit` button that submits a form and lets the flow transition to the `subflow-state` with the `getUser` ID. The web page is called `testPage.jspx`, and is built like this:

```
<?xml version="1.0" encoding="ISO-8859-1" ?>
<jsp:root
    xmlns="http://www.w3.org/1999/xhtml"
    xmlns:jsp="http://java.sun.com/JSP/Page"
    xmlns:form="http://www.springframework.org/tags/form"
                                          version="2.1">
   <jsp:directive.page language="java"
                       contentType="text/html;
                       charset=ISO-8859-1"
                       pageEncoding="ISO-8859-1" />

   <html>
      <head>
         <title>Welcome</title>
      </head>
      <body>
         <p>
         Click to login!
         </p>
         <form:form method="post">
            <input type="submit"
                   name="_eventId_login"
                   value="Login" />
         </form:form>
      </body>
   </html>
</jsp:root>
```

There's only a single button on the web page, which has the name `_eventId_login`. As already explained in Chapter 2, this convention says that an event will be triggered with the `login` ID. In the flow definition we just saw, transition to the `subflow-state` occurs as soon as this event is triggered.

This flow then calls the flow with the name `loginform`, using the `subflow` attribute of the `subflow-state`. This is the actual flow we want to execute, and we have already used it in Chapter 2. We can also say that the subflow "takes a parameter"—we use an `input` element to give the `user` model to the subflow. The subflow can then do whatever operation it needs to do with the model. We do not have to bother about it, because the subflow is some kind of black box, which we might not even know. Alternatively, we can specify a `SubflowAttributeMapper` instead of the `input` and `output` elements, to give parameters to the subflow and receive return values from the subflow.

When the subflow is called, it is processed like any other flow, until it reaches an `end-state`, where it returns to the calling flow. When the subflow returns, we transition to the `end-state welcomeView`, which shows a short welcome message to the logged-in user.

As you can see, using subflows in your own applications is actually not much different from using normal flows, but it greatly enhances the re-usability of your flow definitions.

Spring JavaScript

Spring JavaScript is a new library being shipped, for the first time, along with Spring Web Flow 2. However, Spring JavaScript is completely independent of Spring Web Flow. This means that you can use this library in your web applications, even if you are not using Spring Web Flow or even Spring MVC.

Spring JavaScript helps you integrate modern AJAX technologies in your web applications. It is built on the Dojo toolkit, a very popular open source framework to write AJAX-powered web applications. We will show you in detail how to integrate Spring JavaScript in your applications, and what you can do with the Dojo toolkit. Spring JavaScript is an abstraction layer. Thus, it is perfectly feasible to change the Dojo-based implementation and change it to another JavaScript library.

What is AJAX?

Nowadays, you can read about AJAX all over the Internet. Many recently updated web sites use AJAX technologies. **AJAX** is an acronym that stands for **Asynchronous JavaScript And XML**. It's not known today who mentioned this acronym for the first time. However, Jesse James Garrett had already mentioned this term in his article *Ajax: A New Approach to Web Applications*, in February 18, 2005. Reading his article to get an overview of how AJAX really works is highly recommended. You can find this article at: `http://www.adaptivepath.com/ideas/essays/archives/000385.php`. In a nutshell, AJAX is about not loading a web site completely on every request synchronously, as it is usually done (that is, by sending a request to the server and waiting for the server to respond with the result page). With AJAX, you can send requests to a web server asynchronously via XML. This makes web applications much more responsive and makes them feel like desktop (client) applications, as only a minimum amount of data is requested, which is necessary to render the part of the web site that we want to change. While the data is received, the user interface of the web application stays responsive, and the user can still interact with it.

The `XMLHttpRequest` object is technically responsible for AJAX. It was first introduced in Microsoft® Internet Explorer 4.0 and is available today in all major browsers. The `XMLHttpRequest` object is the requirement for asynchronous communication with a web server.

Of course, it is possible to write the required JavaScript yourself, but others have already done it so many times and have also created various AJAX toolkits. As mentioned already, Spring JavaScript is an abstraction layer on top of these AJAX toolkits. Spring JavaScript makes it easy for you to enhance your web applications with features, which improve the usability and performance of your applications.

But although all current browser releases offer the possibilities to use JavaScript and AJAX, not all users choose to allow these technologies to be executed in their browsers because of the possibility of security threats. Spring JavaScript enables you to *decorate* certain HTML elements in your web site, in a way which does not prevent users using older browsers or users who disabled JavaScript support in their browsers to access your web site. For example, imagine that you want to enable your users to pick a date. Using Spring JavaScript and Dojo, this can be achieved very quickly with the following source code:

```
<?xml version="1.0" encoding="ISO-8859-1" ?>
<jsp:root
    xmlns="http://www.w3.org/1999/xhtml"
    xmlns:jsp="http://java.sun.com/JSP/Page"
    xmlns:form="http://www.springframework.org/tags/form"
    xmlns:c="http://java.sun.com/jsp/jstl/core"
```

```
        version="2.1">

    <jsp:directive.page language="java"
       contentType="text/html; charset=ISO-8859-1"
       pageEncoding="ISO-8859-1" isELIgnored="false"/>

    <html>
       <head>
          <title>Spring JS Example Application</title>
          <style type="text/css">
               @import
             "${pageContext.request.contextPath}/resources/dijit/
                                          themes/tundra/tundra.css";
               @import
             "${pageContext.request.contextPath}/resources/dojo/
                                                resources/dojo.css";
          </style>

          <jsp:element name="script">
             <jsp:attribute name="type">
                text/javascript
             </jsp:attribute>
             <jsp:attribute name="src">
                <c:url value="/resources/dojo/dojo.js" />
             </jsp:attribute>
             <jsp:body> </jsp:body>
          </jsp:element>
          <jsp:element name="script">
             <jsp:attribute name="type">
                text/javascript
             </jsp:attribute>
             <jsp:attribute name="src">
                <c:url value="/resources/spring/Spring.js" />
             </jsp:attribute>
             <jsp:body> </jsp:body>
          </jsp:element>
             <jsp:element name="script">
             <jsp:attribute name="type">
                text/javascript
             </jsp:attribute>
             <jsp:attribute name="src">
                <c:url value="/resources/spring/Spring-Dojo.js" />
             </jsp:attribute>
             <jsp:body> </jsp:body>
          </jsp:element>

       </head>
       <body class="tundra">
```

```
            <h1>Spring JS Example</h1>
            <p>Please fill out the following form:</p>
            <form action="doSomething.do" method="post">
               <p>
                  <input type="text" id="dateField" />
               </p>
            </form>
            <script type="text/javascript">
               Spring.addDecoration(new Spring.ElementDecoration(
               {
                  elementId: "dateField",
                  widgetType: "dijit.form.DateTextBox"
               }));
            </script>
         </body>
      </html>
   </jsp:root>
```

Please note that the widgets from the Dojo toolkit are customizable, so you can adapt them to suit your own web site design. In our example, we are using the so-called *Tundra* theme.

> We are using the XML-style declaration of the `script` tags, including an empty `jsp:body` element. Otherwise, the generated web page is rendered with `script` tags in the following form:
>
> <script type="text/javascript" src="/flowjs/resources/dojo/dojo.js" />
>
> Which is a valid XML, but not a valid (X)HTML. Instead, we use the XML-style, which renders the `script` tags correctly:
>
> <script type="text/javascript" src="/flowjs/resources/dojo/dojo.js">
> </script>

The previous code creates a standard HTML form with one text field, named `dateField`. Then we add a *decoration* to this text field by using JavaScript. We want to add a `DateTextBox`, a widget from Dojo, to display the `dateField` text field.

In JavaScript-enabled browsers, the previous example will appear as shown in the following screenshot:

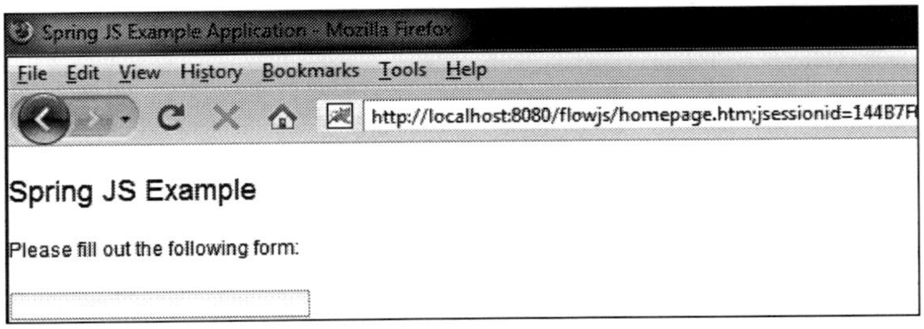

When you click on the text field, a small calendar will appear, which you can use to choose a date:

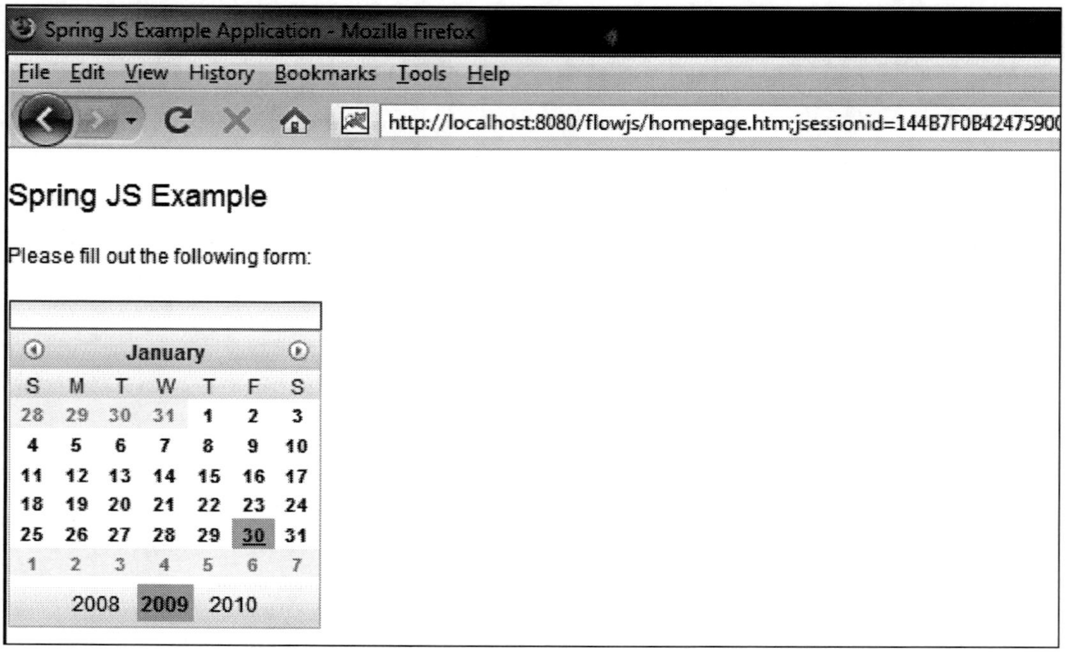

For this widget, a validation is already enabled. If you write random text or an invalid date, you will get a message that tells you about the error. In case you disabled JavaScript support in your browser, the text field will still work and enable you to enter a date, although the calendar and the validation will not work anymore. We recommend writing a custom validation, just in case your users do not have JavaScript enabled on their browsers.

Before we dive into the depth of Spring JavaScript and the Dojo toolkit, we will show you how to install Spring JavaScript.

Installing Spring JavaScript

If you are using Maven, all you have to do to add support for Spring JavaScript in your application is to add the following XML snippet to your `pom.xml`:

```
<dependency>
   <groupId>org.springframework.webflow</groupId>
   <artifactId>org.springframework.js</artifactId>
   <version>2.0.5.RELEASE</version>
</dependency>
```

This will download the Spring JavaScript distribution to your computer automatically and make it available to your application. Because Spring JavaScript is only an abstraction, you also need a concrete implementation of the AJAX functionality. With the current release of Spring Web Flow 2, only the Dojo toolkit is supported. Luckily, Dojo is already included in the Spring JavaScript distribution, so you do not have to do any extra configuration.

The first example with Spring JavaScript

We will show you how to carefully enhance a wizard style application with AJAX components to create a new bug report. The finished form will look like this:

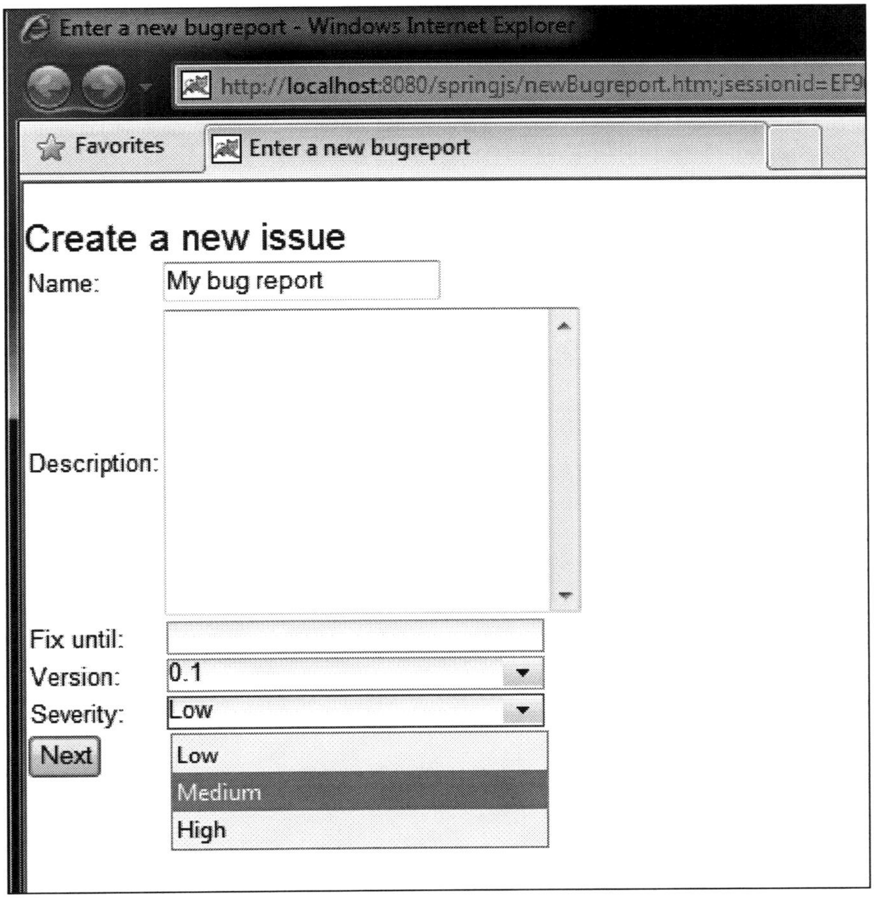

This form includes the title of the bug, the version of the application this bug corresponds to, a detailed description of how the bug happened, what went wrong, and the severity of the bug.

Of course, we also need some information about the user to know at least who is reporting the bug. So we created a second, smaller form which appears as shown here:

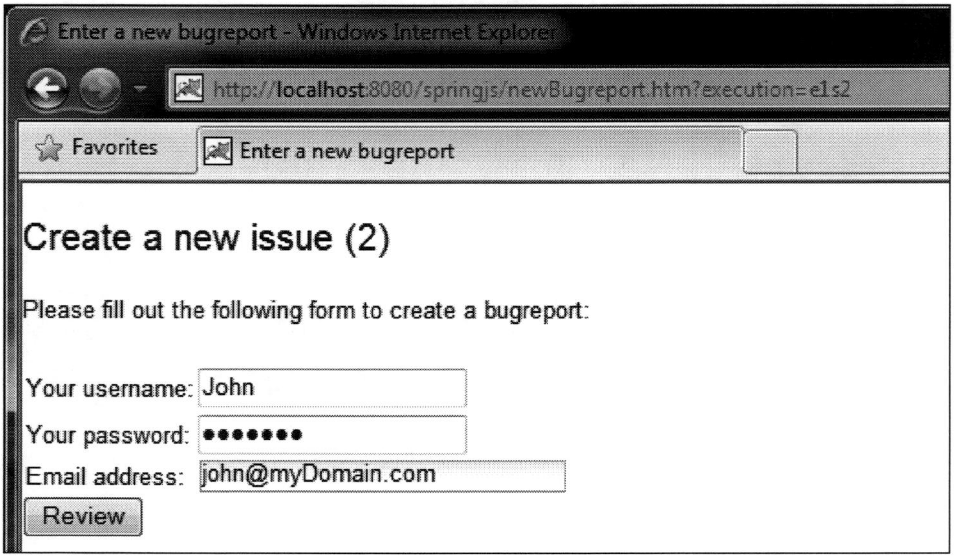

When you click on the **Review** button, all entered information is displayed again so that the user can check if he/she had entered the correct information:

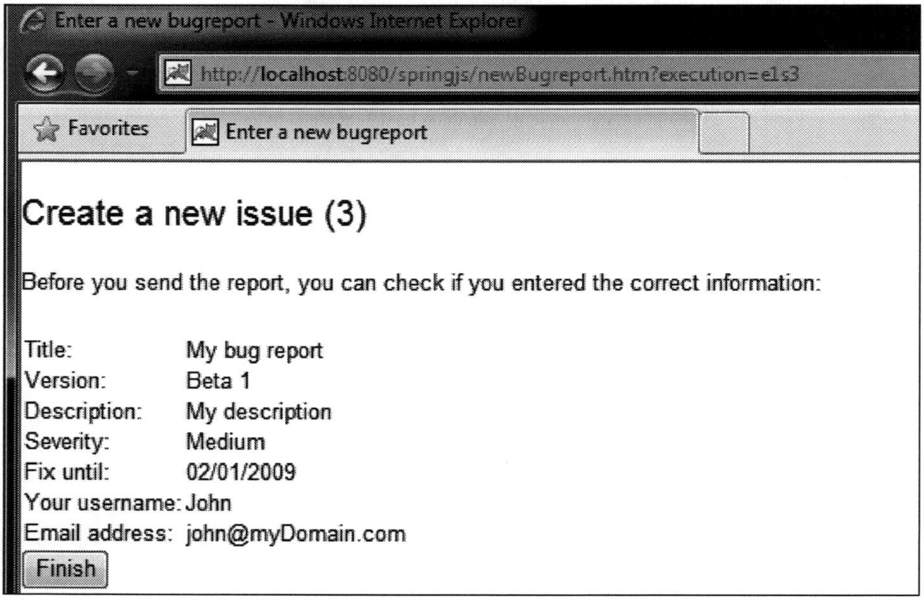

The flow definition for this form looks like this:

```
<?xml version="1.0" encoding="UTF-8"?>
<flow xmlns="http://www.springframework.org/schema/webflow"
   xmlns:xsi="http://www.w3.org/2001/XMLSchema-instance"
   xsi:schemaLocation="http://www.springframework.org/schema/webflow
        http://www.springframework.org/schema/webflow/spring-webflow-
                                                              2.0.xsd">

    <persistence-context />

    <var class="flowtrac.core.model.issue.Issue"
         name="issue" />

    <var class="flowtrac.core.model.user.DBUser"
         name="user" />

   <view-state id="firstPage" model="issue" view="firstPage.jspx">
      <transition on="next" to="secondPage" />
   </view-state>

   <view-state id="secondPage" model="user" view="secondPage.jspx">
      <transition on="review" to="updateIssue" />
   </view-state>

   <action-state id="updateIssue">
      <evaluate expression="issue.setCreatedBy(user)" />
      <transition to="review" />
   </action-state>

   <view-state id="review" model="issue" view="review.jspx">
      <transition on="finish" to="finish" />
   </view-state>

   <action-state id="saveBug">
      <evaluate expression="persistenceContext.persist(issue)" />
      <transition on="success" to="finish" />
      <transition to="onError" />
   </action-state>

   <end-state id="finish" view="firstPage.jspx" commit="true" />
   <end-state id="onError" view="errorPage.jspx" />

</flow>
```

The flow definition we just saw consists of three `view-states`. On the first page (the `firstPage` state), the user is asked to provide some general information concerning the issue he/she wants to report. On the second state, called `secondPage`, the user has to enter his/her username, email address, and password for user identification. Next, an `action-state` will assign the identified user to the just created issue and then proceed to a review page. There the user can take a look at all the information he entered in the wizard, before the data is actually sent to the bug-tracking system. When he/she finishes the wizard, the bug details will be added to the bug database, and the user will again be forwarded to the initial page.

The form of the first page (`firstPage.jspx`) of the wizard is built using the following source code:

```
<form:form method="post" modelAttribute="issue">
        <table>
            <tr>
                <td>
                    Name:
                </td>
                <td>
                    <form:input id="title" path="name" />
                </td>
            </tr>
            <tr>
                <td>
                    Description:
                </td>
                <td>
                    <form:textarea id="description"
                     path="description" cols="25"
                     rows="10" />
                </td>
            </tr>
            <tr>
                <td>
                    Fix until:
                </td>
                <td>
                    <form:input id="fixingDate"
                                path="fixingDate" />
                </td>
            </tr>
            <tr>
                <td>
```

```
                        Version:
                    </td>
                    <td>
                        <form:select id="version" path="version">
                            <form:option value="0.1" />
                            <form:option value="0.2" />
                            <form:option value="0.3" />
                            <form:option value="Beta 1" />
                            <form:option value="1.0" />
                        </form:select>
                    </td>
:
                </tr>
                <tr>
                    <td>
                        Severity:
                    </td>
                    <td>
                        <form:select id="severity"
                                     path="severity">
                            <form:option value="Low" />
                            <form:option value="Medium" />
                            <form:option value="High" />
                        </form:select>
                    </td>
                </tr>
            </table>
            <input type="submit"
                   name="_eventId_next"
                   value="Next" />
</form:form>
     <script type="text/javascript">
         <![CDATA[
             Spring.addDecoration(
                new Spring.ElementDecoration(
                 {
                    elementId: "fixingDate",
                    widgetType: "dijit.form.DateTextBox"
                 }));

             Spring.addDecoration(
                new Spring.ElementDecoration(
             {
                 elementId: "version",
                 widgetType: "dijit.form.FilteringSelect",
                 widgetAttrs: {autoComplete : "true" }
```

```
                    }));

                    Spring.addDecoration(:
new Spring.ElementDecoration(
                    {
                        elementId: "severity",
                        widgetType: "dijit.form.FilteringSelect",
                        widgetAttrs: {autoComplete : "true" }
                    }));
                ]]>
            </script>
```

The HTML of the site is very straightforward. Using the Spring `form` tag library, a form is created that includes the above mentioned fields. No AJAX features are added to the web site at this stage. To enhance the usability of the web site, we decide to add some special features of Dojo: the filtering of select box along with auto-completion. The user can either enter a value in the box (which is already present in the drop-down options), or if he/she prefers the keyboard, they can navigate through the form using the arrow keys, or click on the box to select the value of his choice. If he/she enters a value which is not included in the select box, an error message will be shown:

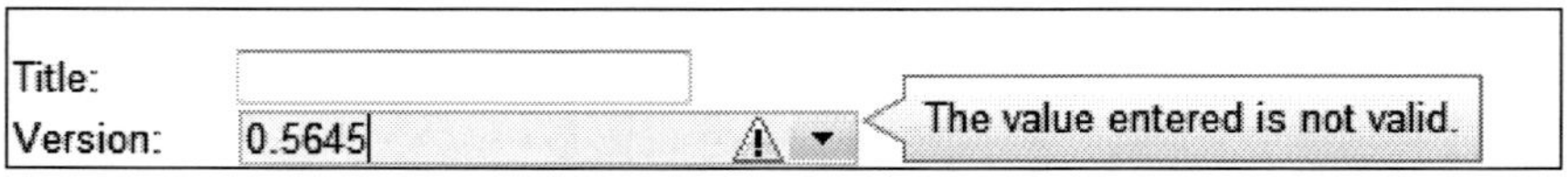

The JavaScript is added as shown in the simple example earlier in this chapter. We are using the `addDecoration()` method to carefully enhance the web site. This time we choose a widget called `dijit.form.FilteringSelect`. We provided additional parameters using the `widgetAttrs` argument. Here, we have enabled auto-completion. This means that the currently entered partial value will be completed and selected as soon as the user uses the *Tab* key on his/her keyboard to go to the next component of the form. Additionally, we have also added a `DateTextBox` again to display a nice calendar widget when the user selects a due date to fix the bug.

The form of the second page (`secondPage.jspx`) is built using the following source code:

```
<form:form method="post" commandName="user">
    <table>
        <tr>
            <td>
                Your username:
            </td>
            <td>
```

```
                <form:input id="username" path="username" />
            </td>
        </tr>
        <tr>
            <td>
                Your password:
            </td>
            <td>
                <form:password id="password" path="password" />
            </td>
        </tr>
        <tr>
            <td>
                Email address:
            </td>
            <td>
                <form:input id="eMail" path="email" />
            </td>
        </tr>
    </table>
    <input type="submit" name="_eventId_review" value="Review" />
</form:form>

<script   type="text/javascript">
Spring.addDecoration(new Spring.ElementDecoration(
                        {
                            elementId: "email",
                            widgetType: "dijit.form.ValidationTextBox",
                            widgetAttrs: {regExp : ".*@.*\.{0,2}" }
                        }));

</script>
```

We have enabled validation again as shown earlier on the first page. This time we want to make sure that the entered email address is valid, so we are using a very simple, regular expression to check this.

Finally, the user can review his/her entered information on the `review.jspx` page. We are using the `core` **JSTL(JSP Standard Tag Library)** tags to display the entered values and the `fmt` tags to format a date appropriately:

```
<form:form method="post" modelAttribute="issue">
            <table>
                <tr>
                    <td>
                        Title:
```

```
                </td>
                <td>
                    <span>
                        <c:out value="${issue.name}" />
                    </span>
                </td>
            </tr>
            <tr>
                <td>
                    Version:
                </td>
                <td>
                    <span>
                        <c:out value="${issue.version}" />
                    </span>
                </td>
            </tr>
            <tr>
                <td>
                    Description:
                 </td>
                <td>
                    <div>
                        <c:out value="${issue.description}" />
                    </div>
                </td>
            </tr>
            <tr>
                <td>
                    Severity:
                </td>
                <td>
                    <span>
                         <c:out value="${issue.severity}" />
                    </span>
                </td>
            </tr>
            <tr>
                <td>
                    Fix until:
                </td>
                <td>
                    <span>
                        <fmt:formatDate pattern="MM/dd/yyyy"
```

```
                        value="${issue.fixingDate}" />
                </span>
            </td>
        </tr>
        <tr>
            <td>
                Your username:
            </td>
            <td>
              <span>
                 <c:out
                   value="${issue.createdBy.username}" />
               </span>
            </td>
        </tr>
        <tr>
            <td>
                Email address:
            </td>
            <td>
              <span>
                <c:out value="${issue.createdBy.email}" />
              </span>
            </td>
        </tr>
    </table>
    <input type="submit"
           name="_eventId_finish"
           value="Finish" />
</form:form>
```

Apache Tiles integration

Although we cannot give you a full introduction to Apache Tiles 2, we want to show you how to integrate this template engine with your web applications. **Apache Tiles** is a template engine that uses the **Composition** pattern. In this case, this pattern means that a web site consists of multiple distinct parts that can be merged to form a complete web site on request. This has two advantages: you greatly enhance the re-usability of your web sites, and with the use of AJAX, you can even improve performance by rendering only those parts of the web sites that change. We recommend reading the tutorials on the Tiles web site at `http://tiles.apache.org`.

Our web application is an Apache Tile integrated version of the "Hello world" application that looks like this:

If you click on the **Next** button, a request to the server will be sent which renders a new web site using Tiles:

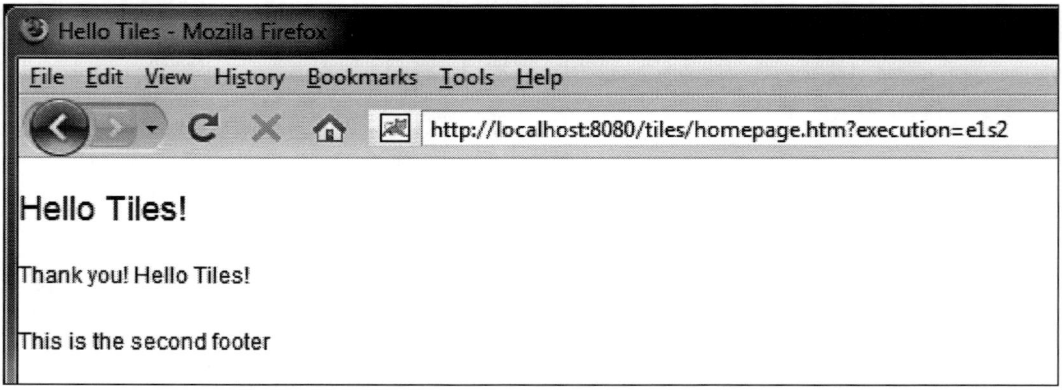

Let's take a look at the main template of this web site. Please note that we have omitted the definitions of the styles and the `script` tags. You can find them in the calendar example given earlier in this chapter.

```
<?xml version="1.0" encoding="ISO-8859-1" ?>
<jsp:root
     xmlns="http://www.w3.org/1999/xhtml"
     xmlns:jsp="http://java.sun.com/JSP/Page"
     xmlns:c="http://java.sun.com/jstl/core"
     xmlns:tiles="http://tiles.apache.org/tags-tiles"
```

```
    xmlns:form="http://www.springframework.org/tags/form"
    version="1.2">
  <jsp:directive.page language="java"
     contentType="text/html; charset=ISO-8859-1"
     pageEncoding="ISO-8859-1" isELIgnored="false" />
  <html>
     <head>
        <title>Hello Tiles</title>
...
     </head>

     <body class="tundra">
        <h1>Hello Tiles!</h1>
        <tiles:insertAttribute name="body" />

        <p><tiles:insertAttribute name="footer" /></p>
     </body>
  </html>
</jsp:root>
```

As you can see, the main page is just a plain JSPX file with only a few new tags. First of all, we include an additional tag library from Apache Tiles with the prefix, `tiles`. With the `insertAttribute` tags, we can define where the content should appear later. You can imagine these tags as named placeholders for the real content.

The flow definition of this flow appears as shown in the following source code listing:

```
<?xml version="1.0" encoding="UTF-8"?>
<flow xmlns="http://www.springframework.org/schema/webflow"
   xmlns:xsi="http://www.w3.org/2001/XMLSchema-instance"
   xsi:schemaLocation="http://www.springframework.org/schema/webflow
                       http://www.springframework.org/schema/webflow
                                           /spring-webflow-2.0.xsd">

   <view-state id="homepage">
      <transition on="next" to="secondPage" />
   </view-state>

   <view-state id="secondPage" />
</flow>
```

We have only two `view-states` in this example. The first one, the `homepage` state, makes the transitions to the `secondPage` state when the `next` event is triggered.

Next, we have to define the views we have and the parts they consist of. We do this using an Apache Tiles definition file:

```
<?xml version="1.0" encoding="UTF-8"?>
<!DOCTYPE tiles-definitions PUBLIC
   "-//Apache Software Foundation//DTD Tiles Configuration 2.0//EN"
   "http://tiles.apache.org/dtds/tiles-config_2_0.dtd">
<tiles-definitions>
   <definition name="homepage"
               template="/WEB-INF/flows/homepage.jspx">
      <put-attribute name="body"
                     value="/WEB-INF/flows/firstPage.jsp" />
      <put-attribute name="footer"
                     value="/WEB-INF/flows/footerOne.jsp" />
   </definition>
   <definition name="secondPage"
               template="/WEB-INF/flows/homepage.jspx">
      <put-attribute name="body"
                     value="/WEB-INF/flows/secondPage.jsp" />
      <put-attribute name="footer"
                     value="/WEB-INF/flows/footerTwo.jsp" />
   </definition>
</tiles-definitions>
```

We have two views, so we have two definitions. We define that the body element of the homepage view should display the content in the firstPage.jsp file.

> Please remember that we added the code <tiles:insertAttribute name="body" /> to the homepage.jspx to indicate where the content should be inserted and how the attribute is called.

We also added a page footer to each definition, because we want to display a different footer on both the pages.

The parts of the web site we referenced from the Tiles definition file are so easy that we only need to show two of them to you—the first body and the first footer. First, the body page:

```
<%@ taglib prefix="form"
           uri="http://www.springframework.org/tags/form"%>
<p>
Hello! Please click the button below to switch to the next page!
<form:form method="post">
   <input type="submit" name="_eventId_next" value="Next" />
</form:form>
</p>
```

Now, the footer:

```
<span style="font-size:9pt">This is the first footer</span>
```

As you can see, these are just HTML fragments to be rendered by the Tiles engine when a user browses your web site.

If you try to execute the example now, you will notice that it doesn't work. You will need some additional configuration to let Spring Web Flow know that you want to use Tiles to render your views. We include the application context file and highlight the additions:

```
<?xml version="1.0" encoding="UTF-8"?>
<beans xmlns="http://www.springframework.org/schema/beans"
       xmlns:xsi="http://www.w3.org/2001/XMLSchema-instance"
       xmlns:webflow="http://www.springframework.org/schema/
                                            webflow-config"
       xsi:schemaLocation="
            http://www.springframework.org/schema/beans
            http://www.springframework.org/schema/beans
                                  /spring-beans-2.5.xsd
            http://www.springframework.org/schema/webflow-config
            http://www.springframework.org/schema/webflow-config
                             /spring-webflow-config-2.0.xsd">

   <!-- Tiles -->
   <bean id="tilesConfigurer"
      class="org.springframework.web.servlet.view.tiles2.
         TilesConfigurer">
      <property name="definitions">
         <list>
            <value>/WEB-INF/flows/tiles-def.xml
            </value>
         </list>
      </property>
   </bean>

   <!-- Spring MVC -->
   <bean id="handlerMapping"
         class="org.springframework.web.servlet.
                      handler.SimpleUrlHandlerMapping">
      <property name="mappings">
         <value>/homepage.htm=flowController
         </value>
      </property>
   </bean>
```

```
    <bean id="tilesViewResolver"
          class="org.springframework.web.servlet
                                .view.UrlBasedViewResolver">
       <property name="viewClass"
                value="org.springframework.web.servlet.view.tiles2
                                                    .TilesView" />
    </bean>

    <bean id="flowController"
       class="org.springframework.webflow.mvc.servlet.FlowController">
       <property name="flowExecutor" ref="flowExecutor" />
    </bean>

    <!-- Spring Web Flow -->

    <bean id="viewFactoryCreator"
          class="org.springframework.webflow.mvc.builder.
                                      MvcViewFactoryCreator">
       <property name="viewResolvers" ref="tilesViewResolver" />
    </bean>

    <webflow:flow-builder-services id="flowBuilderServices"
       view-factory-creator="viewFactoryCreator" />

    <webflow:flow-registry id="flowRegistry"
       flow-builder-services="flowBuilderServices">
       <webflow:flow-location id="homepage"
          path="/WEB-INF/flows/homepage-flow.xml" />
    </webflow:flow-registry>

    <webflow:flow-executor id="flowExecutor"
       flow-registry="flowRegistry" />

</beans>
```

Firstly, we enable Spring MVC support for the Apache Tiles engine by defining a `TilesConfigurer`. This is where we define where our Tiles configuration file is located. We could also specify multiple configuration files, if needed. Next, we define a custom view resolver with a special `viewClass` property. A **view resolver** in Spring MVC is used to connect logical view names to concrete view implementations that can be shown to the user. In our case, we do not want to map JSP sites (we could have used an `org.springframework.web.servlet.view.JstlView` as `viewClass` in that case), but to use Apache Tiles to render our views, so we are using the `TilesView` class instead.

Because we want to inform Spring Web Flow that we are using a custom view resolver, we have to create an `MvcViewFactoryCreator` bean in our configuration file. If we do not specify an object of this class, Spring Web Flow will still use it, but with a default implementation. This implementation assumes that the views to render are JSPs that are relative to the flow folder. For this reason, we always put the JSP files in the same folder as the flow definition file. Here, we tell `MvcViewFactoryCreator` to use the `TilesView`, that we've already defined.

This `MvcViewFactoryCreator` is now added to the so-called Web Flow builder services. Here, the developer can specify custom beans and behavior used to construct flow definitions. Using the builder service, and more specifically the `view-factory-creator` attribute, we can manipulate how Spring Web Flow renders views defined in our flow definition file.

Finally, we have to add the builder services to `flowRegistry`. That's it! We can now use Apache Tiles in our flows.

Tiles and AJAX

Until now, all requests using tiles were re-loading the web site completely. In the AJAX universe, you normally do not want to have a re-load of the entire web site when you click on a link. After all, that is what AJAX is all about. Spring JavaScript allows you to partially update chosen Tiles parts of your web page. The remaining web site will not be reloaded, which can greatly enhance the performance of your web application. The Web Flow developers point out that in theory, any template engine could be used. However, Spring Web Flow 2 ships only with support for Apache Tiles 2 by default. To show this concept to you, we wrote a small example application that generates random numbers.

First, we want to show you the Spring Web Flow configuration file:

```
<?xml version="1.0" encoding="UTF-8"?>
<flow xmlns="http://www.springframework.org/schema/webflow"
   xmlns:xsi="http://www.w3.org/2001/XMLSchema-instance"
   xsi:schemaLocation="http://www.springframework.org/schema/webflow
         http://www.springframework.org/schema/webflow/
spring-webflow-2.0.xsd">

   <view-state id="homepage" />

</flow>
```

For our example, we only need one `view-state` because all processing is done in the `homepage` state.

Next, we create a controller, which does the work of generating random numbers:

```
@Controller
public class ExampleController {
    // Create a pseudo-random number generator
    private static Random randomizer = new Random();

    @RequestMapping("/getNumbers.htm")
    public ModelMap getRandomNumbers() {
        List<Integer> randomNumberList = new ArrayList<Integer>();
        // Create ten new random numbers
        for (int i = 0; i < 10; ++i) {
            randomNumberList.add(randomizer.nextInt());
        }
        // Return the numbers as ModelMap
        return new ModelMap("numberList", randomNumberList);
    }
}
```

This example uses the new annotation based controller configuration, which was introduced in Spring 2.5. Using the `@Controller` annotation, you mark the class as Spring MVC controller. This class includes one method called `getRandomNumbers()`, which creates 10 pseudo-random numbers, and returns a Spring MVC `ModelMap` object that includes these numbers. The method is annotated with the `@RequestMapping` annotation. This annotation causes the method to be called whenever the URL `/getNumbers.htm` is accessed by a user.

The annotation based configuration needs additional configuration options, particularly if you plan to use it with Spring Web Flow. We will show you the configuration options that are need to be added into the Spring context configuration file we used in the previous example:

```
<beans xmlns="http://www.springframework.org/schema/beans"
       xmlns:xsi="http://www.w3.org/2001/XMLSchema-instance"
       xmlns:webflow="http://www.springframework.org/schema
                                                  /webflow-config"
   xmlns:context="http://www.springframework.org/schema/context"
   xsi:schemaLocation="
         http://www.springframework.org/schema/beans
         http://www.springframework.org/schema/beans
                                   /spring-beans-2.5.xsd
         http://www.springframework.org/schema/webflow-config
         http://www.springframework.org/schema
                   /webflow-config/spring-webflow-config-2.0.xsd
         http://www.springframework.org/schema/context
```

```
         http://www.springframework.org/schema/context
                                  /spring-context-2.5.xsd">

   <context:component-scan base-package="com.webflow2book" />

    <!-- For annotated methods and types -->
   <bean class="org.springframework.web.servlet.mvc.annotation
                              .AnnotationMethodHandlerAdapter" />

    <bean class="org.springframework.web.servlet.mvc.annotation
                              .DefaultAnnotationHandlerMapping" />

  <bean id="tilesConfigurer" ...></bean>

  <!-- For FlowController-->
  <bean class="org.springframework.web.servlet.mvc
                              .SimpleControllerHandlerAdapter" />

  <bean id="tilesViewResolver"
        class="org.springframework.js.ajax.AjaxUrlBasedViewResolver">
        <property name="viewClass"
                  value="org.springframework.webflow.mvc.view
                                          .FlowAjaxTilesView" />
   </bean>
    ...
  </beans>
```

First, we define the component-scan element in the context namespace. We've also added it to the beans element. This enables automatic registering of Spring beans for classes that are annotated using annotations such as @Service or @Controller.

> You have to define the <context:annotation-config /> element in addition to the component-scan element if you want to use annotations such as @Autowired and @Required in your classes.

Next, we define the AnnotationMethodHandlerAdapter and the DefaultAnnotationHandlerMapping. These classes are used to enable the usage of the @RequestMapping at the type level (by HandlerMapping) and at the method level (by HandlerAdapter). Usually, the DispatcherServlet already contains the appropriate classes, but as we define custom HandlerMappings, we need to explicitly create these beans. Afterwards, we create a bean instance of the SimpleControllerHandlerAdapter class. This HandlerAdapter is needed to enable usage of the FlowController. Without defining this adapter, we will get an exception that says that no adapter for the FlowController handler is specified.

Finally, we have to change the `tilesViewResolver` from our last example to make it AJAX-aware. For this example, we have used the `AjaxUrlBasedViewResolver` and the `FlowAjaxTilesView` as its view classes. The `AjaxUrlBasedViewResolver` overrides the `createView()` method of the `UrlBasedViewResolver` class. We used `UrlBasedViewResolver` in our last chapter to add some custom code, which handles URLs that contain redirects correctly in an AJAX environment. The `FlowAjaxTilesView` handles partial rendering of the content.

Now that we have finished our configuration, we can write a web page that uses it (saved as `homepage.jspx` in the `src/main/webapps/WEB-INF/flows/` folder):

```
<?xml version="1.0" encoding="ISO-8859-1" ?>
<jsp:root
    xmlns="http://www.w3.org/1999/xhtml"
    xmlns:jsp="http://java.sun.com/JSP/Page"
    xmlns:c="http://java.sun.com/jsp/jstl/core"
    xmlns:tiles="http://tiles.apache.org/tags-tiles"
          version="2.1">
   <jsp:directive.page language="java"
      contentType="text/html; charset=ISO-8859-1"
      pageEncoding="ISO-8859-1" isELIgnored="false" />

   <html>
      <head>

         ...

         <title>Enter a new bugreport</title>
      </head>

      <body class="tundra">
            <h1>Hello Tiles!</h1>

            Hello! Please click the link below to load random numbers
               on demand <br />

            <a id="loadNumbers"
               href="${pageContext.request.contextPath}
                                          /getNumbers.htm">
               Load numbers
            </a>
            <script type="text/javascript">
                Spring.addDecoration(
                    new Spring.AjaxEventDecoration( {
                    elementId: "loadNumbers",
                    event: "onclick",
                    params: { fragments: "number" }
```

```
                })); 
            </script>
            <br />
            <tiles:insertAttribute name="number" />
        </body>
    </html>
</jsp:root>
```

This web page includes the same style and script elements of the earlier examples; therefore, we do not mention it again. In the body of the page, we add a link that accesses the controller that we had written earlier. Usually, this would trigger a new request that will cause the page to reload and show the new content. This happens even if the user has disabled support for JavaScript in his/her browser so that your web site stays usable even if the user does not want to use JavaScript. If JavaScript is enabled, the code in the following `script` tag is executed. This code adds an `AjaxEventDecoration` to the link we've just defined. This will cause the link to submit an AJAX request instead of a normal request, when the event `onclick` is triggered. As soon as the user clicks on the link, an AJAX request is submitted. We also specify which parts of the web page should be rendered partially. In our example, we want the fragment `number` to be rendered using this code:

```
<tiles:insertAttribute name="number" />
```

We can define where the fragment should be rendered, and how it is to be called. Of course, we also need a Tiles configuration file (`tiles-def.xml`):

```
<?xml version="1.0" encoding="UTF-8"?>
<!DOCTYPE tiles-definitions PUBLIC
   "-//Apache Software Foundation//DTD Tiles Configuration 2.0//EN"
   "http://tiles.apache.org/dtds/tiles-config_2_0.dtd">

<tiles-definitions>
   <definition name="homepage"
               template="/WEB-INF/flows/homepage.jspx">
      <put-attribute name="number"
                     value="/WEB-INF/flows/emptyPage.jsp" />
   </definition>
   <definition name="getNumbers"
               template="/WEB-INF/flows/homepage.jspx">
      <put-attribute name="number"
                     value="/WEB-INF/flows/numberList.jsp" />
   </definition>
</tiles-definitions>
```

The definition `homepage` will be used when we enter the web page with the `/homepage.htm` URL. This will tell the `insertAttribute` element to render the `emptyPage.jsp`, which has to be saved alongside the other JSP(X) files in the `src/main/webapp/WEB-INF/flows` folder path. The code for `emptyPage.jsp` looks like this:

```
<div id="numberDiv">
    No numbers loaded yet!
</div>
```

This will render the page as shown in the following screenshot:

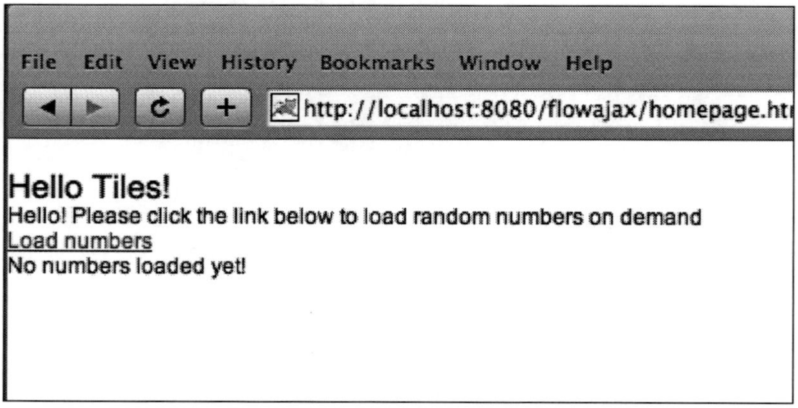

As soon as the link on our page is clicked, the `ExampleController` is called, and then a list of random numbers generated. Tiles will then take the `getNumbers` definition into account and uses the `numberList.jsp` to render the output. This file is displayed in the following source code listing:

```
<%@ taglib prefix="c" uri="http://java.sun.com/jstl/core"%>

<div id="numberDiv">
    <c:forEach items="${numberList}" var="item">
    <li>
        <c:out value="${item}" />
    </li>
    </c:forEach>
</div>
```

The output should appear similar to this (the numbers might be different):

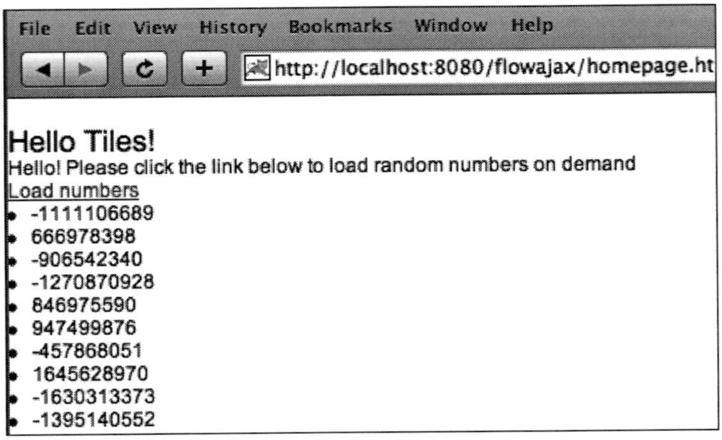

If you click on the **Load numbers** link more often, you will get new numbers without having the complete page re-rendered.

The Web Flow configuration

In the previous chapters, we already mentioned the Web Flow configuration file quite often for our examples and even showed you the basic elements in Chapter 3. In this chapter, we want to give you an in-depth look into the file and its elements. We recommend reading this chapter and using it as a reference afterwards. We learned that it is very important to know which elements are allowed in the Spring Web Flow configuration file and which attributes they have. It will also make it easier to understand how the XML Schema definition file works, in case you have to take a look at the file of Spring Web Flow while you're configuring your flow.

Let's take a look at the **XML Schema Definition** (**XSD**) file of the Spring Web Flow configuration file. To make the file more compact and easier to read, we removed documentation and similar additions from the file. The complete file is downloadable from `http://www.springframework.org/schema/webflow/spring-webflow-2.0.xsd`.

> An **XSD** file (**XML Schema Definition**) is a file that is used to describe an XML Schema, which in itself is a W3C recommendation to describe the structure of XML files. In this kind of definition files, you can describe which elements can or must be present in an XML file. XSD files are primarily used to check the validity of XML files that are supposed to follow a certain structure. The schema can also be used to automatically create code, using code generation tools.

The elements of the configuration file are:

flow

The root element of the Spring Web Flow definition file is the `flow` element. It has to be present in all configurations because all other elements are sub-elements of the `flow` tag, which defines exactly one flow. If you want to define more than one flow, you will have to use the same amount of `flow` tags. As every configuration file allows only one root element, you will have to define a new configuration file for every flow you want to define.

attribute

Using the `attribute` tag, you can define metadata for a flow. You can use this metadata to change the behavior of the flow.

secured

The `secured` tag is used to secure your flow using Spring Security. The element is defined like this:

```
<xsd:complexType name="secured">
   <xsd:attribute name="attributes"
                  type="xsd:string"
                  use="required" />
   <xsd:attribute name="match"
                  use="optional">
      <xsd:simpleType>
         <xsd:restriction base="xsd:string">
            <xsd:enumeration value="any" />
            <xsd:enumeration value="all" />
         </xsd:restriction>
      </xsd:simpleType>
   </xsd:attribute>
</xsd:complexType>
```

If you want to use the `secured` element, you will have to at least define the `attributes` attribute. You can use the `attributes` element to define roles that are allowed to access the flow, for example. The `match` attribute defines whether all the elements specified in the `attributes` attribute have to match successfully (`all`), or if one of them is sufficient (`any`). For more information on using this tag and Spring Security in general, refer to Chapter 7 of this book.

persistence-context

Used in Chapter 2 of this book, the `persistence-context` element enables you to use a persistence provider in your flow definition. This lets you persist database objects in `action-states`.

> To use `persistence-context` tag, you also have to define a data source and configure the persistence provider of your choice (for example, Hibernate or the Java Persistence API) in your Spring application context configuration file.

The `persistence-context` element is empty, which means that you just have to add

```
<persistence-context />
```

to your flow definition, to enable its features.

var

As already mentioned in Chapter 3, you can use the `var` element to define instance variables, which are accessible in your entire flow. These variables are quite important, so make sure that you are familiar with them. Using `var` elements, you can define `model` objects. Later, you can bind these `model` objects to the forms in your JSP web sites and can store them in a database using the persistence features enabled with the `persistence-context` element. Nevertheless, using instance variables is not mandatory, so you do not have to define any, unless required in your flow. The element is defined as shown in the following snippet from the XSD file:

```
<xsd:element name="var" minOccurs="0" maxOccurs="unbounded">
   <xsd:complexType>
      <xsd:attribute name="name" type="xsd:string" use="required" />
      <xsd:attribute name="class" type="type" use="required" />
   </xsd:complexType>
</xsd:element>
```

The element has two attributes that are both `required`. The instance variable you want to define needs a `name`, so that you can reference it later in your JSP files. Spring Web Flow also needs to know the type of the variable, so you have to define the `class` attribute with the class of your variable.

input

You can use the input element to pass information into a flow. When you call a flow, you can (or will have to, depending on whether the input element is required or not) pass objects into the flow. You can then use these objects to process your flow. The XML Schema definition of this element looks like this:

```
<xsd:complexType name="input">
   <xsd:attribute name="name" type="expression" use="required" />
   <xsd:attribute name="value" type="expression" />
   <xsd:attribute name="type" type="type" />
   <xsd:attribute name="required" type="xsd:boolean" />
</xsd:complexType>
```

The input element possesses certain attributes, of which only the name attribute is required. You have to specify a name for the input argument, which you can use to reference the variable in your flow. The value attribute is used to specify the value of the attribute, for example, if you want to define a default value for the variable. You can also define a type (for example int or long) for the variable if you want a specific type of information. A type conversion will be tried if the argument passed to the flow does not match the type you expect. With the required attribute, you can control if the user of your flow has to pass in a variable, or if the input attribute is optional.

output

While you can define input parameters with the input element, you can specify return values with the output element. These are variables that will be passed to your end-state as the result value of your flow. Here's the XML Schema definition of the output element:

```
<xsd:complexType name="output">
   <xsd:attribute name="name" type="expression" use="required" />
   <xsd:attribute name="value" type="expression" />
   <xsd:attribute name="type" type="type" />
   <xsd:attribute name="required" type="xsd:boolean" />
   </xsd:attribute>
</xsd:complexType>
```

The definition is quite similar to the input element. You can also see that the name of the output element is required. Otherwise, you have no means of referencing the variable from your end-state. The value attribute is the value of your variable, for example, the result of a computation or a user returned from a database. Of course, you can also specify the type you expect your output variable to be. As with the input element, a type conversion will be attempted if the type of the variable does not match the type specified here. The required attribute will check if nothing was specified, or the result of a computation is null. If it is null, an error will be thrown.

actionTypes

Per se, this is not an element which you can use in your flow definition, but it is a very important part of the XML Schema definition, referenced by many other elements. The definition is quite complex and looks like this:

```
<xsd:group name="actionTypes">
   <xsd:choice>
      <xsd:element name="evaluate">
         <xsd:complexType>
            <xsd:sequence>
               <xsd:element name="attribute"
                            type="attribute"
                            minOccurs="0"
                            maxOccurs="unbounded" />
            </xsd:sequence>
            <xsd:attribute name="expression"
type="expression" use="required" />
            <xsd:attribute name="result"
                           type="expression"
                           use="optional" />
            <xsd:attribute name="result-type"
                           type="type"
                           use="optional" />
         </xsd:complexType>
      </xsd:element>
      <xsd:element name="render">
         <xsd:complexType>
            <xsd:sequence>
               <xsd:element name="attribute"
                            type="attribute"
                            minOccurs="0"
                            maxOccurs="unbounded" />
            </xsd:sequence>
            <xsd:attribute name="fragments"
                           type="xsd:string"
                           use="required" />
         </xsd:complexType>
      </xsd:element>
      <xsd:element name="set">
         <xsd:complexType>
            <xsd:sequence>
               <xsd:element name="attribute"
                            type="attribute"
                            minOccurs="0"
                            maxOccurs="unbounded" />
```

```
                <//xsd:sequence>
                <xsd:attribute name="name"
                               type="expression"
                               use="required" />
                <xsd:attribute name="value"
                               type="expression"
                               use="required" />
                <xsd:attribute name="type" type="type" />
            </xsd:complexType>
        </xsd:element>
    </xsd:choice>
</xsd:group>
```

actionTypes is a group of sub-elements, namely evaluate, render, and set. Let's go through the single elements to understand how the whole definition works.

evaluate

With the evaluate element, you can execute code based on the expression languages explained in Chapter 3. Please see the explanations there to learn how the expression attribute of the evaluate element works. As described by the previous source code, the element has three attributes; one of them is required. The expression attribute is required and executes the code that you want to run. The result value of the expression, if present, can be stored in the result attribute. Using the result-type attribute, you can convert the result value in the specified type, if needed. Additionally, you can define attributes using a sub-element of the attribute element.

render

Use the render element to partially render content of a web site. Using the required fragments attribute, you can define which fragments should be rendered. Please see the information concerning Spring JavaScript and Apache Tiles integration earlier in this chapter to learn how to partially render web sites. As is the case with the evaluate element, you can also specify additional attributes using the attribute sub-element.

set

The set element can be used to set attributes in one of the Spring Web Flows scopes. With the name attribute you can define where (in which scope) you want to define the attribute, and how it should be called. The following short source code illustrates how the set element works:

```
<set name="flowScope.myVariable" value="myValue" type="long" />
```

As you can see, the `name` consists of the name of the scope and the name of your variable, delimited by a dot (`.`). Both the `name` attribute and the `value` attribute are required. The `value` is the actual value of your variable. The `type` attribute is optional and describes the type of your variable. As before, you can also define additional attributes using the `attribute` sub-element.

on-start

You can think of the `on-start` state as a constructor or initialization method, actions which are executed as soon as the flow starts. The `on-start` element has no attributes, but sub-elements which define what to do when the flow starts. The XML Schema definition looks like this:

```
<xsd:element name="on-start" minOccurs="0">
   <xsd:complexType>
      <xsd:group ref="actionTypes" maxOccurs="unbounded" />
   </xsd:complexType>
</xsd:element>
```

As you can see, the `on-start` element references the `actionTypes` definition in the definition file. We recommend reading about the `actionTypes` definition we just saw.

on-end

In contrast with the `on-start` element, the `on-end` element is called as soon as the flow ends. Here's the XML Schema definition of the `on-end`-element:

```
<xsd:element name="on-end" minOccurs="0">
   <xsd:complexType>
      <xsd:group ref="actionTypes" maxOccurs="unbounded" />
   </xsd:complexType>
</xsd:element>
```

The definition is almost identical to the definition of the `on-start` element; it also references the `actionTypes` group described earlier. This means that the `on-start` and the `on-end` elements work similarly; but they are called at different times.

transition

The `transition` element is used to move from one state of your flow to another. Without transitions, you can't really call it a flow, because the word "flow" implies that there is some kind of movement. The `transition` element is used throughout the configuration file and is quite complex. It has several attributes and sub-elements. Here's the corresponding Schema definition:

```
<xsd:complexType name="transition">
   <xsd:sequence>
      <xsd:element name="attribute"
                   type="attribute"
                   minOccurs="0"
                   maxOccurs="unbounded" />
      <xsd:element name="secured" type="secured" minOccurs="0" />
      <xsd:group ref="actionTypes"
                 minOccurs="0"
                 maxOccurs="unbounded" />
   </xsd:sequence>
   <xsd:attribute name="on" type="transitionCriteria" />
   <xsd:attribute name="on-exception" type="xsd:string" />
   <xsd:attribute name="to"
                  type="targetStateResolver"
                  use="optional" />
</xsd:complexType>
```

As the code shows, the `transition` element can have several sub-elements, namely `attribute`, `secured`, and all the items defined by the `actionTypes` group including `evaluate`, `render`, and `set` (all of which have already been explained). The attributes of this element are much more interesting. The first one, `on`, defines when the transition should occur. For example, in the following source code:

```
<view-state id="firstPage">
   <transition on="next" to="secondPage" />
</view-state>
```

The transition to the `secondPage` state will occur, when the `next` event has been triggered. This usually happens when the user clicks on a button with the correct event ID:

```
<input type="submit" name="_eventId_next" value="Next" />
```

The `on-exception` attribute can be used to specify to which state the flow should transition if a certain exception (or one of the exceptions' super classes) is thrown in the application.

> The name of the exception class must be fully qualified (for example: `java.lang.Exception`).

Also, it cannot be used together with the `secured` element. It is recommended to use a `transition` tag with either the `on` attribute or the `on-exception` attribute, but not both together in one tag.

Finally, the `to` attribute defines which state the flow should transit to when either the `on` attribute or the `on-exception` attribute matches.

global-transitions

You can use the `global-transitions` element to define transitions that are shared between all your states. Thus, you can define global transitions such as `onError` or `onSuccess`, for example, transitions which redirect to an `end-state` that shows error or success messages. Let's take a look at the XML Schema Definition of the `global-transitions` element:

```
<xsd:element name="global-transitions" minOccurs="0">
   <xsd:complexType>
      <xsd:sequence>
         <xsd:element name="transition"
                      type="viewTransition"
                      maxOccurs="unbounded" />
      </xsd:sequence>
   </xsd:complexType>
</xsd:element>
```

The element only allows sub-elements of the type, `transition`, which we have explained earlier in this chapter.

exception-handler

This element helps you define custom exception handlers, either global handler for the whole flow or for a single state. The definition of the element looks like this:

```
<xsd:complexType name="exception-handler">
   <xsd:attribute name="bean" type="beanName" use="required" />
</xsd:complexType>
```

As you can see, the Schema definition of the `exception-handler` element is very simple. It only has one required attribute called `bean`. This attribute is a reference to a bean in your Spring application context file, where you have defined your custom exception handler. This handler has to be a class implementing the `FlowExecutionExceptionHandler` interface. Here's an example implementation of the interface:

```
public class CustomExceptionHandler implements
   FlowExecutionExceptionHandler {

   @Override
   public boolean canHandle(FlowExecutionException ex) {
      return ex.getCause().getClass().isAssignableFrom(
                                  IllegalStateException.class);
   }

   @Override
   public void handle(FlowExecutionException ex,
      RequestControlContext ctx) {

      TargetStateResolver resolver = new
         DefaultTargetStateResolver("onError");
      Transition targetTransition = new Transition(resolver);
      ctx.execute(targetTransition);
   };
}
```

This simple implementation checks if the exception that was thrown is assignable from the `IllegalStateException` class. If that is the case, the `handle()` method is called next. We ask a `DefaultTargetStateResolver` to prepare a transition to the `onError` state, which of course has to exist in your flow definition. Next, we create a new `Transition` using the `resolver` we just created. Finally, we execute the operation. The transition will complete and the page defined in the `onError` state will be shown.

bean-import

Use the `bean-import` element to import any beans defined in a Spring context configuration into your flow. All the beans that are imported are accessible from any expression you choose to use in your flow. This element is defined like this:

```
<xsd:element name="bean-import" minOccurs="0" maxOccurs="unbounded">
   <xsd:complexType>
      <xsd:attribute name="resource"
                     type="resource"
                     use="required" />
   </xsd:complexType>
</xsd:element>
```

The element has one required attribute that is called `resource`. This attribute describes the file where your bean definitions are specified.

action-state

An `action-state` is used to execute code within your flow. You can, for example, save an object to a database using an `action-state` like this:

```
<action-state id="updateUser">
      <evaluate expression="flowScope.resultUser.setLastLogin(
                                        new java.util.Date())" />
      <evaluate expression="persistenceContext.merge(
                                           flowScope.resultUser)" />
      <transition to="welcomeView" />
</action-state>
```

This example is from Chapter 2, where we developed a small login form web application. The XML Schema definition of the `action-state` element looks like this:

```
<xsd:element name="action-state">
   <xsd:complexType>
      <xsd:sequence minOccurs="0">
         <xsd:element name="attribute"
                      type="attribute"
                      minOccurs="0"
                      maxOccurs="unbounded" />
         <xsd:element name="secured" type="secured" minOccurs="0" />
         <xsd:element name="on-entry" minOccurs="0">
            <xsd:complexType>
               <xsd:group ref="actionTypes" maxOccurs="unbounded" />
            </xsd:complexType>
         </xsd:element>
         <xsd:group ref="actionTypes"
                    minOccurs="0"
                    maxOccurs="unbounded" />
         <xsd:element name="transition"
                      type="transition"
                      minOccurs="0"
                      maxOccurs="unbounded" />
         <xsd:element name="on-exit"
                      minOccurs="0">
            <xsd:complexType>
               <xsd:group ref="actionTypes" maxOccurs="unbounded" />
            </xsd:complexType>
         </xsd:element>
```

```
            <xsd:element name="exception-handler"
                         type="exception-handler"
                         minOccurs="0"
                         maxOccurs="unbounded" />
         </xsd:sequence>
         <xsd:attribute name="id" type="xsd:ID" use="required" />
         <xsd:attribute name="parent" type="stateParent" />
      </xsd:complexType>
   </xsd:element>
```

view-state

The `view-state` element is very complex. Therefore, the definition in the XML Schema file is also quite long. As it is one of the most important and heavily used elements in Spring Web Flow, we quote the definition here. Because it is so long, we will split the definition into pieces and explain it step-by-step.

```
   <xsd:element name="view-state">
      <xsd:complexType>
         <xsd:sequence>
            <xsd:element name="attribute"
                         type="attribute"
                         minOccurs="0"
                         maxOccurs="unbounded" />
            <xsd:element name="secured" type="secured" minOccurs="0" />
            <xsd:element name="var"
                         minOccurs="0"
                         maxOccurs="unbounded">
               <xsd:complexType>
                  <xsd:attribute name="name"
                                 type="xsd:string"
                                 use="required" />
                  <xsd:attribute name="class"
                                 type="type"
                                 use="required" />
               </xsd:complexType>
            </xsd:element>
```

This should not be completely new to you. The `view-state` element has several sub-elements. Three of them are: the `attribute` , the `secured`, and the `var` elements, which we have already explained earlier in this chapter. You can secure not only the entire flow, but also single states, using a `secured` tag in your state. The same is also true for attributes and variables. They are **local** in this state. As such, they are created as soon as the flow enters the state and destroyed as soon as the state ends.

```
            <xsd:element name="binder"
                         minOccurs="0"
                         maxOccurs="unbounded">
```

```
   <xsd:complexType>
      <xsd:sequence>
         <xsd:element name="binding"
                      minOccurs="1"
                      maxOccurs="unbounded">
            <xsd:complexType>
               <xsd:attribute name="property"
                              type="xsd:string"
                              use="required" />
               <xsd:attribute name="converter"
                              type="xsd:string" />
               <xsd:attribute name="required"
                              type="xsd:boolean" />
            </xsd:complexType>
         </xsd:element>
      </xsd:sequence>
   </xsd:complexType>
</xsd:element>
```

The `binder` element is a new element which we haven't described yet. Using the `binder` element, you can configure how and what properties from your model are bound to the UI of your view. The `binder` element itself has one sub-element called `binding`. The `binding` element has three properties: `property`, `converter`, and `required`. The `property` attribute is required. This attribute is used to specify which property of the model you want to bind the values of your UI to. Using the `converter` attribute, you can define how the model property should appear in the UI. Custom converters can be registered using an implementation of the `ConversionInterface`. Spring Web Flow already includes a default implementation called `GenericConversionService`. This class includes an `addConverter()` method that takes an ID for the converter and an object of type `Converter`:

As you can see, the `Converter` interface is not very difficult to implement and performs a conversion between two objects.

Last, but not the least, the `required` attribute tells Spring Web Flow to check if the object bound to the property is empty or null. If the attribute is set to `true` and the value is empty or null, an error will occur.

```
            <xsd:element name="on-entry" minOccurs="0">
               <xsd:complexType>
                  <xsd:group ref="actionTypes" maxOccurs="unbounded" />
               </xsd:complexType>
            </xsd:element>
            <xsd:element name="on-render" minOccurs="0">
               <xsd:complexType>
                  <xsd:group ref="actionTypes" maxOccurs="unbounded" />
               </xsd:complexType>
            </xsd:element>
            <xsd:element name="transition"
                         type="viewTransition"
                         minOccurs="0"
                         maxOccurs="unbounded" />
            <xsd:element name="on-exit" minOccurs="0">
               <xsd:complexType>
                  <xsd:group ref="actionTypes" maxOccurs="unbounded" />
               </xsd:complexType>
            </xsd:element>
```

All the sub-elements have additional sub-elements of the `actionTypes` group including `evaluate`, `render` and `set`, explained earlier in this chapter. You can use the `on-entry` element to execute actions as soon as the flow enters this state. The `on-render` element is called shortly before the view is finally rendered. We have already explained the `transition` element, which lets the flow continue to the next state. Before the state is left and the flow continues, the `on-exit`-element, if present, is called:

```
            <xsd:element name="exception-handler"
                         type="exception-handler"
                         minOccurs="0"
                         maxOccurs="unbounded" />
         </xsd:sequence>
```

This element helps you define custom exception handlers, specific to this state.

```
         <xsd:attribute name="id" type="xsd:ID" use="required" />
         <xsd:attribute name="parent" type="stateParent" />
         <xsd:attribute name="view" type="viewFactory" />
         <xsd:attribute name="redirect" type="xsd:boolean" />
         <xsd:attribute name="popup" type="xsd:boolean" />
         <xsd:attribute name="model" type="expression" />
      </xsd:complexType>
   </xsd:element>
```

The remaining attributes are very straightforward, and are explained in the following table:

Attribute name	Description
`id`	The ID of this state; each state needs a unique name that enables referencing, for example, referencing this state in transition elements
`parent`	Use this attribute to define a parent state for your `view-state`
`view`	This is the name of the view (or the file) that Spring Web Flow is supposed to render, for example, `welcomePage.jsp`; the `view` can also be an evaluated expression
`redirect`	It will trigger a redirect before the `view-state` is rendered
`model`	The `model` object to be used in this view; it can be used together with form-binding to display values from the object, and to change the values of the `model` object
`popup`	Opens a new pop up dialog and displays the view in this dialog

decision-state

The `decision` state can be used as a simple if-else construct in your flow definition if you have to make evaluation dependent decisions in your flow.

```
<xsd:element name="decision-state">
   <xsd:complexType>
      <xsd:sequence>
         <xsd:element name="attribute"
                      type="attribute"
                      minOccurs="0"
                      maxOccurs="unbounded" />
         <xsd:element name="secured" type="secured" minOccurs="0" />
         <xsd:element name="on-entry" minOccurs="0">
            <xsd:complexType>
               <xsd:group ref="actionTypes" maxOccurs="unbounded" />
            </xsd:complexType>
         </xsd:element>
```

These are the same elements that were used in the `view-state` element. Read the paragraph concerning the `view-state` for details about these tags.

```
         <xsd:element name="if" minOccurs="0" maxOccurs="unbounded">
            <xsd:complexType>
               <xsd:attribute name="test"
                              type="expression"
                              use="required" />
               <xsd:attribute name="then"
```

```
                              type="targetStateResolver"
                              use="required">
                <xsd:attribute name="else"
                              type="targetStateResolver">
            </xsd:complexType>
        </xsd:element>
```

This is the most important definition in the `decision-state`. It has a sub-element called `if` that has three attributes, of which two of them are required (`test` and `then`). The `test` attribute executes an expression that checks a certain condition. If the condition is evaluated to `true`, the `then` attribute will be executed. As it is of type, `targetStateResolver`, you can enter the name of any state here. The flow will transition to this state. You can specify an `else` attribute if the condition is evaluated to `false`; it will transition the flow to a different state.

```
        <xsd:element name="on-exit" minOccurs="0">
            <xsd:complexType>
                <xsd:group ref="actionTypes" maxOccurs="unbounded" />
            </xsd:complexType>
        </xsd:element>
        <xsd:element name="exception-handler"
                     type="exception-handler"
                     minOccurs="0"
                     maxOccurs="unbounded" />
    </xsd:sequence>
    <xsd:attribute name="id" type="xsd:ID" use="required" />
    <xsd:attribute name="parent" type="stateParent" />
  </xsd:complexType>
</xsd:element>
```

These elements are identical to the ones found in the `view-state`.

subflow-state

The `subflow-state` is used to create a reference to another flow, which is then executed as a subflow. For more detailed information, please see *Subflows* section in this chapter. The XML Schema definition is again quite similar to the one of the states we have seen earlier:

```
<xsd:element name="subflow-state">
    <xsd:complexType>
        <xsd:sequence minOccurs="0" >
            <xsd:element name="attribute"
                         type="attribute"
                         minOccurs="0"
                         maxOccurs="unbounded" />
```

```
            <xsd:element name="secured" type="secured" minOccurs="0" />
            <xsd:element name="on-entry" minOccurs="0">
               <xsd:complexType>
                  <xsd:group ref="actionTypes" maxOccurs="unbounded" />
               </xsd:complexType>
```

These are the same elements used in the `view-state` element. Refer to the paragraph concerning the `view-state` for details about these tags.

```
            <xsd:element name="input"
                         type="input"
                         minOccurs="0"
                         maxOccurs="unbounded" />
            <xsd:element name="output"
                         type="output"
                         minOccurs="0"
                         maxOccurs="unbounded" />
```

These elements of the `subflow-state` are used to create `input` and `output` variables. Every `input` variable you define will be accessible from the subflow. When the subflow returns, it can return multiple results. These subflow results can be saved in the variables specified by the `output` elements, and are accessible in the remaining flow.

```
            <xsd:element name="transition"
                         type="transition"
                         minOccurs="0"
                         maxOccurs="unbounded" />
            <xsd:element name="on-exit" minOccurs="0">
               <xsd:complexType>
                  <xsd:group ref="actionTypes" maxOccurs="unbounded" />
               </xsd:complexType>
            </xsd:element>
            <xsd:element name="exception-handler"
                         type="exception-handler"
                         minOccurs="0"
                         maxOccurs="unbounded" />
         </xsd:sequence>
         <xsd:attribute name="id" type="xsd:ID" use="required" />
         <xsd:attribute name="parent" type="stateParent" />
```

These elements are identical to the ones found in the `view-state`.

```
         <xsd:attribute name="subflow" type="flowId" />
         <xsd:attribute name="subflow-attribute-mapper"
                        type="beanName" />
      </xsd:complexType>
   </xsd:element>
```

Finally, you can specify which flow should be executed as subflow by using the `subflow` attribute. It is of type `flowId`, which can be any flow you have in your application. Instead of `input` and `output` elements, you can also use a so-called `SubflowAttributeMapper` to give attributes to the subflow and receive return values from the subflow. `SubflowAttributeMapper` is an interface which looks like this:

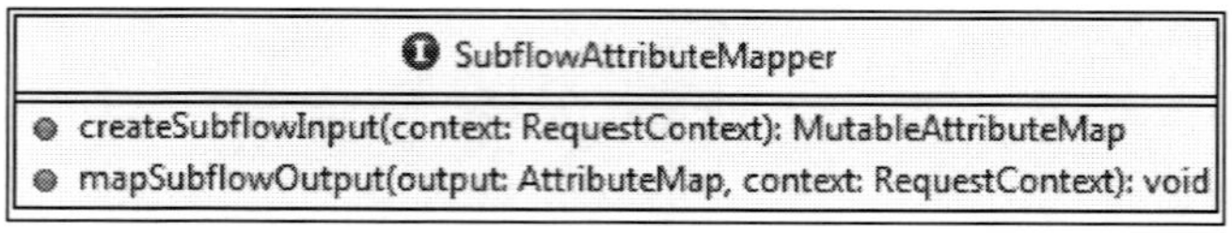

In the `createSubflowInput()` method, you can get the data you want to pass into the subflow from the `RequestContext` argument. From this data, you have to create a map which you can return afterwards. The method returns an object of type, `MutableAttributeMap`, which is another interface that you have to implement. You can also use the default implementation `LocalAttributeMap`, which is included in Spring Web Flow.

The `mapSubflowOutput()` method works in the opposite direction. You get the return values from the subflow in the first parameter from the method and can save them in the `RequestContext`.

end-state

Every flow definition can have one or more `end-states`. An `end-state` defines a possible ending point of your flow.

```
<xsd:element name="end-state">
   <xsd:complexType>
      <xsd:sequence>
         <xsd:element name="attribute"
                      type="attribute"
                      minOccurs="0"
                      maxOccurs="unbounded" />
         <xsd:element name="secured" type="secured" minOccurs="0" />
         <xsd:element name="on-entry" minOccurs="0">
            <xsd:complexType>
               <xsd:group ref="actionTypes" maxOccurs="unbounded" />
            </xsd:complexType>
         </xsd:element>
         <xsd:element name="output"
                      type="output"
                      minOccurs="0"
                      maxOccurs="unbounded" />
         <xsd:element name="exception-handler"
```

```
                        type="exception-handler"
                        minOccurs="0"
                        maxOccurs="unbounded" />
        </xsd:sequence>
        <xsd:attribute name="id" type="xsd:ID" use="required" />
        <xsd:attribute name="parent" type="stateParent" />
        <xsd:attribute name="view" type="viewFactory" />
        <xsd:attribute name="commit" type="xsd:string" />
    </xsd:complexType>
</xsd:element>
```

Most of the `end-state` elements have already been explained. Only one attribute is new—the `commit` attribute of the `end-state` element. If you are using a `persistence-context` in your flow, and the `commit` attribute is set to `true`, all changes made to entities will be flushed to the database. If the attribute is set to `false`, no flush to the database will happen.

Summary

In this chapter, we first explained to you in detail what subflows are, and how to use them efficiently in Spring Web Flow. We created a simple example application and re-used the login form from Chapter 2. We showed you that using subflows in Spring Web Flow is both easy and advantageous for the re-usability of flow definition.

Afterwards, we showed you the new JavaScript abstraction framework shipped along with Spring Web Flow, called Spring JavaScript or Spring JS. Again, we developed a small example which showed client-side validation of your web forms. We also explained what Apache Tiles 2 is, and how to use it as template engine in your applications, including using the AJAX features of Spring JavaScript and Tiles to partially render web pages.

Finally, we delved into the depth of the flow configuration file by explaining all the important elements of the Spring Web Flow XML Schema.

In the next chapter, we will show you how to test your flows using unit tests and mocking technologies.

6
Testing Spring Web Flow Applications

Testing is an important aspect in every software development process. Applications written with Spring Web Flow are no exception. Luckily, the authors of Spring Web Flow thought the same way and included comprehensive support for unit testing.

How to test a Spring Web Flow application

Testing your flows requires the JUnit library, version 3.8.x or higher. In the current version of Spring Web Flow (2.0.5), there is no support for testing your flows with TestNG instead of JUnit (see `http://forum.springframework.org/showthread.php?t=54914`).

You can download JUnit at `www.junit.org` or use the Maven build tool to download the library automatically. Just add the following tags to your `pom.xml`:

```
<dependency>
<groupId>junit</groupId>
<artifactId>junit</artifactId>
<version>3.8.2</version>
</dependency>
```

The first example

Do you remember the login page example from Chapter 2? We will use the same example to implement our unit tests. Here is the flow definition file again, in case you forgot what it looks like:

```
<?xml version="1.0" encoding="UTF-8"?>
<flow xmlns="http://www.springframework.org/schema/webflow"
      xmlns:xsi="http://www.w3.org/2001/XMLSchema-instance"
```

```
      xsi:schemaLocation=
   "http://www.springframework.org/schema/webflow
        http://www.springframework.org/schema/webflow/
   spring-webflow-2.0.xsd">
      <persistence-context />
      <var name="user" class="com.webflow2book.User"/>
   <view-state id="loginPage" model="user" view="loginPage.jspx">
               <transition on="login" to="getUser" />
      </view-state>
      <action-state id="getUser">
         <evaluate
            expression="userservice.getUserByUsername(user.username)"
            result="flowScope.resultUser" />
         <transition to="checkCredentials" />
      </action-state>
      <decision-state id="checkCredentials">
         <if test="flowScope.resultUser == null" then="failedView" />
         <if test="flowScope.resultUser.password.equals(user.password)"
            then="updateUser" else="failedView" />
      </decision-state>
      <action-state id="updateUser">
         <evaluate expression="flowScope.resultUser.setLastLogin(
   new java.util.Date())" />
         <transition to="welcomeView" />
      </action-state>
      <end-state id="welcomeView" view="welcomeView.jspx"
    commit="true" />
      <end-state id="failedView" view="failedView.jspx" />
   </flow>
```

A look into the source code

The `AbstractXmlFlowExecutionTests` abstract class includes everything to test your flows. You can see the relationship between the classes in the `org.springframework.webflow.test.execution` package in the following diagram:

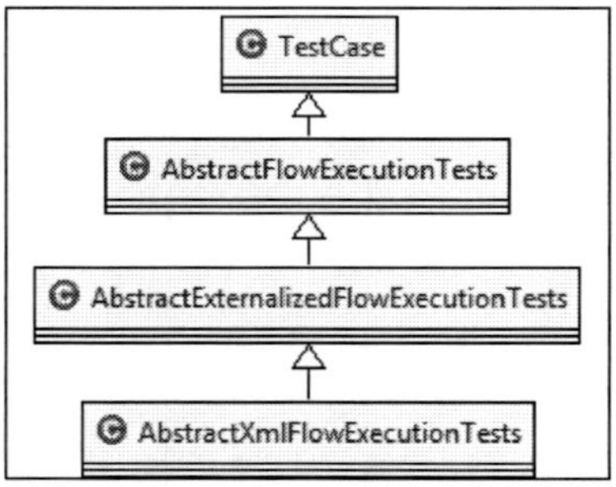

As you can see, the class ultimately inherits from JUnit's `TestCase` class. So all you need to do is write your own test class that extends `AbstractXmlFlowExecutionTests` and write your tests. The `AbstractFlowExecutionTests` base class provides us with the necessary methods to test flow executions, transitions, and subflows, and also includes methods like `startFlow()`, `resumeFlow()`, and `setCurrentState()`. These methods are necessary to test our flows with unit tests.

When writing unit tests for Spring Web Flow, we have to implement at least the `getResource()` method of the `AbstractExternalizedFlowExecutionTests` abstract class. This method is used to find the flow definition file that specifies the flow we want to test:

```
@Override
protected FlowDefinitionResource getResource(
          FlowDefinitionResourceFactory resourceFactory) {
       return resourceFactory.createFileResource
("src/main/webapp/WEB-INF/flows/loginform.xml");
}
```

As shown in the source code above, you can use the `FlowDefinitionResourceFactory` object handed into the method by Spring Web Flow to specify the path to your flow definition file. The `getResource()` method is called from the `AbstractExternalizedFlowExecutionTests` class to set up the flow you want to test.

First steps in testing

We would like to test if the login works correctly, to make sure no user without the correct credentials can log in to our web application. More specifically, this means that we have to test the `UserService` class that we had written in Chapter 2.

To be able to test the `UserService` class, we would normally provide an entry in the Spring configuration file. As we do not have such a file in our test environment, because we want to make unit tests as isolated as possible, we have to override the `configureFlowBuilderContext()` method instead. This method gives us a `MockFlowBuilderContext` object, which we can use to register all dependencies needed in our flow:

```
@Override
protected void configureFlowBuilderContext(
          MockFlowBuilderContext builderContext) {
   builderContext.registerBean("userservice", new UserServiceImpl());
builderContext.registerBean("persistenceExceptionHandler",
   this.persistenceExceptionHandler);
}
```

We also added a custom exception handler, which we implemented like this:

```
public class PersistenceExceptionHandler implements
      FlowExecutionExceptionHandler {

   @Override
   public boolean canHandle(FlowExecutionException ex) {
      // Check if error happened while evaluating an expression
      return ex.getCause().getClass()
.isAssignableFrom(EvaluationException.class);
  }

   @Override
   public void handle(FlowExecutionException ex,
      RequestControlContext ctx) {

      TargetStateResolver resolver = new
         DefaultTargetStateResolver("failedView");
      Transition targetTransition = new Transition(resolver);
      ctx.execute(targetTransition);
   };
}
```

If an `EvaluationException` is thrown while executing `action-states`, we automatically make a transition to `failedView` `view-state` with this exception handler.

We can now proceed to write our actual test cases. First of all, we want to test if the initialization of our flow works:

```
   public void testStartLoginFlow() {
      MockExternalContext context = new MockExternalContext();

      startFlow(context);

      assertFlowExecutionActive();
      assertCurrentStateEquals("loginPage");
   }
```

Let's go through this test case step-by-step:

1. First, we create a `MockExternalContext` object, which is a mock implementation of the `ExternalContext` interface defined in Spring Web Flow. An external context is a pointer to the environment calling your flow and is required for flow execution. For instance, if your flow is called from a servlet, `ServletExternalContext` is used.
2. We then start flow execution by giving the `context` object to the `startFlow()` method.

3. As usual in JUnit test cases, we use `assert*()` methods to check if we got the results we expected. We are using custom `assert*()` methods that ship with the Spring Web Flow distribution. In this case, we check if the flow execution is active and if the flow continues to `loginPage` state.

Next, we test the possible outcomes of the login process:

```
public void testValidLogin() {
   this.setCurrentState("loginPage");

   User user = this.createValidUser();

   this.getFlowScope().put("user", user);

   MockExternalContext context = new MockExternalContext();
   context.setEventId("login");
   this.resumeFlow(context);

   assertFlowExecutionOutcomeEquals("welcomeView");
   assertFlowExecutionEnded();
}
public void testInvalidLogin() {
   this.setCurrentState("loginPage");
   User user = this.createInvalidUser();

   this.getFlowScope().put("user", user);

   MockExternalContext context = new MockExternalContext();
   context.setEventId("login");
   this.resumeFlow(context);

   assertFlowExecutionOutcomeEquals("failedView");
   assertFlowExecutionEnded();
}
```

Again, let's take a look at the test cases step-by-step:

1. We are using the convenience `setCurrentState()` method to set the state we want the flow to be in. As we want to test the login process, we set the current state to `loginPage`.
2. Next, we create an appropriate `User` object.
3. Afer that, we use the `getFlowScope()` method to return a reference to a `MutableAttributeMap`, representing the `flow` scope in our flow. We are adding the `User` object to the map and thus saving it in the `flow` scope.
4. We continue by creating a `MockExternalContext` object again and setting the event id to `login`. This simulates setting the `EventId` by clicking on the **login** button on our web site.
5. Finally, we resume flow execution using the just created external context.

These two test cases only differ in user creation and assertion checking. In the `testValidLogin` test case, the `createValidUser()` method is used, which creates a user with the correct credentials:

```
private User createValidUser() {
   User user = new User();
   user.setUsername("John");
   user.setPassword("myPass!");
   return user;
}
```

In the other test case, we use the `createInvalidUser()` method to create a user with wrong credentials. Just copy the above method, rename it to `createInvalidUser()`, and change the username and password to random words or names.

After we resumed the execution of the flow, we can check for the expected results. In case of the `testValidLogin` test case, we expect that the flow outcome is `welcomeView`, as defined in our flow configuration file:

```
<end-state id="welcomeView" view="welcomeView.jspx" />
```

For this, we are using the `assertFlowExecutionOutcomeEquals` method. We also expect the flow to be finished, as we arrived at an end state (`assertFlowExecutionEnded`). The `testInvalidLogin` test case is very similar; we are just expecting a different outcome, namely `failedView`.

Testing Persistent Contexts

If you try the tests above yourself, you will notice that they do not work yet. The above defined exception handler will be called and the test will fail, as the flow transitioned to `failedView` instead of `welcomeView`:

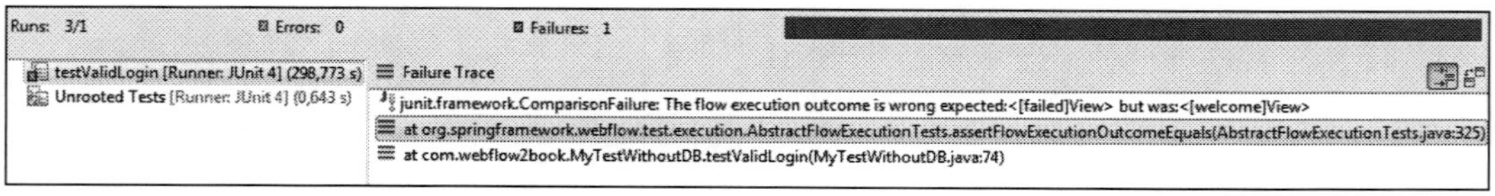

Please note that this test actually hits a bug in the current release of Spring Web Flow 2 (2.0.5). The arguments in `assertFlowExecutionOutcomeEquals` are reversed, as can be seen in the following source code from the current release:

```
    protected void assertFlowExecutionOutcomeEquals(String outcome) {
 assertNotNull("There has been no flow execution outcome",
 flowExecutionOutcome);
      assertEquals("The flow execution outcome is wrong",
         flowExecutionOutcome.getId(), outcome);
    }
```

In the `assertEquals()` method, the outcome of the test is the second parameter, not the third, as it is in the above case. The actual outcome should be in the third place. This also explains why the output of the above test is wrong:

```
junit.framework.ComparisonFailure: The flow execution outcome is wrong
   expected:<[failed]View> but was:<[welcome]View>
```

The correct output should be `welcomeView`, but `failedView` is the outcome.

The reason for this is that we used *Persistent Contexts* to develop our example in Chapter 2. In our test case, we created a new `UserService` object without any reference to a persistence context. As such, the `EntityManager` called in the service is null. Of course, we do not want our test cases to access our database, so we need to write so-called *mock* objects. Mock objects deliver a fake implementation of an interface. This way the test case can access every method of the interface, but you can define what happens when the methods are called.

If you have plenty of objects, writing mock objects can be a very long and daunting task. Luckily, there are tools that help the developer write mock objects for themselves. In this book, we will be using EasyMock (see `http://www.easymock.org/`) for this task.

A short introduction to EasyMock

EasyMock is an open-source project under the MIT license (see also `http://www.easymock.org/License.html`), developed by Tammo Freese et al. EasyMock uses Java's proxy pattern features to automatically create implementations of our interfaces. Using only a few static methods, we can test if our methods were called at all, return the correct objects, or throw exceptions. Test cases with EasyMock usually follow the pattern outlined in the schema below:

1. We call the methods we expect to be called by the class we want to test (in our case, the `UserService` object) on our mock objects (the mock implementation of the `EntityManager` interface). Optionally, EasyMock can check if they are called in the order we expect them to be called.
2. Call the static `replay` method on the mocked object. Until the call to `replay`, EasyMock records all method calls to our object. After the call to `replay`, the object begins acting as a mock object. This means that we can now use the class tested and EasyMock checks if the expectations we recorded earlier are met, for example, that we use the correct arguments for our methods.
3. When all our tests are done, we call the static `verify` method. This method checks if we recorded expected method calls which are not actually used by the class we want to test.

Now that you know the basic theory, we can implement additional tests in our test cases. If you want to learn more about EasyMock, please refer to the excellent documentation on the project's web site. Please note that EasyMock works only with Java versions 5.0 and higher.

We start by defining two members in our test class and overriding the `setUp()` method from the `TestCase` class:

```
import static org.easymock.EasyMock.expect;
import static org.easymock.EasyMock.replay;
import static org.easymock.EasyMock.verify;
import static org.easymock.EasyMock.createStrictMock;
public class MyTest extends AbstractXmlFlowExecutionTests {
   private UserService userService;
   private EntityManager entityManager;
   private PersistenceExceptionHandler persistenceExceptionHandler;
   /**
    * @see junit.framework.TestCase#setUp()
    */
   @Override
   protected void setUp() throws Exception {
      this.entityManager = createStrictMock(EntityManager.class);
      this.userService = new UserServiceImpl();
      this.userService.setEntityManager(this.entityManager);
      this.persistenceExceptionHandler =
 new PersistenceExceptionHandler();
     }
```

We initialize our mock object by calling the static `createStrictMock()` method. As we want to create a mock object of the `EntityManager` interface, we hand in the `Class` object, which corresponds to the `EntityManager` interface, to the method. The `createStrictMock()` method performs additional checks, such as to check the order in which the methods are called. If you do not want EasyMock to do this, just import and use the `createMock()` method instead.

Afterwards, we create a new instance of the `UserService` class and set the reference to the `EntityManager` to the mock object we just created. We also created an instance of our own exception handler again. Next, we have to make some adjustments to the `configureFlowBuilderContext()` method we created earlier in this chapter:

```
@Override
protected void configureFlowBuilderContext(
      MockFlowBuilderContext builderContext) {
   builderContext.registerBean("userservice", this.userService);
   builderContext.registerBean("persistenceExceptionHandler",
      this.persistenceExceptionHandler);
}
```

Instead of creating a new `UserService` instance, we use the one we created in the `setUp()` method.

Finally, we can change our test cases to actually test if everything works as expected:

```
public void testValidLogin() {
   // Create user
   User user = this.createValidUser();
   // EasyMock
   Query query = createMock(Query.class);
   expect(this.entityManager.createQuery("select user from " +
      " com.webflow2book.User user where user.username " +
      " like :username")).andReturn(query);
   expect(query.setParameter("username",
      user.getUsername())).andReturn(query);
   expect(query.getSingleResult()).andReturn(user);
   replay(this.entityManager, query);
   // Standard Web Flow tests
   this.setCurrentState("loginPage");
   this.getFlowScope().put("user", user);
   MockExternalContext context = new MockExternalContext();
   context.setEventId("login");
   this.resumeFlow(context);
   assertFlowExecutionOutcomeEquals("welcomeView");
   assertFlowExecutionEnded();
   verify(this.entityManager, query);
}
```

As explained in the schema above, we first call the methods we expect to be called by the `UserService` class (the class we want to test). We use the `expect()` method to tell EasyMock that we expect a call to the `createQuery()` method of the `EntityManager` with the specified arguments. Additionally, we expect to get a concrete instance of the `Query` interface from the `EntityManager` with the query we just created. We also expect that a parameter is set using the `setParameter()` method of `Query`. Finally, we expect to get a `User` object with the username as `John` and password as `myPass!` in return. In this case, we can reuse the `User` object created by the `createValidUser()` method as this object has the username and password we expect.

The call to `replay()` "arms" the mock object. When the `resumeFlow()` method is called, the flow resumes to the `action-state` defined in our flow definition. The `action-state` calls the `getUserByUsername()` method on the `UserServiceImpl` class, which in turn calls our mocked methods of the `EntityManager` interface.

The final call to `verify()` checks if we expect methods to be called which are not actually called by the `UserServiceImpl` class.

The `testInvalidLogin()` method looks very similar, but we expect a `NoResultException` to be thrown by the call to `getSingleResult()`:

```
public void testInvalidLogin() {
    User user = this.createInvalidUser();

Query query = createMock(Query.class);

expect(this.entityManager.createQuery("select user from " +
    " com.webflow2book.User user where user.username " +
" like :username")).andReturn(query);
expect(query.setParameter("username", user.getUsername())).
andReturn(query);
    expect(query.getSingleResult()).andThrow(new NoResultException());
    replay(this.entityManager, query);
    ...
}
```

Testing subflows

When you are using subflows in your application, you will wonder if there is a way to test them as well. There is! Spring Web Flow includes support for testing your subflows.

In Chapter 5, we have shown you the following flow that calls a subflow:

```
<?xml version="1.0" encoding="UTF-8"?>
<flow xmlns="http://www.springframework.org/schema/webflow"
    xmlns:xsi="http://www.w3.org/2001/XMLSchema-instance"
    xsi:schemaLocation="http://www.springframework.org/schema/webflow
         http://www.springframework.org/schema/webflow/spring-webflow-
          2.0.xsd">

    <var name="user" class="com.webflow2book.User"/>

    <view-state id="testPage" view="testPage.jspx">
        <transition on="login" to="getUser" />
    </view-state>

    <subflow-state id="getUser" subflow="loginform">
        <input name="user" />
        <transition on="success" to="welcomeView" />
    </subflow-state>

    <end-state id="welcomeView" view="welcomeView.jspx" />
</flow>
```

As we explained in Chapter 5, the subflow which is called is exactly the same as that which we used and tested in Chapter 2. We only changed `end-state` from

```
<end-state id="welcomeView" view="welcomeView.jspx"
 commit="true" />
<end-state id="failedView" view="failedView.jspx" />
```

to

```
<end-state id="success" commit="true" />
<end-state id="failedView" view="failedView.jspx" />
```

To test this subflow, we first create a unit test:

```
public void testLoginSubflow() {
   this.setCurrentState("testPage");

   User user = this.createValidUser();
   this.getFlowScope().put("user", user);

   this.getFlowDefinitionRegistry().registerFlowDefinition(this.
       createMockLoginFlow(user));

   MockExternalContext context = new MockExternalContext();
   context.setEventId("login");
   this.resumeFlow(context);

   assertFlowExecutionEnded();
   assertFlowExecutionOutcomeEquals("welcomeView");
}
```

Let's go through this test step-by-step again:

1. We set the current state to the `testPage` state. As can be seen in the above flow definition, this is the first `view-state` in our flow.
2. We create a user we will pass into the subflow as `input` variable. Afterwards, we store the user in the `flow` scope.
3. We create the subflow using the `createMockLoginFlow()` method and register it in our flow definition registry. The `createMockLoginFlow()` method is described after that.
4. The remaining test is already familiar; we create `MockExternalContext`, trigger the `login` event which will make the flow transit to `getUser subflow-state`, and resume the flow.

The `createMockLoginFlow()` method is described in the following source code listing:

```
private Flow createMockLoginFlow(final User user) {
      Flow loginFlow = new Flow("loginform");
      loginFlow.setInputMapper(new Mapper() {
         @Override
         public MappingResults map(Object source, Object target) {
            assertEquals(user, ((AttributeMap)source).get("user"));
            return null;
         }
      });
      new EndState(loginFlow, "success");
      return loginFlow;
   }
```

First of all, we create a new flow. We pass the ID of the subflow into the constructor of the `Flow` class. Next, we create an input mapper for our subflow. For our unit test, we want to make sure the `User` object passed into our subflow is really the `User` we actually wanted to pass into the flow. We can check this using the `assertEquals()` method of JUnit. Now, we create the `end-state`, which is `view-state success`. This state ends the subflow and returns to the calling flow.

Now, we just have to check if the calling flow really ended and if we reached the state we expected:

```
assertFlowExecutionEnded();
assertFlowExecutionOutcomeEquals("welcomeView");
```

More testing with EasyMock

Because we think testing is such an important aspect in the software development lifecycle, we decided to show you another example, which you can try immediately because it consists of easy-to-follow step-by-step instructions. We will create unit tests for a shopping-cart application without actually writing the logic and using a test-driven development approach.

First, create a new project in your favourite IDE. We recommend using a Maven plugin in your IDE, because this will make dependency management much easier. Of course, you can use any dependency management tool, but for the remainder of this example we will assume a Maven-style directory layout. This will usually look as shown in the following screenshot:

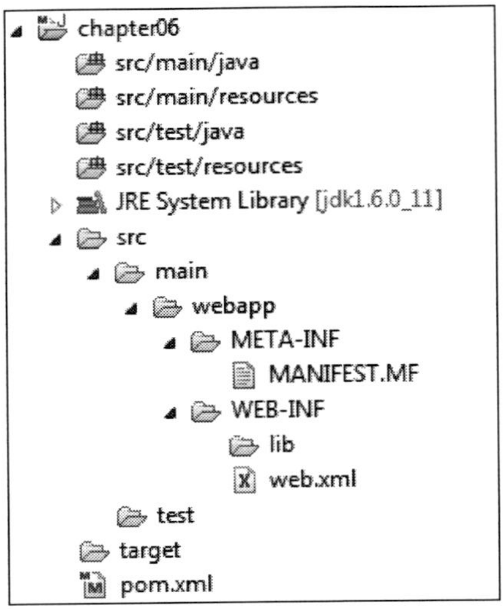

Open up `pom.xml` and add a few dependencies as shown below:

```
<project xmlns="http://maven.apache.org/POM/4.0.0" xmlns:xsi="http://
www.w3.org/2001/XMLSchema-instance" xsi:schemaLocation="http://maven.
apache.org/POM/4.0.0 http://maven.apache.org/maven-v4_0_0.xsd">
  <modelVersion>4.0.0</modelVersion>
  <groupId>com.webflow2book</groupId>
  <artifactId>chapter06</artifactId>
  <packaging>war</packaging>
  <name>EasyMock example</name>
  <version>0.0.1-SNAPSHOT</version>
  <description>Example project for unit testing with
   EasyMock</description>
  <dependencies>
    <dependency>
      <groupId>org.springframework.webflow</groupId>
      <artifactId>org.springframework.webflow</artifactId>
      <version>2.0.5.RELEASE</version>
    </dependency>
    <dependency>
      <groupId>ognl</groupId>
      <artifactId>ognl</artifactId>
      <version>2.7.3</version>
    </dependency>
    <dependency>
      <groupId>junit</groupId>
```

```
            <artifactId>junit</artifactId>
            <version>4.5</version>
            <scope>test</scope>
        </dependency>
        <dependency>
            <groupId>org.easymock</groupId>
            <artifactId>easymock</artifactId>
            <version>2.4</version>
        </dependency>
    </dependencies>
</project>
```

Now create a new folder `flows` in your `src/main/webapp/WEB-INF` directory and create a new file in it, which will be called `shoppingcart-flow.xml` and is displayed in the following source code listing:

```
<?xml version="1.0" encoding="UTF-8"?>
<flow xmlns="http://www.springframework.org/schema/webflow"
   xmlns:xsi="http://www.w3.org/2001/XMLSchema-instance"
   xsi:schemaLocation="http://www.springframework.org/schema/webflow
        http://www.springframework.org/schema/webflow/
spring-webflow-2.0.xsd">

   <var name="cart" class="com.webflow2book.ShoppingCart"/>

   <view-state id="homepage">
      <transition on="order" to="shoppingCartContents" />
   </view-state>

   <view-state id="shoppingCartContents">
      <transition on="next" to="payment" />
      <transition on="cancel" to="homepage" />
   </view-state>

   <view-state id="payment">
      <transition on="next" to="checkValidPayment" />
      <transition on="cancel" to="homepage" />
   </view-state>

   <action-state id="checkValidPayment">
      <evaluate expression=
          "paymentservice.checkPayment(flowScope.chosenPaymentOption)"
         result="flowScope.paymentValid"
          result-type="boolean" />
      <transition to="isValidPayment" />
   </action-state>
```

```
    <decision-state id="isValidPayment">
        <if test="paymentValid == true" then="review" else="payment" />
    </decision-state>

    <view-state id="review">
        <transition on="order" to="success" />
        <transition on="cancel" to="homepage" />
    </view-state>

    <end-state id="success" />
</flow>
```

First, a homepage is displayed. When the user clicks on the button that triggers the `order` event, the flow transitions to the `shoppingCartContents` flow, where they can take a look at everything that is included in their shopping carts. When the user triggers the `next` event, they have to choose a payment option, which is afterwards validated in the `checkValidPayment` state. If the validation succeeds, the user can take another look at their orders (in the `review` state) before they actually submit them. Now, we will start writing tests for this flow.

Create a new class in `src/test/java`, called `ShoppingCartTests`, which inherits from the `AbstractXmlFlowExecutionTests` class. Eclipse automatically adds a stub implementation of the `getResource()` method. Implement the method as shown below:

```
public class ShoppingCartTests extends AbstractXmlFlowExecutionTests {

    protected FlowDefinitionResource getResource(
            FlowDefinitionResourceFactory resourceFactory) {
        return resourceFactory
.createFileResource(
"src/main/webapp/WEB-INF/flows/shoppingcart-flow.xml"
);
class}

}
```

We also know that we will need a mocked implementation of the `PaymentService` interface. Please note that we have not yet written the classes and interfaces needed for our example. Just ignore the errors in your IDE for now, we will resolve them later.

```
public class ShoppingCartTests extends AbstractXmlFlowExecutionTests {

    private PaymentService paymentService;

    @Override
    public void setUp() {
```

```
        this.paymentService = createMock(PaymentService.class);
    }

    protected void configureFlowBuilderContext(
            MockFlowBuilderContext builderContext) {
        builderContext.registerBean("paymentservice",
            this.paymentService);
    }
...
}
```

Now you can begin writing your unit tests. We provide some basic tests; feel free to add more tests when you try the example:

```
    public void testStartShoppingCartFlow() {
        MockExternalContext context = new MockExternalContext();

        startFlow(context);

        assertFlowExecutionActive();
        assertCurrentStateEquals("homepage");
    }

    public void testSuccessfulTransitionToContents() {
        this.setCurrentState("homepage");
        MockExternalContext context = new MockExternalContext();
        context.setEventId("order");
        this.resumeFlow(context);

        assertFlowExecutionActive();
        assertCurrentStateEquals("shoppingCartContents");
    }

    public void testSuccessfulTransitionToPayment() {
        this.setCurrentState("shoppingCartContents");
        MockExternalContext context = new MockExternalContext();
        context.setEventId("next");
        this.resumeFlow(context);

        assertFlowExecutionActive();
        assertCurrentStateEquals("payment");
    }
```

In the `testStartShoppingCartFlow` test, we check if the flow is started correctly. In the two other tests, we check if the flow makes correct transitions when an event is triggered. Before we try to run the tests, let's continue and write a test for `checkValidPayment` `action-state`:

```
public void testValidPayment() {
   Payment validPayment = createMock(Payment.class);

   expect(this.paymentService.checkPayment(validPayment))
  .andReturn(true);

   replay(this.paymentService);

   this.setCurrentState("payment");

   MockExternalContext context = new MockExternalContext();
   context.setEventId("next");
   this.getFlowScope().put("chosenPaymentOption", validPayment);
   this.resumeFlow(context);

   boolean paymentValid =
      (Boolean)this.getFlowScope().get("paymentValid");

   assertTrue(paymentValid);
   assertFlowExecutionActive();
   assertCurrentStateEquals("review");

   verify(this.paymentService);
}
```

This test will first create a new mock object of the `Payment` interface. Next, we expect a call to the `checkPayment()` method of the `PaymentService` interface that returns `true` and thus indicates a valid payment option. We arm EasyMock by calling `replay()` and let our flow transit to the `checkValidPayment` state by storing the payment in the `flow` scope and resuming to the next state. Finally, we check if the `flow` scope contains the result of the `checkPayment()` method and if it equals `true`. We also check if the flow execution is still active and if the current state equals `review`.

If you try to let the tests run now, they will of course fail. Neither have we defined the `ShoppingCart` class, nor the interfaces in the above source code. This is what test-driven development is all about. We created the test classes and therefore already know how we expect the system to behave before having written the components we want to test. Again, feel free to add more test cases if you like.

We will implement the basic classes which we need for our tests to run now. Let's start by creating the `ShoppingCart` class:

```
public class ShoppingCart implements Serializable {

   private static final long serialVersionUID
= -4928926176100893795L;

   private List<Item> itemList;

   public ShoppingCart() {
      this.itemList = new ArrayList<Item>();
   }

   public List<Item> getItemList() {
      return itemList;
   }

   public void setItemList(List<Item> itemList) {
      this.itemList = itemList;
   }
}
```

As you can see, our shopping cart only consists of a list of items. The `Item` class is defined like this:

```
public class Item implements Serializable {

   private static final long serialVersionUID = 2401655063039143584L;

   private String title;
   private double price;

   public String getTitle() {
      return title;
   }

   public void setTitle(String title) {
      this.title = title;
   }

   public double getPrice() {
      return price;
   }

   public void setPrice(double price) {
      this.price = price;
   }
}
```

Next, we write the interfaces for our `PaymentService` and `Payment`:

```
public interface PaymentService {
   boolean checkPayment(Payment payment);
}

public interface Payment {
   // Empty for now
}
```

If you run the tests now, they will succeed and you can start creating concrete implementations of your interfaces:

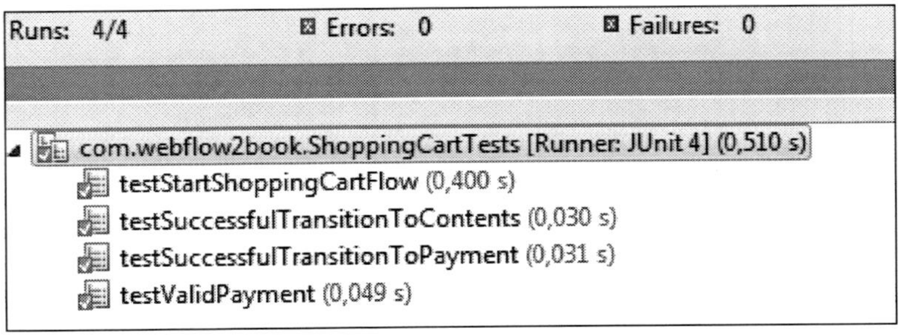

Summary

In this chapter, we explained how to efficiently test your Spring Web Flow applications. We showed you the inheritance hierarchy of Spring Web Flow's test-related classes and how they relate to each other. Then, we began to implement some simple unit tests using these classes.

This involved the following steps:

1. Creating a `MockExternalContext`
2. Starting the flow using the `startFlow()` method and the context we created in Step 1
3. Using `assert()` methods to check if the assumptions we have are valid or if the application behaves differently
4. Setting the event ID of the flow to the state you want to transit to next and call `resumeFlow()` to switch to this state

We also explained how you can use EasyMock to create mock implementations of your interfaces to test your services and how to test subflows you created in your applications. Finally, we provided you with an easy-to-follow example that explains how to integrate a test-driven development approach in your work with Spring Web Flow.

7
Security

Throughout this book, we explained how to use Spring Web Flow using a simple login example. But we never showed you what is actually protected by the login application. In this chapter, we will describe how to secure your Spring Web Flow applications using Spring Security.

For this, we instance a web application which our users can employ to change their password. The finished application is shown in the following screenshot:

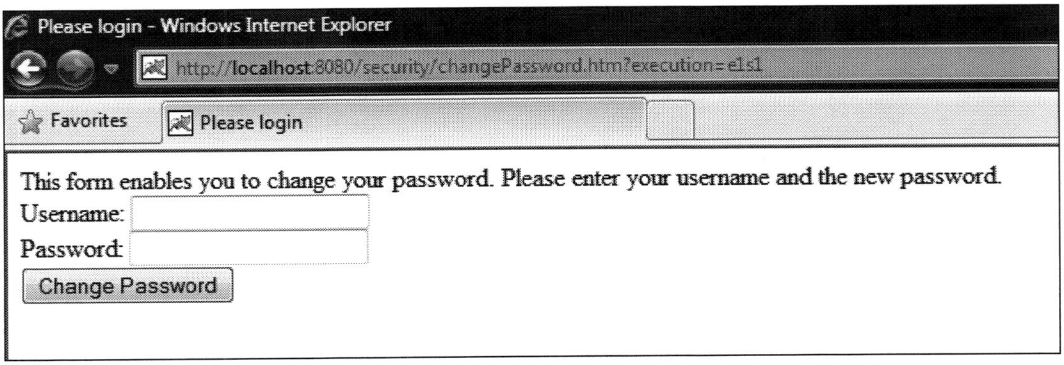

As in the previous chapters, the application consists of a JSP page with a small HTML form. Of course, not everybody who is using the Internet should be able to change the password of any user. Imagine someone guesses a username and changes it to a password of his or her choice. Then the intruder would be able to use all elements of our application. That would be particularly dangerous if we would maintain a web shop, where the users can buy their favorite books, DVDs, etc. To make sure only our registered users can access the application above, we will integrate Spring Security into it.

Introducing Spring Security

Spring Security is part of the Spring framework portfolio. Originally named Acegi Security, Spring Security is a flexible framework for securing all kinds of applications, including rich-clients and, of course, web applications. First of all, we want to show you how to get started with Spring Security. Afterwards, we want to dig a bit deeper into the technology and show you how to write your own authentication provider.

Spring Security can be used for both common goals of security frameworks, *authentication* and *authorization*. Authentication means the process of checking credentials of a user to make sure the user is exactly the one he or she claims to be. Authorization means the process of deciding whether the user has access to certain parts of the web application. Depending on which *roles* are assigned to a user, we can decide, on a very detailed level, who has access to which parts.

In this chapter, we chose the same configuration file layout and filenames you can find in the examples distributed with Spring Web Flow. We hope that makes it easier for you to understand this chapter and get accustomed to the layout of the examples.

Installing Spring Security

To install Spring Security, you can again choose from several alternatives. If you are using Maven in your build process, you just have to add the following dependency to your `pom.xml` file:

```
<dependency>
   <groupId>org.springframework.security</groupId>
   <artifactId>spring-security-core</artifactId>
   <version>2.0.4</version>
</dependency>
```

If you are using version 5 of the JDK (codename "Tiger") or better, you can also get some benefit from several convenient features (such as annotations for authorizing access to methods) by adding a further dependency called `spring-security-core-tiger`:

```
<dependency>
   <groupId>org.springframework.security</groupId>
   <artifactId>spring-security-core-tiger</artifactId>
   <version>2.0.4</version>
</dependency>
```

If you are interested in the Spring Security source code, you can check it out from the projects Subversion repository at `http://acegisecurity.svn.sourceforge.net/svnroot/acegisecurity/spring-security/trunk/` or download the source code of a specific release from `http://sourceforge.net/project/showfiles.php?group_id=73357`. We highly recommend downloading the source code, as it is very helpful to understand this chapter and to debug your applications in case there are problems integrating Spring Security into your own applications.

If you are not using Ant instead of Maven, you have to download the required libraries yourself, unless you are using a dependency manager like Apache Ivy. Please refer Chapter 2 for a more detailed explanation about how Apache Ivy works.

As you now have a working project, we will fade into the explanation about how Spring Security works.

Basic authentication with Spring Security

There are only a few settings necessary in your application context file to be able to use Spring Security. First of all, you have to add an additional XML namespace to your Spring application context file to be able to use tags from the `security` namespace.

```
<?xml version="1.0" encoding="UTF-8"?>
<beans xmlns="http://www.springframework.org/schema/beans"
      xmlns:xsi="http://www.w3.org/2001/XMLSchema-instance"
      xmlns:security="http://www.springframework.org/schema/security"
      xsi:schemaLocation="
          http://www.springframework.org/schema/beans
          http://www.springframework.org/schema/beans/spring-beans-
2.5.xsd
          http://www.springframework.org/schema/security
          http://www.springframework.org/schema/security/spring-
security-2.0.xsd">
```

Then you have to add at least an authentication provider and, to be able to use web security, an `http` element.

```
<security:http auto-config="true" />

<security:authentication-provider>
   <security:user-service>
      <security:user name="John" password="myPass!"
         authorities="ROLE_USER" />
   </security:user-service>
</security:authentication-provider>
```

In this first example, we enable `auto-config`. This provides us with a default login page, so we do not have to create one. If the user wants to access a secured web page, the login page will appear and it will not be possible for the user to access the web site without entering his or her credentials first. We also specify a very simple, default authentication provider and add the users of the application to the configuration file. This is sufficient for now. Of course, you usually have an existent data repository (like a database or LDAP) where you store the credentials of your users, like the one we used in the earlier chapters. Later in this chapter, we will show you how to write your own authentication provider that works with the familiar database schema we used before.

Setting up your web.xml

You also need some settings in your `web.xml` to enable filtering of the URLs you want to secure with Spring Security.

```
    <context-param>
       <param-name>contextConfigLocation</param-name>
       <param-value>
          /WEB-INF/config/web-application-config.xml
       </param-value>
    </context-param>

    <filter>
       <filter-name>springSecurityFilterChain</filter-name>
       <filter-class>
 org.springframework.web.filter.DelegatingFilterProxy
 </filter-class>
    </filter>

    <filter-mapping>
       <filter-name>springSecurityFilterChain</filter-name>
       <url-pattern>/*</url-pattern>
    </filter-mapping>

    <listener>
       <listener-class>
 org.springframework.web.context.ContextLoaderListener
 </listener-class>
    </listener>

    <servlet>
       <servlet-name>dispatcherServlet</servlet-name>
       <servlet-class>
 org.springframework.web.servlet.DispatcherServlet
 </servlet-class>
```

```
        <init-param>
            <param-name>contextConfigLocation</param-name>
            <param-value></param-value>
        </init-param>
        <load-on-startup>1</load-on-startup>
    </servlet>
    <servlet-mapping>
        <servlet-name>dispatcherServlet</servlet-name>
        <url-pattern>*.htm</url-pattern>
    </servlet-mapping>
```

First of all, we specify a `DelegatingFilterProxy` filter, which we call `springSecurityFilterChain`. It is mandatory that the filter is named this way because the name is used internally in Spring Security. `DelegatingProxyFilter` is a class from the core Spring framework and delegates to a Spring bean implementing the `filter` interface. We do not have to write this bean ourselves as it is already implemented by Spring Security. We just have to tell the filter which URLs to filter. In our case, we tell it to filter all URLs (`/*`) so that every access to your application will be handled by Spring Security.

Next, we set up the Spring `ContextLoaderListener`, which is necessary for `DelegatingFilterProxy`. We will describe it later. It is used to conveniently create an `ApplicationContext` for web applications, so the developer doesn't have to take care of creating one. The `ContextLoaderListener` needs an additional parameter telling it where to find the Spring configuration file. We specify the location of the configuration file using `context-param` tags.

Advanced Spring Security configuration

Now that we've managed to authenticate the user, we have to decide if he/she has access to certain parts of the application. For this, Spring Security offers `AccessDecisionManagers`. They decide if the current user has permission to invoke the method, before a method gets called. Spring Security already includes several different `AccessDecisionManager` implementations, which are based on a voting concept. The user can specify several voters (implementations of the `AccessDecisionVoter` interface), which are called one after the other. Each implementation can either choose to vote for granting the user access to a resource, deny access, or abstain from voting. The `AccessDecisionManager` then makes the final decision whether to grant or deny access to the requested resource by looking at the voting results of its `AccessDecisionVoters`.

The following UML diagram shows what the `AccessDecisionManager` interface looks like:

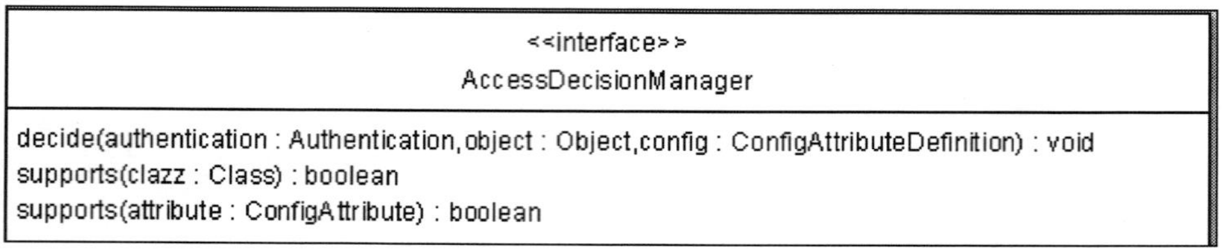

Three `AccessDecisionManagers` are already included in the Spring Security distribution:

- `AffirmativeBased`: This decision manager grants the user access to the requested resource if at least one voter returns a positive result. Negative results will be ignored as long as at least one voter granted access.
- `ConsensusBased`: This decision manager allows access to the resource when there are more positive than negative voting results.
- `UnanimousBased`: This requires a unanimous vote by the participating voters. If any vote has been negative, the access is denied.

In most use cases, the above decision managers are sufficient. You can, of course, provide your own decision managers.

The most often used `AccessDecisionVoter` is `RoleVoter`, which is also already included in the Spring Security distribution. RoleVoter expects `a ConfigAttribute` to start with the `ROLE_` prefix by default, although this can be changed to whatever prefix you like. A `ConfigAttribute` is, as the name suggests, a simple configuration parameter which has a special meaning in certain classes in Spring Security, for example `AccessDecisionManager`.

Let's take a quick look at the source code of the `ConfigAttribute` interface (in Spring Security 2.0.4). As you can see in the following code listing, it is fairly simple:

```
public interface ConfigAttribute extends Serializable {
    String getAttribute();
}
```

The `ConfigAttribute` interface requires classes to implement only the `getAttribute()` method, which is the value of the parameter. A very easy to understand implementation is the `SecurityConfig` class, also a part of Spring Security:

```
public class SecurityConfig implements ConfigAttribute {
    private String attrib;

    public String getAttribute() {
```

```
            return this.attrib;
        }
        public String toString() {
            return this.attrib;
        }
    }
```

We left out some information from the class (such as the constructor, the `equals()`, and the `hashCode()` method) and only provided you with the important code. The `SecurityConfig` class stores the attribute as a simple Java `String` object.

Now let's come back to our `AccessDecisionManager` interface. As you can see in the figure above, `ConfigAttribute` is used in one of the two `supports()` methods. In the `RoleVoter` class, the method returns `true` if the `ConfigAttribute` parameter is not null and the attribute starts with the specified prefix.

To write your own `AccessDecisionVoter`, you just have to implement the `AccessDecisionVoter` interface, which you can see in the following figure:

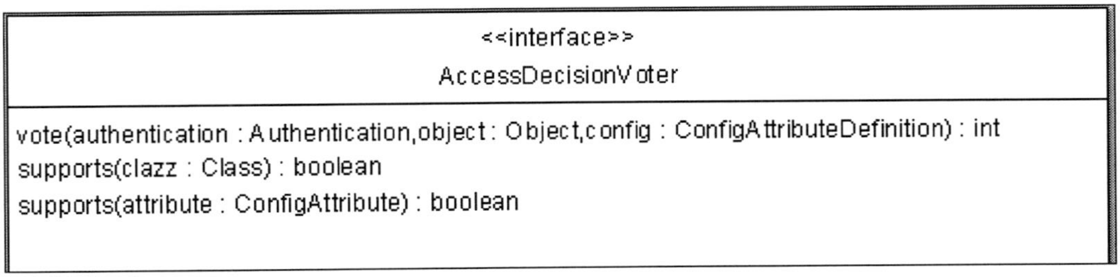

For example, if you do not want to use roles for your users, you would have to implement your own voter. In the following example, we chose to ask for specific rights. If the user is assigned this right, he/she gets access to the resource:

```
public class SimpleRightsVoter implements AccessDecisionVoter {
@Override
public boolean supports(ConfigAttribute arg0) {
   return true;
}
@Override
public boolean supports(Class arg0) {
   return true;
}
@Override
public int vote(Authentication authentication, Object object,
      ConfigAttributeDefinition config) {
```

```
        // Step through the config attributes
        for(Iterator<ConfigAttribute> it =
           config.getConfigAttributes().iterator(); it.hasNext();) {
  ConfigAttribute attribute = it.next();
           // No credentials, access is denied
           if(authentication == null) {
              return ACCESS_DENIED;
           }
           // Check if the authenticated principal has the necessary
           // rights
           GrantedAuthority[] authorities =
              authentication.getAuthorities();
           int length = authorities.length;
           for(int i = 0; i < length; ++i) {
              // Grant access, if the user does have
            // the correct rights
              if(authorities[i].getAuthority().equals(
              attribute.getAttribute())) {
                 return ACCESS_GRANTED;
              }
           }
        }
        return ACCESS_ABSTAIN;
  }
  }
```

We do not differentiate between classes and configuration attributes, so we let the two `supports()` methods just return `true`. The most important piece of the code is included in the `vote()` method. First of all, we iterate through all configuration attributes and then check if the authenticated principal has one of the rights specified in the attributes. If yes, the method returns the `ACCESS_GRANTED` constant and the user will have access to the resource. If not, the method returns `ACCESS_DENIED` and denies access. We also return `ACCESS_DENIED` if no authentication information was given to the method.

As you can see, the concept of different voters is extremely powerful and flexible, but nevertheless very easy to understand and implement.

Now we have to tell Spring Security to use our new `SingleRightsVoter` instead of the default `RoleVoter`. We need a couple of new configuration options for this:

```
<bean id="simpleRightsVoter"
 class="com.webflow2book.SimpleRightsVoter" />
<bean id="myAccessDecisionManager"
   class="org.springframework.security.vote.ConsensusBased">
   <property name="decisionVoters">
      <list>
```

```
            <ref bean="simpleRightsVoter" />
         </list>
      </property>
   </bean>
   <security:http
access-decision-manager-ref="myAccessDecisionManager"
      auto-config="true" />
   <security:authentication-provider>
      <security:user-service>
         <security:user name="John" password="myPass!"
            authorities="ALL_RIGHTS" />
      </security:user-service>
   </security:authentication-provider>
```

First, we configure a new Spring bean with our voters' class. Next, we need to create a custom access decision manager as we need to give it our voter. As can be seen in the example above, we chose a `ConsensusBased` access decision manager. Its `decisionVoters` property expects a list of voters (references to Spring beans), which will be asked sequentially if the principal should have the right to access the web site or not. We will need to give the `http` element a hint as to which bean is used as the access decision manager; this is done via the `access-decision-manager-ref` attribute. Now only the authorities need to be changed. We changed them from `ROLE_USER to ALL_RIGHTS.`

UserDetails

A very important part in Spring Security is played by the `UserDetails` interface. If you query an `Authentication` object to return the principal, it is very likely that you get an object that is actually an instance of the `UserDetails` interface. The following figure shows what the interface includes:

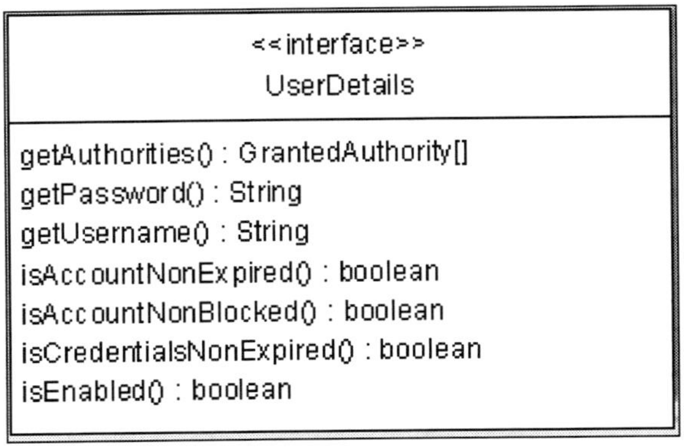

The interface is very straightforward. You can get a list of all authorities (rights or roles) the user possesses using the `getAuthorities()` method. You can also ask for the username and the password using the methods from the interface. The remaining methods are important for checking if the account and the credentials are still valid or if they have expired or were locked.

The reference implementation of the `UserDetails` interface is the `User` class in the `org.springframework.security.userdetails` package. The class is too long to be quoted in this book, but we highly recommend taking a look at it to understand how Spring Security works.

An object of the `UserDetails` interface is usually provided to you by a `UserDetailsService`, which is also an interface that looks as in the following figure:

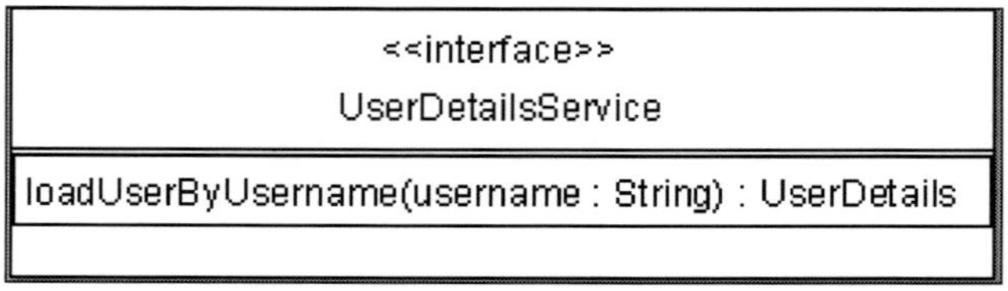

This interface is even simpler than the `UserDetails` interface shown previously. The developer has to write only one method to implement the interface. Spring Security comes with a couple of implementations of this interface, but many users write their own implementation. In this way you can use your existing persistence layer (for example, implemented with Hibernate or the Java Persistence API) or other technologies you are using for your data access (like LDAP).

Using database access to retrieve users

If you have plenty of users, defining them all in the Spring configuration file is very inconvenient and error-prone. Usually, you have all your users stored in a database or in an LDAP directory. For our example, we are using a database, a strategy we have used throughout the book until now. We want to show you how easy it is to use Spring Security with a database instead of a configuration file.

Basically, all we have to do is change our definition of the authentication provider from a `user-service` to a `jdbc-user-service` like this:

```
<bean id="dataSource" destroy-method="close"
   class="org.springframework.jndi.JndiObjectFactoryBean">
   <property name="jndiName"
      value="java:comp/env/jdbc/chapter02db" />
```

```
    <property name="resourceRef" value="true" />
</bean>

<security:authentication-provider>
    <security:jdbc-user-service data-source-ref="dataSource" />
</security:authentication-provider>
```

The data source is the same we used in earlier chapters. As a reminder, we included it in the previous code. Spring Security will now try to receive the principals from the database. It has several requirements on the database schema though, which are usually not impedimentary if you create a database from scratch. If you want to use Spring Security in an already existing environment, it might be difficult to change the schema to the one Spring Security expects. The following figure shows what the schema has to look like:

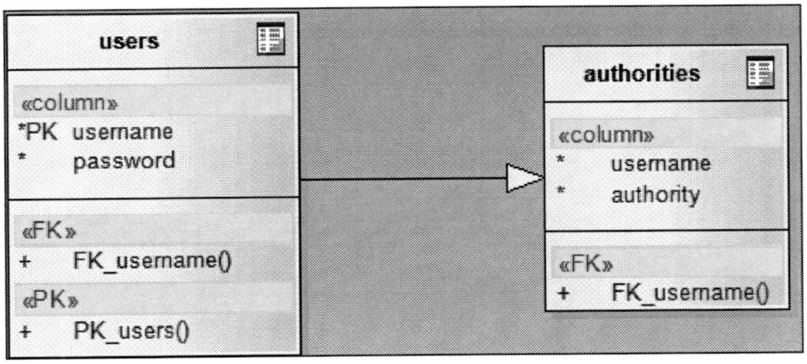

If you do not want to, or can't, change the database schema, you can still use the built-in functionality of `jdbc-user-service` by overriding the queries that are used to get the user and his or her authorities. As we do not have authorities in the database yet, we had to create a new database table. For this example, we created a new table, which does not comply with the default schema expected by Spring Security:

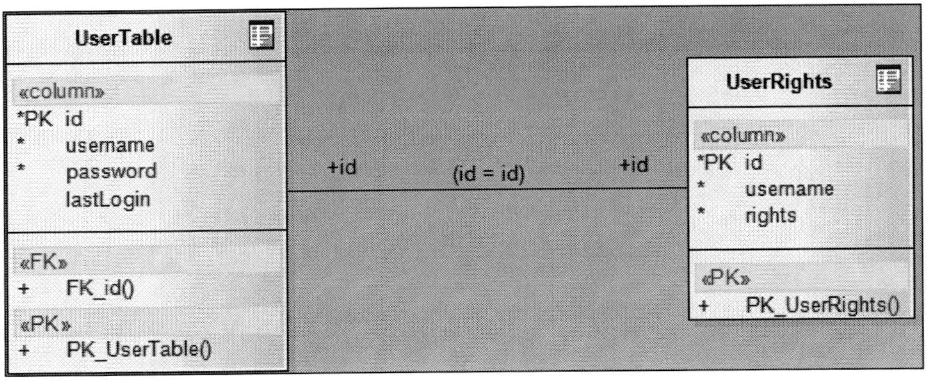

The corresponding Spring configuration looks like this:

```
    <security:authentication-provider>
       <security:jdbc-user-service data-source-ref="dataSource"
          users-by-username-query="select username, password,
 1 as enabled from UserTable where username = ?"
          authorities-by-username-query="select username,
 rights as authority from UserRights where username = ?"
    />
```

As you can see, we "simulate" the default database schema by returning the information the responsible classes expect. For example, we do not have a field that shows if an account is disabled or not, so we just return the value `1` for every dataset.

If you have a much more complicated database schema, the above solution might not be enough. In this case, you still have the possibility to write your own implementation of `UserDetailsService`.

Securing parts of a web page

Spring Security includes a tag library that you can use to secure certain parts of a JSP. For example, if you want only authorized users to see a specific part of a web page, such as a link for an administrative interface, you can implement this use case very easily with the tag library.

If you want to use it, you have to define an additional dependency in your dependency manager (e.g. Maven or Ivy):

```
<dependency>
<groupId>org.springframework.security</groupId>
<artifactId>spring-security-taglibs</artifactId>
<version>2.0.4</version>
</dependency>
```

In the JSP you want to secure, you can afterwards add a new `taglib` directive:

```
<%@ taglib prefix="sec"
uri="http://www.springframework.org/security/tags" %>
```

Now you can use the `authorize` tag to secure parts of your web page. The tag itself has multiple attributes you can use to decide whether the user has to own all rights you enter in the attribute, any of the specified rights, or none of them at all:

Attribute	Meaning
`ifAllGranted`	Shows the secured part of the page if the user owns every right defined in the attribute.
`ifAnyGranted`	If the user owns one of the rights defined in the attribute, the secured part of the page is rendered and shown to the user.
`ifNotGranted`	The user must not possess any of the rights defined.

Each of these attributes is a list of multiple roles. You can separate each role by using commas or entering only a single role.

To implement the above mentioned use case of securing the link of an administrative interface, you can use a tag like this:

```
<sec:authorize ifAllGranted="ADMIN_RIGHTS">
<a href="<c:url value="/admin.htm" />">Admin interface</a>
</sec:authorize>
```

Only users who own the `ADMIN_RIGHTS` right can see the link to the web page. All other users will not see the link. Remember that you can freely define the available rights. For example, with the appropriate `AccessDecisionVoter`, you can decide for yourself if you want to call the `ADMIN_RIGHTS` or `ADMIN_ROLE` right.

There are a few other tags available in the tag library, which are listed in the following table:

Tag	Usage
`authorize`	As just explained, this tag is used to secure parts of your web page using roles or rights.
`authentication`	Provides access to the `Authentication` object that is currently used.
`acl`	Uses ACLs (Access Control Lists) to determine if the secured part of the web page should be displayed or not. Please see the Spring Security reference documentation for details.
`accesscontrollist`	Also uses ACLs, but a different implementation in Spring Security. Please consult the Spring Security reference documentation for details.

Securing method invocations

As you have already seen, Spring Security is extremely powerful. You can define how the framework decides how access is granted using custom voters. You also learned how to access your database to gather required information like usernames and passwords. In the last section, we have shown you how to secure specific parts of your web pages. Now we want to have a look at how you can secure method invocations. Using these techniques, only users with the correct credentials can call secured methods.

Spring Security does support its own annotation, `@Secured`, which you can apply to any method you want to secure, as well as the annotations specified in JSR-250 (Common Annotations for the Java Platform), like `@RolesAllowed`. For more information concerning JSR-250, please access the web site at `http://jcp.org/en/jsr/detail?id=250`. To enable these annotations, you have to add a new tag in your Spring configuration:

```
<security:global-method-security secured-annotations="enabled"
   jsr250-annotations="enabled" />
```

This requires the `security` namespace, mentioned earlier in this chapter.

Let's take a look at how you can secure your method invocations. As an example, we are using the following controller and JSR-250-based annotations:

```
@Controller
public class AdminController {

   @Autowired
   @Qualifier(value = "adminService")
   private AdminService adminService;

   @RequestMapping("/admin.htm")
   public String getStrings(ModelMap model) {
      List<String> resultList = new ArrayList<String>();

      resultList.addAll(this.adminService.getSecretStrings());
      resultList.addAll(this.adminService.getPublicStrings());
      model.addAttribute("resultList", resultList);

      return "adminInterface";
   }}
```

We are using the new annotation-based configuration for Spring MVC applications, available since Spring 2.5, which we also used in Chapter 5. Please take a look at Chapter 5 to learn how to configure the annotation-based Spring MVC configuration in conjunction with Spring Web Flow.

With the @Controller annotation, we define that the AdminController class should act as Spring MVC controller. We inject an object of the AdminService interface, which is displayed in the following diagram, using the auto-wiring features of the Spring framework:

Next, we declare a method, which we annotate using the @RequestMapping annotation. This tells Spring MVC that this method should be called if the URL in the annotation is accessed by the user. We call two methods of the service class and return the resulting List object.

Now we want to show you how the service class is implemented:

```
@Service(value = "adminService")
public class AdminServiceImpl implements AdminService {

   @RolesAllowed(value = "SPECIAL_ADMIN_RIGHTS")
   public List<String> getSecretStrings() {
      List<String> stringList = new ArrayList<String>();
      stringList.add("This is secret");
      return stringList;
   }

   public List<String> getPublicStrings() {
      List<String> stringList = new ArrayList<String>();
      stringList.add("This is public");
      return stringList;
   }
}
```

Again, we are using the annotation-based configuration of the Spring framework. This time, we declare AdminServiceImpl as @Service. We call it adminService, and as you can see in the controller class, this is exactly how we inject the service implementation into the controller. We annotate the getSecretStrings() method with the @RolesAllowed annotation and define that only users with the SPECIAL_ADMIN_RIGHTS role are allowed to access this method.

If we try to access a web page which is secured that way without the correct rights, we will not be able to see it:

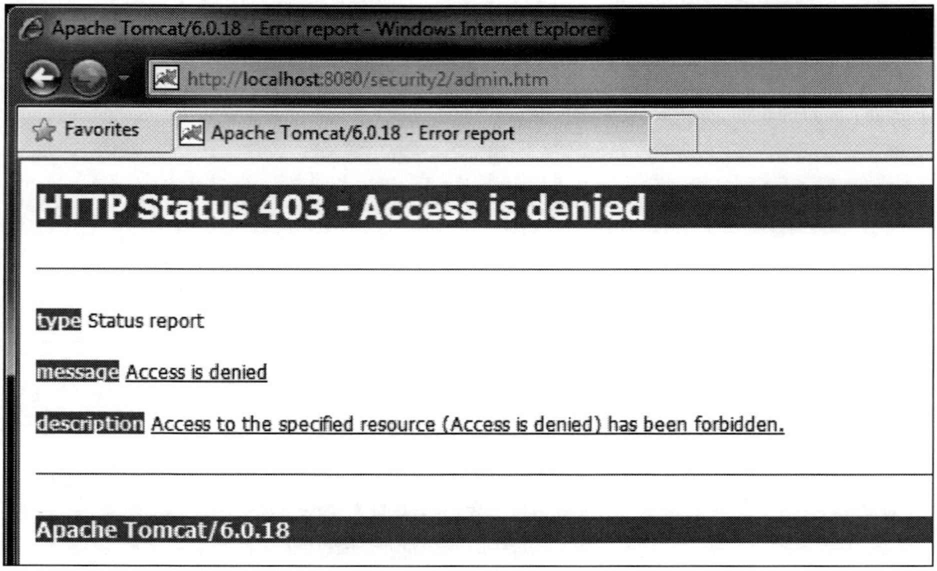

As you can see, securing your methods with Spring Security is not black magic. Please see the Spring Security reference documentation for more examples on how you can secure your web applications.

Using Spring Security with Spring Web Flow

You should now have a basic understanding of how Spring Security works. Integrating Spring Security into our flows is very easy. Now, in the remaining section, we can finally show you how the example from the beginning of this chapter was built.

Changing the user's password

For our example, we are using the following Web Flow definition:

```
<?xml version="1.0" encoding="UTF-8"?>
<flow xmlns="http://www.springframework.org/schema/webflow"
       xmlns:xsi="http://www.w3.org/2001/XMLSchema-instance"
  xsi:schemaLocation="http://www.springframework.org/
```

```
schema/webflow
        http://www.springframework.org/schema/webflow/spring-webflow-
        2.0.xsd">
   <secured attributes="ALL_RIGHTS" />
   <persistence-context />
   <var class="com.webflow2book.User" name="user"/>
   <view-state id="changePassword" model="user">
      <transition on="doChange" to="doChange" />
   </view-state>
   <action-state id="doChange">
      <evaluate expression="userservice.changePassword(
      user.username, user.password)" />
      <transition to="successView" />
      <transition on-exception=
      "javax.persistence.NoResultException" to="failedView" />
   </action-state>
   <end-state id="successView" view="successView.jsp"
   commit="true" />
   <end-state id="failedView" view="failedView.jsp" />
</flow>
```

This flow enables the user to change his or her password. The `changePassword` view is a simple web form, written as a JSP file, which prompts for the username of the user and a new password:

```
<?xml version="1.0" encoding="ISO-8859-1" ?>
...
<html xmlns="http://www.w3.org/1999/xhtml">
<head>
<meta http-equiv="Content-Type" content="text/html; charset=ISO-8859-
1" />
<title>Change Password</title>
</head>
<body>
This form enables you to change your password. Please enter your
username and the new password.
<form:form method="post" modelAttribute="user">
   Username: <form:input path="username" />
   <br />
   Password: <form:password path="password" />
   <br />
   <input type="submit" name="_eventId_doChange" value="Change
Password" />
</form:form>
</body>
</html>
```

When the user clicks on the **Change Password** button, the flow will transit to the doChange state. This state is an action-state that calls the changePassword() method in our UserService. The UserService just delegates the method call to the persistence layer. The persistence layer is making the database call to change the password of the user:

```
public void changePassword(String username, String newPassword) {
   Query query = this.getEntityManager().createNamedQuery(
         "User.findByUsername");
   User user = (User)query.setParameter("username",
      username).getSingleResult();
   user.setPassword(newPassword);
}
```

We are using a Java Persistence API, like we did in earlier chapters, so we ask the EntityManager to create a new named query. We are using the same query we wrote in Chapter 2:

```
<named-query name="User.findByUsername">
   <query>
   select user from com.webflow2book.User user
   where user.username like :username
   </query>
</named-query>
```

This query finds a user in our database by his/her username. The changePassword() method then sets the new password for the user. When the transaction is committed, the change will be made in the database.

To configure the usage of Spring Security in our flow, all we have to do is add a secured tag on top of our flow configuration file, like we did in the previous configuration file:

```
<secured attributes="ALL_RIGHTS" />
```

This enables security for our flow and required the user who wants to use the application to have at least the ALL_RIGHTS authority.

Then we need to add an additional listener to our application context file:

```
<bean id="securityFlowExecutionListener"
   class="org.springframework.webflow.security.
    SecurityFlowExecutionListener" />

<webflow:flow-executor id="flowExecutor"
   flow-registry="flowRegistry">
   <webflow:flow-execution-listeners>
```

```
        <webflow:listener ref="jpaFlowExecutionListener" />
        <webflow:listener ref="securityFlowExecutionListener" />
    </webflow:flow-execution-listeners>
</webflow:flow-executor>
```

We add a new listener to the flow executor, a `SecurityFlowExecutionListener`. This listener includes a reference to an `AccessDecisionManager`, which is responsible for deciding if the request from the user should be granted or denied.

If the user now tries to access the sample application, he/she will be presented by a login screen:

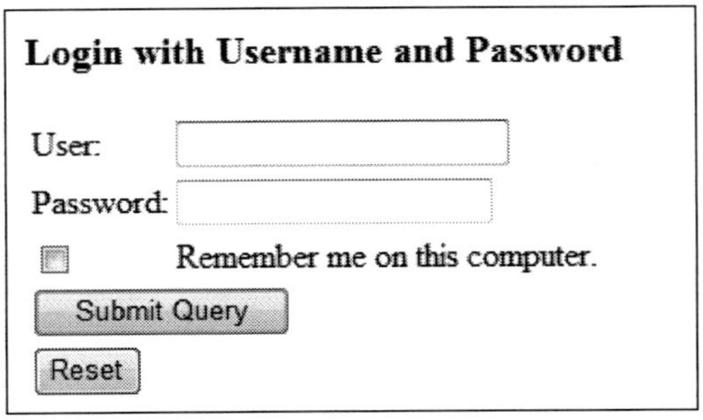

This is the default login screen provided by Spring Security. Only if the user enters the correct credentials, the form to change his/her password will be shown. If the user enters a wrong username or password, an `AccessDeniedException` will be thrown and the user will see an error message:

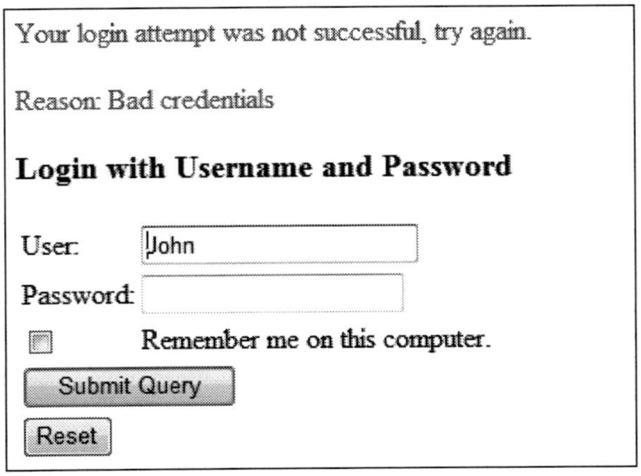

Summary

In this chapter, we showed you what Spring Security is, how it works, and how to integrate it into your flows. You learned that Spring Security is a part of the Spring portfolio and a very flexible and easy-to-use security framework that you can use for all your security needs. This is true not only for web applications, but also for your rich-client applications which are based on Spring.

We explained how to configure Spring Security, the different types of `AccessDecisionManagers`, and how to write your own `AccessDecisionVoter`.

The chapter ended with a small example, which showed you how to use Spring Security in your own projects. All you have to do for this is:

1. Set up Spring Security. This includes your `web.xml` file and your application context configuration file. Think about which `AccessDecisionManager` you want to use and is suitable for your use case. By default, an `AffirmativeBased` manager will be used.
2. Add the `secured` element to your flow definition and include all roles or other authorities that should have access to the flow.
3. Add `SecurityFlowExecutionListener` to your application context.

A
flow.trac:The Model for the Examples

In the previous chapters, we used the `model` classes from our sample project with the name, **flow.trac-core**. This project provides classes which could be used to implement a simple bug tracker application. In this appendix, we want to give you a short overview of the mentioned `model` classes. With this information, it is possible to understand the usage of the classes in the examples of this book.

flow.trac

The `flow.trac` model is separated into three packages, which are shown in the following figure. The classes in the project, `flow.trace.core`, are independent of Spring Web Flow 2.

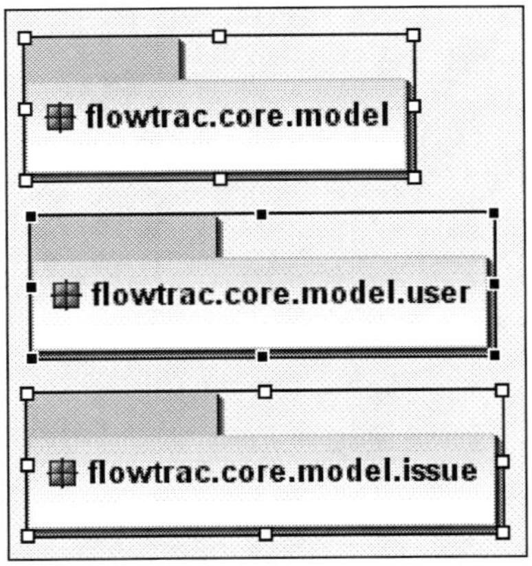

The classes defined in `flow.trac.core` are listed here.

Item

Each element, which can be stored into a database, is of type `Item`, is a simple marker interface.

An `Item` has some meta information which is enumerated as follows:

- The date on which the item is created (Method: `getCreationDate()`)
- The date on which the item was last modified (Method: `getLastModified()`)
- The user who created the item (Method: `getCreatedBy()`)
- The user who has done the last modification on the item (Method: `getLastModifiedBy()`)

Additionally, the interface `Item` extends the marker interface, `java.io.Serializable`.

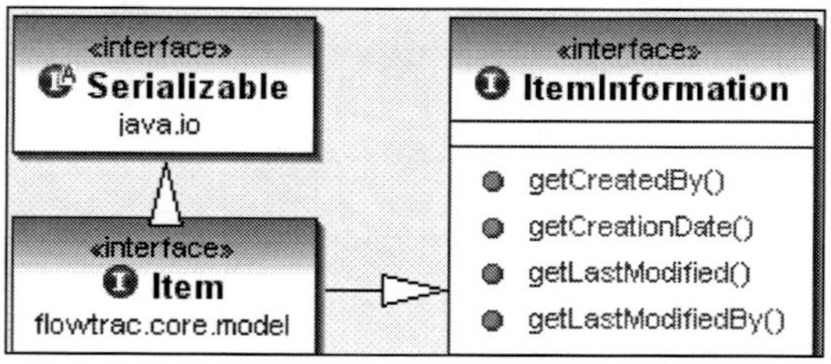

User

There are users inside a bug tracker system. In our case, the users are represented as an instance from `flowtrac.core.model.User`.

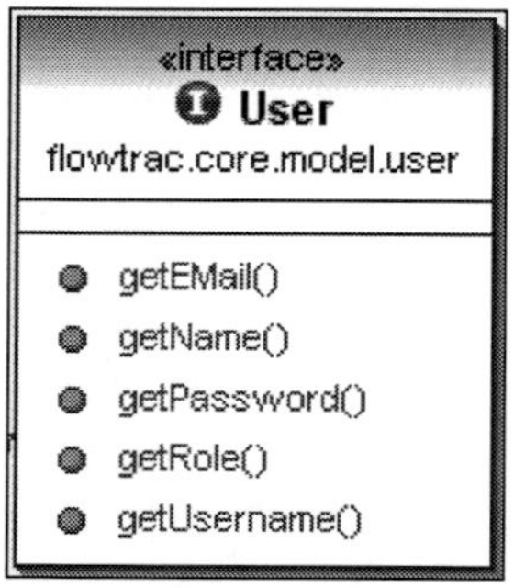

For the `User` instance, it is worth mentioning that our examples use the name of the user as the identifier. Therefore, the username is unique in our examples.

Role

Each user has a role of type, `flowtrac.core.model.user.Role`. At the time of first contact with the system (the login mask) each user possesses the role, `Anonymous`. The role itself is modeled as an `enumeration` type. We have implemented the following five roles:

- `Anonymous`
- `Guest`
- `NamedUser`
- `ProjectAdministrator`
- `Administrator`

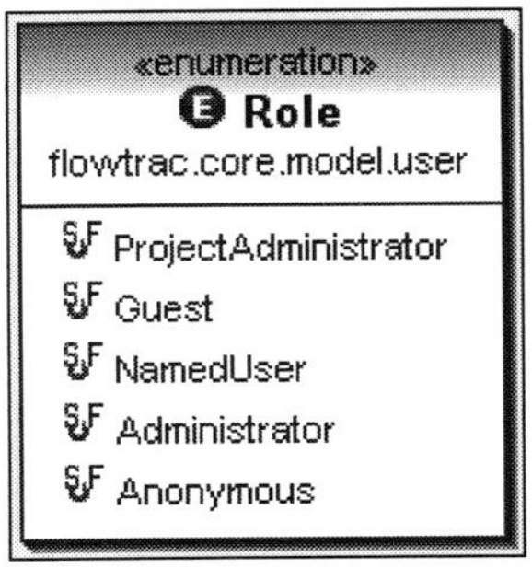

Project

After a user is logged in, the role of the user changes to a `NamedUser`. Inside the bug tracker, an issue belongs to a project. The project is realized as an interface from the type, `flowtrace.core.model.Project`. The interface `Project` extends from `flowtrac.core.model.Item`.

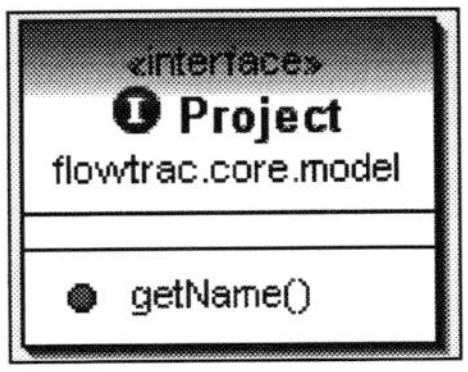

Issue

The central element of the system is of the type `Issue`. This element contains all information about a bug or a requirement. The `Issue` is annotated with elements from the JPA (Java Persistence API) to store it into a relational database.

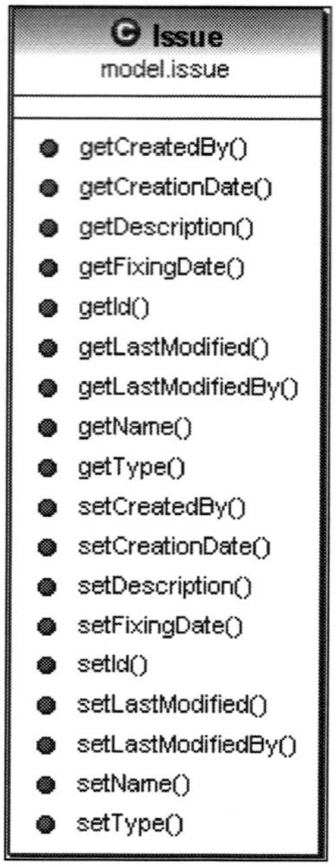

In the following listing, we show the complete implementation of the class `flowtrac.core.model.issue.Issue`.

```
package flowtrac.core.model.issue;

import java.util.Date;

import javax.persistence.Entity;
import javax.persistence.GeneratedValue;
import javax.persistence.Id;

import flowtrac.core.model.Item;
import flowtrac.core.model.user.User;

@Entity
public class Issue implements Item {

    /**
     * Generated by eclipse.
     */
    private static final long serialVersionUID = 5711325923341961421L;
```

```
    private String name;
    private String description;
    private Long id;
    private Date fixingDate;
    private Date lastModifed;
    private Date creationDate;

    /**
     * @see flowtrac.core.model.issue.Issue#getFixingDate()
     */
    public Date getFixingDate() {
        return this.fixingDate;
    }

    /**
     * @see flowtrac.core.model.issue.Issue#getId()
     */
    @Id
    @GeneratedValue
    public Long getId() {
        return this.id;
    }

    /**
     * @see flowtrac.core.model.issue.Issue#getName()
     */
    public String getName() {
        return this.name;
    }

    /**
     * @see flowtrac.core.model.issue.Issue#setName(java.lang.String)
     */
    public void setName(String name) {
        this.name = name;
    }

    /**
     * @see flowtrac.core.model.issue.Issue#setId(long)
     */
    public void setId(long id) {
        this.id = id;
    }

    /**
     * @see flowtrac.core.model.issue.Issue#setFixingDate(java.util.
Date)
     */
```

```
public void setFixingDate(Date fixingDate) {
   this.fixingDate = fixingDate;
}

/* (non-Javadoc)
 * @see flowtrac.core.model.issue.ItemInformation#getCreatedBy()
 */
public User getCreatedBy() {
   // TODO Auto-generated method stub
   return null;
}

/**
* @see flowtrac.core.model.issue.ItemInformation#getCreationDate()
 */
public Date getCreationDate() {
   return this.creationDate;
}

/**
 * @see flowtrac.core.model.issue.ItemInformation#getLastModified()
 */
public Date getLastModified() {
   return this.lastModifed;
}

/* (non-Javadoc)
 * @see flowtrac.core.model.issue
        .ItemInformation#getLastModifiedBy()
 */
public User getLastModifiedBy() {
   // TODO Auto-generated method stub
   return null;
}

/* (non-Javadoc)
 * @see flowtrac.core.model.issue.ItemInformation#setCreatedBy(
                                 flowtrac.core.model.user.User)
 */
public void setCreatedBy(User createdBy) {
   // TODO Auto-generated method stub
}

/**
 * @see flowtrac.core.model.issue.
                  ItemInformation#setCreationDate(java.util.Date)
 */
```

```
    public void setCreationDate(Date creationDate) {
        this.creationDate = creationDate;
    }
    /**
     * @see flowtrac.core.model.issue.
                      ItemInformation#setLastModified(java.util.Date)
     */
    public void setLastModified(Date lastModified) {
        this.lastModifed = lastModified;
    }
    /* (non-Javadoc)
     * @see flowtrac.core.model.issue.
      ItemInformation#setLastModifiedBy(flowtrac.core.model.user.User)
     */
    public void setLastModifiedBy(User lastModfiedBy) {
        // TODO Auto-generated method stub
    }
    /**
     * @see flowtrac.core.model.issue.Issue#getDescription()
     */
    public String getDescription() {
        return this.description;
    }
    /**
     * @see flowtrac.core.model.issue.
                Issue#setDescription(java.lang.String)
     */
    public void setDescription(final String description) {
        this.description = description;
    }
    private Type type;
    /**
     * @return type type of the issue.
     */
    public Type getType()  {
        return this.type;
    }
    public void setType(final Type type)  {
        this.type = type;
    }
}
```

Type

An issue can have a `Type`. The type is encapsulated as `enumeration`. Currently, we have implemented the following three types:

- `Feature`
- `Bug`
- `Task`

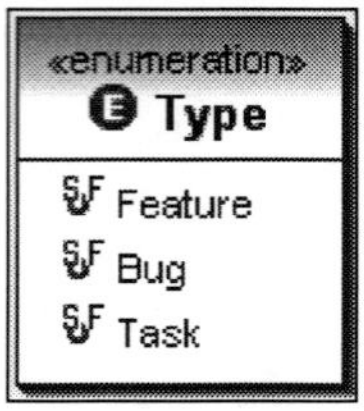

Priority

Each issue has a priority. The priority is encapsulated as `enumeration`. We have implemented the following three priorities:

- `Minor`
- `Major`
- `Critical`

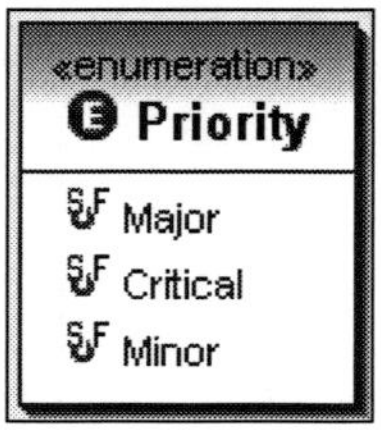

Comment

A user can enter a comment for an issue. A `Comment` is an `Item` and only consists of some text. An `Issue` can have more than one `Comment`.

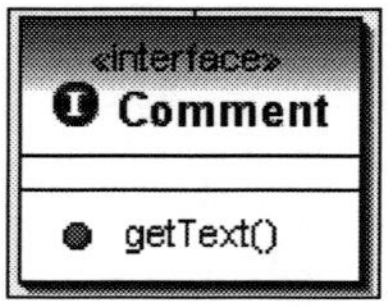

Attachment

A user can attach one or more files to an issue. The attachment itself is encapsulated with the interface, `Attachment`.

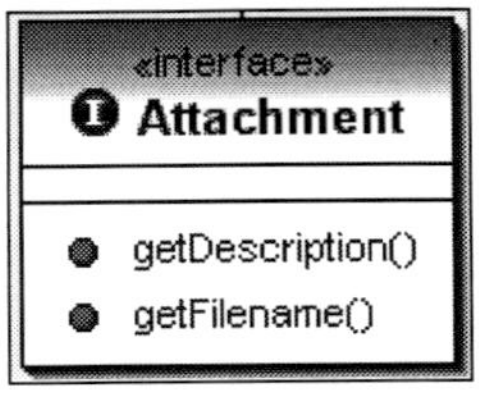

Summary

In this appendix, we described the `model` classes which are used inside the chapters of this book. Most of the elements are realized as interfaces. For the examples it is sufficient to have a full implementation of the class `Issue`, which we have shown in this appendix. Feel free to use the shown source code.

B

Running on the SpringSource dm Server

The **SpringSource dm Server** is a modular **OSGi** (**Open Services Gateway initiative**) -based Java server, which is designed to run Spring-based applications. This means the SpringSource dm Server is the first server which is dedicated to Spring Framework-based applications. This server acts as an application server for Spring applications.

> The web page of the OSGi alliance is `http://www.osgi.org`. Maybe you heard about OSGi from the development environment Eclipse (`http://www.eclipse.org`) because the plug-in technology of Eclipse is built on OSGi.

The SpringSource dm Server is based on the Spring Dynamic Module Kernel (dm-kernel). The first part of this appendix explains the architecture of the SpringSource dm Server and gives you a short introduction to the installation of the current distribution. At the time of this writing, Version 1.0.0 was the latest version. Therefore, our explanations are only valid for this release. This appendix will guide you on how to run your Spring Web Flow 2 applications on the SpringSource dm Server. We want to show you this because when you build your applications on the top of Spring Framework, it can be a good choice to run your applications on the SpringSource dm Server. As you can download the server for free, it is worth giving it a try.

Introduction to the SpringSource dm Server

The SpringSource dm Server is the runtime part of the SpringSource **Application Platform** (AP).

> The SpringSource Application Platform is a combination of SpringSource Enterprise and SpringSource dm Server. The SpringSource Enterprise is a support package from SpringSource, including an IDE with the name, SpringSource Tool Suite. For more information about SpringSource AP, visit `http://www.springsource.com/products/suite/applicationplatform`.

The SpringSource dm Server is built on the following technologies:

- Spring Framework.
- Tomcat, which is used as JEE web container.

  The selection of Apache Tomcat (`http://tomcat.apache.org`) as servlet container is obvious because of the acquisition of the company Covalent from SpringSource. Covalent is known in the community as an important supporter of the Tomcat project.
- OSGi R4.1.
- Equinox as an implementation of the OSGi specification.

  Equinox (`http://www.eclipse.org/equinox/`) is also used in Eclipse as the OSGi container.
- Spring Dynamic Modules for OSGi.

  This module acts as a glue between OSGi and Spring. This means that with this module, you can leverage the full functionality of Spring inside an OSGi kernel.
- SpringSource Tool Suite.
- Spring Application Management Suite.

> It is important to know that the **SpringSource Tool Suite** (**STS**) and the Spring Application Management Suite is only available through the commercial SpringSource Enterprise program. The STS is an IDE based on Eclipse to develop Spring applications, especially applications for the SpringSource dm Server. The Spring Application Management Suite is a web based console for managing Spring applications. The base protocol of this console is **Java Management Extensions** (**JMX**).

The following figure shows the architecture of the SpringSource dm Server. The heart of the server is the **SpringSource Dynamic Module Kernel** (**dm Kernel**). The dm Kernel is built on Equinox, which is shown as a layer under the dm Kernel. The applications that are running inside the SpringSource dm Server are modular, and each module has a personality. The personality of the application describes the type (web, batch, web service, and so on) of the application.

> The Release 1.0.0 of the SpringSource dm Server supports the bundle, web, and WAR personalities. This helps you run web applications in an easy way on the Spring Source dm Server. The future versions of this server will support more personalities.

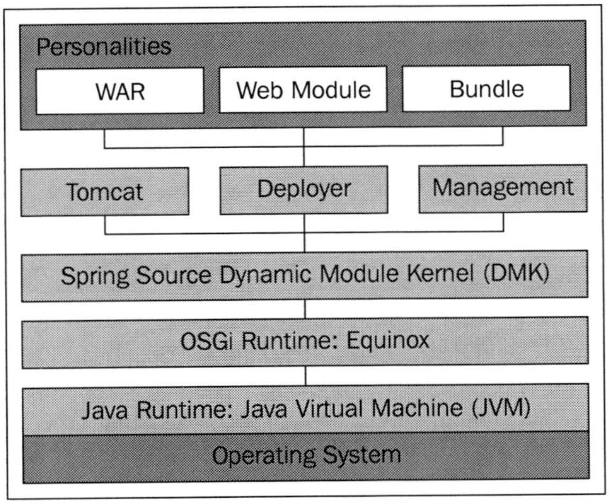

Installation of the SpringSource dm Server

In this appendix, we want to describe the prerequisites, which are essential to install the SpringSource dm Server. These prerequisites for installation may change for future versions. This guide is for the release Version 1.0.0. The first step is to download the latest release of the SpringSource dm Server. You can download the latest version directly from the SpringSource at: `http://www.springsource.com/download/dmserver`. The first page on the download web site only offers the zip-archive (the name of the archive is `springsource-dm-server-sources-1.0.0.RELEASE.zip`) which contains the sources; the archive has a size of about 3.4 MB. The sources are available under the GNU General Public License Version 3. The license is available online at `http://www.gnu.org/licenses/gpl-3.0.html`. For the build of the archive, you need an installed JDK of the Version 1.5 or higher.

> Until the process of the SpringSource dm Server is built, the essential libraries for that build are downloaded with the help of Apache Ivy (`http://ant.apache.org/ivy`). The libraries are stored inside an S3 storage.

Additionally, you need an installed version of the build system Apache ANT (`http://ant.apache.org`) of the Version 1.7, or higher. It is recommended that you read the provided file, `readme.txt`, which contains a step-by-step instruction for the build of the SpringSource dm Server.

If you want to download a binary release, press on the **Download Now!** link.

Before you can finally download the binary release, you have to accept the **SpringSource dm Server 1.0 LICENSE AGREEMENT**. After you have accepted the mentioned license, you can download the binary ZIP archive. The name of the archive is **springsource-dm-server-1.0.0.RELEASE.zip**. For the installation of the SpringSource dm Server, just extract the archive inside an arbitrary folder. After the extraction, the folder looks like this:

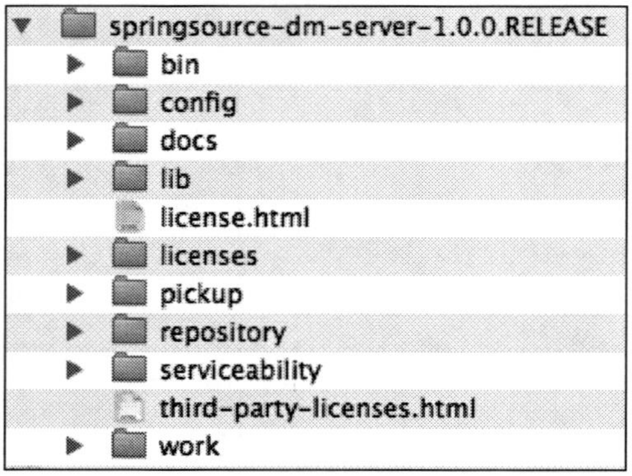

To start the server, there is a script with the name `startup.sh` inside the `bin` folder of the SpringSource dm Server. To stop the server, you can use the script `shutdown.sh` inside the `bin` folder. After the start on the console, the script prints some messages. If there is an error on the startup, ensure that you have set the environment variable `SERVER_HOME`. The standard configuration needs four ports to run. The ports are used for the services which are listed in the following table:

Port	Name of the service
2401	The OSGi telnet console For the first steps, you can use the `help` command inside the console; that command displays the available commands with their description; the command to close the console is exit
8009	The AJP/1.3 connector; that connector is for integration of the tomcat webcontainer inside the Apache HTTP server
8443	The connector which is used for HTTPS
8080	The connector which is used for HTTP

After the SpringSource dm Server is started, you can visit the start page with your favorite web browser. For that, just type `http://localhost:8080` into the address line of the browser. The following screenshot shows the start page:

The distribution of the SpringSource dm Server comes with a link list to the following four documentation sets:

- **SpringSource dm Server - User Guide (1.0.x)**. Available online at: `http://static.springsource.com/projects/dm-server/1.0.x/user-guide/html/`.
- **SpringSource dm Server - Programmer Guide (1.0.x)**. Available online at: `http://static.springsource.com/projects/dm-server/1.0.x/programmer-guide/html/`.
- **Spring Framework (2.5.x)**. Available online at: `http://static.springframework.org/spring/docs/2.5.x/reference/`.
- **Spring Dynamic Modules Reference Guide (1.1.x)**. Available online at: `http://static.springframework.org/osgi/docs/1.1.0-m2/reference/html/`.

> The distribution of the SpringSource dm Server contains the User Guide (in the `user-guide` folder) and the Programmer Guide (in the `programmer-guide` folder) inside the `docs` folder of the distribution.

The folder layout of the `docs` folder is as shown in the following screenshot:

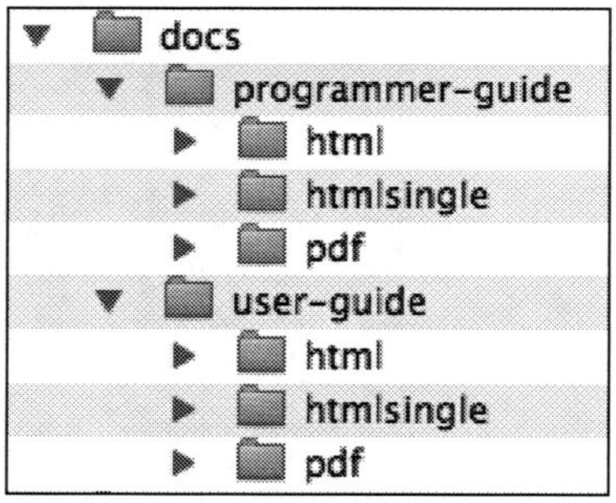

Beside the mentioned set of links on the start page, it contains a link to the **admin console**. If you want to directly start the admin console, just type the URL `http://localhost:8080/admin` in the address line of your browser. The username for the console is `admin`, and the password is `springsource`. After a successful login, the console will be shown. The screenshot of the admin console is shown here:

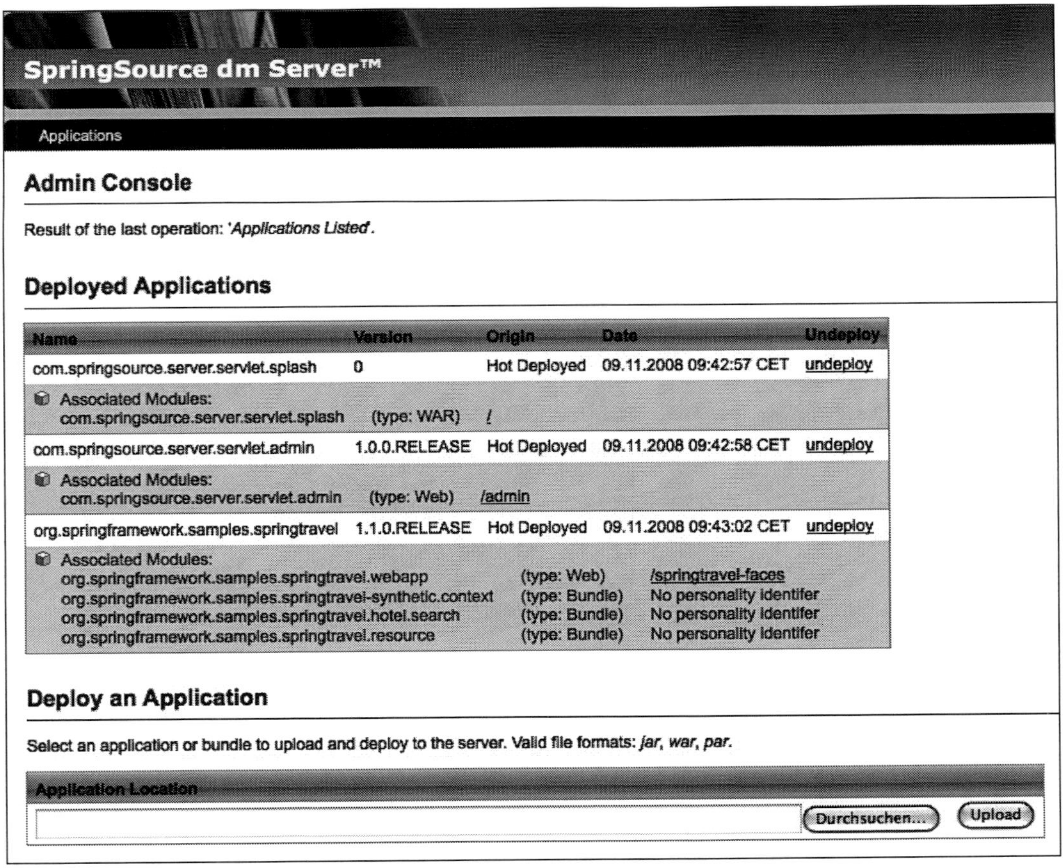

You can use the console to deploy new applications or to see the state of your existing applications. For each application, the URL of the application is shown as a link. Therefore, you can directly go to the specific application.

Beside the admin console, which is a very important feature, there is also the information part. This part contains the following two information blocks:

- **Server Properties**
- **Serviceability Destinations** (The serviceability summarizes the information as to where to find the log files for the specific applications.)

The following screenshot shows you the information part of the admin console. Both the screenshots shown here are in the same HTML page.

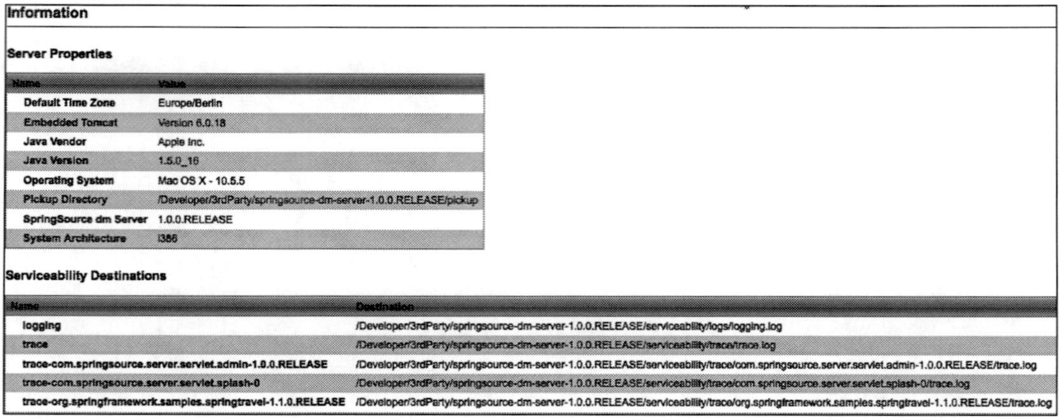

Information

Server Properties

Name	Value
Default Time Zone	Europe/Berlin
Embedded Tomcat	Version 6.0.18
Java Vendor	Apple Inc.
Java Version	1.5.0_16
Operating System	Mac OS X - 10.5.5
Pickup Directory	/Developer/3rdParty/springsource-dm-server-1.0.0.RELEASE/pickup
SpringSource dm Server	1.0.0.RELEASE
System Architecture	i386

Serviceability Destinations

Name	Destination
logging	/Developer/3rdParty/springsource-dm-server-1.0.0.RELEASE/serviceability/logs/logging.log
trace	/Developer/3rdParty/springsource-dm-server-1.0.0.RELEASE/serviceability/trace/trace.log
trace-com.springsource.server.servlet.admin-1.0.0.RELEASE	/Developer/3rdParty/springsource-dm-server-1.0.0.RELEASE/serviceability/trace/com.springsource.server.servlet.admin-1.0.0.RELEASE/trace.log
trace-com.springsource.server.servlet.splash-0	/Developer/3rdParty/springsource-dm-server-1.0.0.RELEASE/serviceability/trace/com.springsource.server.servlet.splash-0/trace.log
trace-org.springframework.samples.springtravel-1.1.0.RELEASE	/Developer/3rdParty/springsource-dm-server-1.0.0.RELEASE/serviceability/trace/org.springframework.samples.springtravel-1.1.0.RELEASE/trace.log

If you want to use the SpringSource dm Server, there are three examples provided for a testdrive of the server. These examples can be downloaded from the same page as the binary distribution of the SpringSource dm Server. The examples are:

- Spring Travel Sample Application 1.1.0
- Petclinic Sample Application 1.5.0
- Formtags Sample Application 1.4.0

The examples are provided as a ZIP archive. Before we go further with the migration of an exisiting application, we want to show how to install one of the samples. We choose the `Spring Travel Sample Application 1.1.0`.

1. Download the 11.3 MB archive with the name, `spring-travel-1.1.0.RELEASE.zip`. Now, you can extract the archive into a temporary (it is not advisable to extract the archive directly inside the folder of the installed SpringSource dm Server) folder. The following screenshot shows the folder layout of the extracted archive of the sample application.

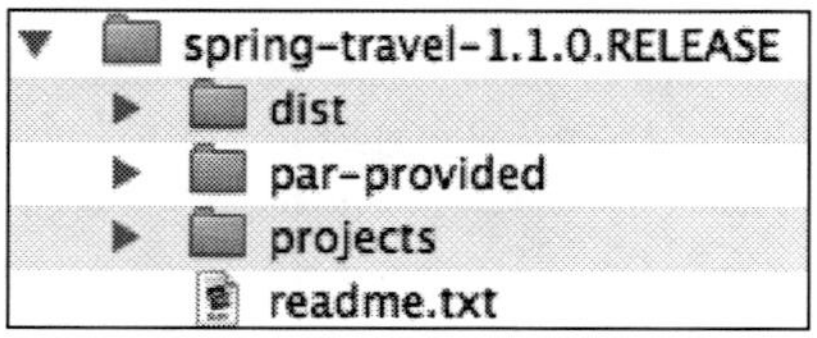

As you can see, the folder contains a file, `readme.txt`, which contains valuable information about the installation process of the **Spring Travel Application** inside the SpringSource dm Server.

2. Copy all the files (the Version 1.1.0 contains 31 files) from the `par-provided/bundles` folder (bundles from a specific par archive) of the sample application into the `repository/bundles/usr` folder (folder for bundles which are provided from the user) of the SpringSource dm Server. It is wise to stop the SpringSource dm Server before you start with the second step of the installation process of the Spring Travel Application.
3. Copy all the files (the Version 1.1.0 contains 2 files) from the `par-provided/libraries` folder into the `repository/libraries/usr` folder of the SpringSource dm Server.
4. Copy the **Platform Archive** (**PAR**) from the `dist` folder into the `pickup` folder of the SpringSource dm Server. A platform archive is a standard JAR, which contains all the modules of your application.
5. Now, start your SpringSource dm Server with the script `startup.sh` and visit the admin console on your local machine with the URL `http://localhost:8080/admin`. The console should now have an entry for the installed **Spring Travel Application**. The following screenshot shows this entry. A hot deployment of the application is also possible.

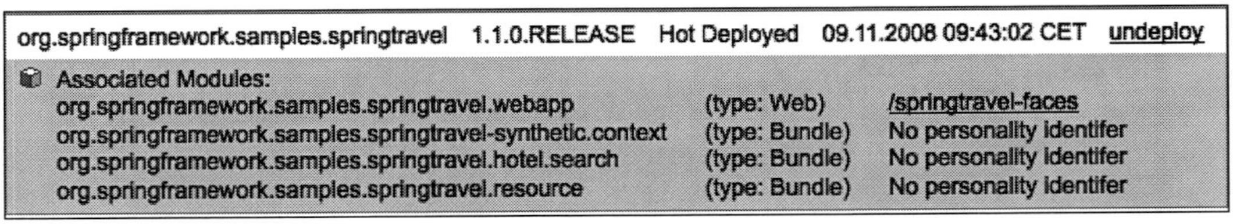

As you can see, the entry contains a link to the installed application. You can directly click on that link. Alternatively, you can call the application by typing the URL `http://localhost:8080/springtravel-faces` in the address line of your browser. After that, the application is presented as illustrated in the following screenshot.

The application, which we have installed, is the reference application of Spring Web Flow 2. Therefore, now you have a running Spring Web Flow 2 application inside the Spring Source dm Server. The reference application can be tested online at `http://richweb.springframework.org/swf-booking-faces/spring/intro`.

Migrating an application

If you have a running Spring Web Flow 2 application, there is the question on how to run it on the SpringSource dm server. The documentation of the SpringSource dm Server contains a detailed instruction on how to migrate a web application to a proprietary PAR archive. With the proprietary PAR format, you save some of the necessary configuration. In this appendix, we show you the important steps.

> Chapter 7 of the documentation inside the programmer-guide of the SpringSource dm Server is an important chapter. The chapter is available online at `http://static.springsource.com/projects/dm-server/1.0.x/programmer-guide/html/ch07.html`.

1. Because one of the cornerstones of the SpringSource dm Server is the Tomcat Servlet Engine, you can directly run your WAR archive on that server. But you still cannot profit from all the benefits of the SpringSource dm Server. To run your WAR archive, simply copy the archive into the `pickup` folder of the SpringSource dm Server.
2. The next step towards OSGi is to remove the libraries from the WAR file and get the dependencies from the container. That is described in Chapter 7.3 of the programmer-guide of SpringSource dm Server at `http://static.springsource.com/projects/dm-server/1.0.x/programmer-guide/html/ch07s03.html`.

> **Where to get a library that can be used inside the OSGi container?**
>
> If you want to use a library in an OSGi container, the library must provide some important information inside the manifest, `MANIFEST.MF`, which is located in the `META-INF` folder of a JAR archive. For your own libraries, it is not a big task to provide that information in the manifest. Mostly, the manifest is created through your build process. But for external libraries, it is recommended not to add the information manually. The solution is the **SpringSource Enterprise Bundle Repository** which is located at `http://www.springsource.com/repository/app/`. That web application contains hundreds of open source libraries, which contain the essential information inside the manifest and can therefore be used inside an OSGi container. Therefore, if you search a library, use that repository. By the way, the SpringSource Enterprise Bundle Repository runs on the SpringSource dm Server, and is therefore one of the first productive applications on that server.

3. After you have removed the libraries from your WAR archive and used the libraries directly from the SpringSource dm Server, the next step is to externalize the services. That step is described in Chapter 7.4 of the programmer-guide. The URL of that chapter is `http://static.springsource.com/projects/dm-server/1.0.x/programmer-guide/html/ch07s04.html`.
4. The last step towards the PAR archive is described inside the Chapter 7.5 of the programmer-guide. The URL of that chapter is `http://static.springsource.com/projects/dm-server/1.0.x/programmer-guide/html/ch07s05.html`.

Summary

In this appendix, we gave you a small introduction into the SpringSource dm Server. This server provides an OSGi kernel in conjunction with the Spring Framework. The SpringSource dm Server is therefore more than only OSGi, or only the Spring Framework. After the introduction, we showed you how to install the binary distribution of the server on your local machine.

We also described the installation of the Spring Web Flow 2 sample application Spring Travel on the SpringSource dm Server. The last section gave you hints for migrating your application to an OSGi application.

If you want to get more information about the SpringSource dm Server, you can read the following provided guides:

- SpringSource dm Server User Guide
- SpringSource dm Server Programmer Guide

Index

Symbols

A

B

C

D

O

P

R

S

3156297

Made in the USA